LONG WAY FROM HOME

MYRNA KOSTASH

*The story of the
Sixties generation
in Canada*

LONG
WAY
FROM
HOME

James Lorimer & Company, Publishers
Toronto, 1980

ISBN 0-88862-380-1 cloth

Design: Don Fernley

6 5 4 3 2 1   80 81 82 83 84 85 86

Canadian Cataloguing in Publication Data
Kostash, Myrna.
  Long way from home
Bibliography: p.294
ISBN 0-88862-380-1 bd.
1. Youth – Canada – Attitudes. 2. Youth – Canada – Political activity. 3. Canada – Social conditions – 1945–1965.* 4. Canada – Social conditions – 1965 – *
I. Title.
HQ799. C3K67   305.2'3'0971   C80-094675-8

James Lorimer & Company, Publishers
Egerton Ryerson Memorial Building
35 Britain Street
Toronto M5A 1R7, Ontario

Printed and bound in Canada

CONTENTS

For Mort Newman, keeping the faith

ACKNOWLEDGEMENTS

The author wishes to acknowledge the assistance of the Explorations Program of the Canada Council in the preparation of this book; and of the following people who gave so generously of their time, memories and ideas:

Sally Albert, Hugh Armstrong, Pat Armstrong, Rose Auger, Pam Barrett, Sarah Berger, Bernie Bloom, Anne Boody, Peter Boothroyd, Barry Boyd, Viola Braun, Caroline Brown, Duane Burton, June Callwood, Maria Campbell, Gerry Cannon, Tim Christian, Bob Collins, Patrick Connell, John Conway, Bill Coull, Gary Craig, Diane Crawford, Claire Culhane, Betty Deegan, Roger Deegan, Mark Dolgoy, Reevan Dolgoy, Daniel Drache, Gordon Drever, Corky Evans, Jeff Eyre, Derek Fox.

Gerry Gilbert, Cy Gonick, Fred Haake, Lynn Hanley, Nancy Hanum, Michael Harcourt, James Harding, Ray Harper, Robin Hedley-Smith, Bill Hoffer, Kay Hohn, Patricia Hughes, Robin Hunter, Steve Jones, John Juliani, Peter Katadotis, Alan Kellog, Roy Koob, Don Kossick, Milly Lamb, Rob Landreth, Victoria Langton, Marc Laurendeau, David Leadbeater, Dolores Macfarlane, Cam Mackie, Sally Mahood, Bruce McLellan, George Melnyk, Michel Mill.

Don Mitchell, Bill Monro, Joann Monro, Richard Moore, Sheila Moore, Graeme Moorhouse, Muck & Linda, Bill Nimtin, Arthur Pape, Ken Pappes, Kathy Payne, Bob Perkins, Jean Perrault, Stan Persky, Holger Petersen, Kevin Peterson, Tom Pocklington, Mitch Podaluk, Helen Potrebenko, Gail Price, Richard Price, Liora Proctor, Chris Purdy, Tom Radford, Jean Rands, Harry Rankin, Robert Reece, Jim Robb, Ann Roberts, Sean Rooney, Russ Rothney, Dimitri Roussopoulos, Clayton Ruby.

Rick Salter, Donaleen Saul, Andreas Schroeder, Lydia Semotuk, Verna Semotuk, Harvey Shepherd, Mark Slipp, Brett Smiley, Joan Smith, Jerry Sperling, Evelyn St.-Croix, Allan Stein, Terry Sulyma, Reg Sylvester, Linda Taylor, Laura Tiberti, Martha Tracey, Peter Turner, Bronwen Wallace,

Doug Ward, Mel Watkins, Andy Wernick, Anne Wheeler, Don Whelan, Peter White, Jim Woodward, Kathy Woodward, Dale X, Irene Zalinsky.

Thanks also to Jane Gutteridge of Canadian Filmmakers Distribution Centre; to the staff of the University of Alberta Archives for their cooperation; and to Mark Budgen.

And to Howard Davidson, Laura Hargrave and Wm. Kostash for their inestimable labours on behalf of this book, a special thanks.

FOREWORD

In a screening room in Toronto, I am watching, one after the other, three Canadian films made during the Sixties. What I'm after is the sights and sounds of a historical period that shook up me and thousands of others in Canada, and that some of us strain now to recall in all its vivid and explicit alarm and excitement. I stare at the screen, waiting for the Sixties I grew up in to be evoked.

Here are the movies. *Breathing Together.* Allen Ginsberg, the American poet, is feeding his chickens oyster shells. His poem, "Moloch," is intoned over a scene of traffic in Chicago. Jerry Rubin, the American yippie, is jumping up and down on the black robes of a court judge. "We accuse America of boredom!" Abbie Hoffman, another yippie, is giving a lecture. "As you can see, the odds have shifted 7 to 5 in favour of the kangaroos." *Neon Palace.* The Apollo moon shot. The Beach Boys. Rin Tin Tin. The inauguration of President Nixon. Poodles dancing to "America the Beautiful." *The Sixties.* Nixon and Kennedy are on television, Adlai Stevenson is at the United Nations, the Beatles are in New York. Martin Luther King meets the cops on a civil rights march. Stokely Carmichael is in Selma, Alabama. An army man says, "We have a substantial military superiority" in Vietnam. The Tet Offensive and a military graveyard. Bobby Kennedy is assassinated. The Beatles sing "We Can Work It Out."

My question was: what did Canada look and feel like in the Sixties? The answer the films gave me was: it didn't look like anything. The Sixties took place in the United States of America. Let's pretend, they say, we were all Americans.

Although I was well into my research by the time I saw those films, they confirmed me in my project: to superimpose on their images ones of our own experience; to throw light on the featureless memory that is confined like the idiot-cousin in the attic of the Americanized mental household. "The Sixties?" some friends have responded. "We've heard all about that. SDS, Bob Dylan, Haight-Ashbury, Black Panthers. . . ." So they have said, in Edmonton, Vancouver, Toronto, in the houses and streets and parks where not so long ago they grew up in the middle of the clamorous, exhilarating, even outrageous disturbances of *right here.* The power of American events and personalities of the period is not to be denied — it was felt throughout the world — inasmuch as the centrality of the American *imperium* is not to be denied. But alongside it is the story of young people in a different country: as I argue in this book, the "facts of life" in Canada (the presences of Quebec, the NDP and the multinational) mean that to know about Berkeley and Chicago and Columbia, about Panthers and Vietnam veterans and rock 'n' roll stars, is not to know everything. At the same time, of course, the two national experiences are not unrelated. Where they touch and where they veer off from each other is one of the things this book is about.

It is also about the fact that we forget so fast. It used to take a generation of time to lose the story of our collective accomplishments (my generation at the dinner table, mouths hanging open as the stories of the Depression and Spain and Hitler came out), but now I meet people a mere ten or fifteen years younger than me who don't know what I'm talking about when I exclaim: "SUPA! FLQ! the SFU 114! Abortion Caravan!" It is very distressing to confront the fact that mine is a generation of amnesiacs failing to pass on the story and its meaning.

There is a discernible tendency among us to dismiss the period of the Sixties as the historical equivalent of our own romance-besotted youth, as though to have been young in a period of international upheaval is to have been histrionic, untenably idealistic, and, well, ridiculous. If this is true, it can only be by contrast, it seems to me, with the constricting compromises and shabby bargains one has struck with life in one's maturity. It is, however, the evaluation that various pundits of the media have delivered on the Sixties. "Where are all the hotheads now?" they ask rhetorically, implying that if the hotheads have now been tamed by the exigencies of life as it is (and ever shall be), then their earlier rebelliousness can only have been spurious. It is interesting to ask the question, in return, whose interests such an evaluation and such amnesia serve? For they are lies. In the course of doing this book, it was brought home to me that there are thousands of people in Canada who have not forgotten how they grew up and what they learned then, and who are continuing to refine and apply this learning in their everyday work and family lives, in their emotional, political and cultural lives. Everyday life in 1980 is not as spectacular as it was in 1968 — the whole world has changed since then — but there is no law, either, that says the times will never again erupt into revolt, or that there will never again be a generation of hotheads.

Finally, I wrote this book because I am in love with the Sixties, with the passions and ideas, friendships and loves, music and dance and poetry, stoned highs and sorrows the period generated. I "came of age" in 1965: I turned twenty-one, and threw myself into the great learning about camaraderie, war, imperialism, rock 'n' roll, the Godhead, vagabonding, lust, appetite and woman power; and I consider myself blessed to have been young in a period when the vision of the good and the true was up for grabs. In seeking our re-vision, thousands and thousands of us wandered very far from "home," from our families, our communities, the values with which we were bred, the ideals with which we were entrusted, the country we were to inherit. Along the way we experienced corruption, disillusion, pain and death, as well as joy, but these were tracks to another "home," lives of our own construction. This is true for every generation, of course; what is special about having grown up in the Sixties is how close our learning came to being revolutionary. You can't get much luckier than that.

A word about how I wrote this book. I ransacked new and used book stores from Montreal to Berkeley (it was a poignant experience to come across literally *bins* of discarded copies of *The Thoughts of Chairman Mao* and *The Medium Is the Message)* in search of both contemporary and recent writings on the Sixties period. (For the limitations of this material, see the Bibliography.) I pounced on whatever people had mouldering in cardboard boxes in their basements: old movement newspapers, posters, letters, photographs, scrapbooks, newsletters and magazines. I spent hours over yellowing university newspapers and going through back issues of magazines and journals that took seriously the events of the period. Most importantly, I interviewed people, for I counted on them to fill the gaps and draw a map through the written material. And to tell the stories, idiosyncratic and passionate and full of character, that are subsumed within scholarly generalizations. Because of the sensitive nature of the details of people's lives from that period, and because there were so many individuals interviewed, I have not used their names in the text. All unattributed quotes come from them.

I have also told the story from the point of view of anglophone Canada. Therefore, the history of Quebec in the Sixties has been told as it was perceived by anglophones.

This book represents the most difficult labour of my life, not least because to this point so few Canadians have sat down to write about and make sense of the Sixties. I like to think my book is only one volume in a Sixties encyclopedia to come.

M.K.
Edmonton
July 1980

INTRODUCTION

The Sixties, as forecast by *Maclean's* magazine in 1959: no war but no real peace either, and "grave defeats for the Free World"; man on the moon by 1966; two-thirds of Canadian business profits to American corporations by 1969; Montreal and Toronto as "megalopolises, traffic-choked, water-short snarls of humanity"; a substantial proportion of workers on a thirty-five-hour week; the family living "more as a unit" with no change in the divorce and abortion laws; the United States as "our greatest and most dependable friend," the Soviet Union "our most dangerous enemy." "Conformity will continue to be a cherished goal."[1]

The way we were, *circa* 1960: supermarkets, laundromats, parking lots and television sets had redesigned the landscape and interior of North American life. The year 1954 had seen the introduction of the electronic digital computer (there would be thirty thousand in North America by 1966), the transistorized portable radio and automation at Ford plants. Sociologists, pop and academic, addressed themselves to the consequences — abundance, leisure — of the anticipated freedom of the "post-scarcity" society. The Canadian birthrate was dropping off, and the boys and girls of the celebrated "baby boom" of the Forties were teenagers: the hope, promise and dread of an earlier generation who had had no choice but to defer their gratifications during Depression and war.

The family consuming the automatic washers, record-players, four-door sedans and frozen Chinese dinners was a model of sexual repression, female subservience and the sexual division of labour. When the model didn't work, it produced the bugaboo of the Fifties, the "juvenile delinquent." Better the kids should be at home, watching television. By the time of their adolescence they had consumed twenty thousand hours of it — Ozzie and Harriet, Milton Berle, Hopalong Cassidy — had become stupid, stupified.

All this and the assembly line, the file-card cabinet and the briefcase too.

Yet it was, even as the mythology has it, an expansionist time. From the Fifties through to the mid-Sixties, incomes were rising faster than prices, and corporate profits were rising fastest of all.[2] The unemployment rate was hovering around 4 percent. Investment of foreign capital in the resource and manufacturing sectors of the Canadian economy proceeded with alacrity. By 1962, 63 percent of the petroleum and natural gas industry, 62 percent of the mining industry and 54 percent of the manufacturing industry were foreign owned.[3]

By 1964 the Montreal subway was under construction, the Winnipeg airport had a mural, Charlottetown had a new theatre and library, Dartmouth had a refinery, and the government of Ontario decided to build at Pickering a nuclear power station.

The self-employed worker or professional was a vanishing type. In 1960, 78 percent of the labour force was earning a wage or salary, compared to 65 percent in 1946. As the percentage of the Gross National Product (GNP) represented by government revenue grew greater and greater, so did the percentage of the labour force employed by the state: 12.6 percent in 1956, 16.3 percent in 1962 and 19.1 percent in 1966.[4] Besides the professionals, these workers were the clerical staffs and the service and support staffs. By 1964 the Canadian Union of Public Employees would be the second largest union in Canada after the United Steelworkers of America.

The data are Canadian but the phenomenon, advanced capitalism, the "new" capitalism, is global — which is to say, American. Coinciding with the creation of the European Common Market and with the regime of C.D. Howe, minister of trade and commerce in Ottawa, American foreign investment expanded between 1958 and 1964 as it had never done before. While the American share of the GNP in Western nations was declining from its immediately post-war peak, it still represented half that wealth: a staggering productivity.[5]

This was a capitalism dominated by the expansive, multinational corporation, by flexibility and self-correcting mechanisms, by dependence on sales and investments abroad and by the coincidental monopolization of markets, centralized government and the decline of small businesses.[6] Unrestrained in their home base by a docile labour force and spurred on by a belligerent Cold War foreign policy, the American multi-nationals deployed their wealth on arms manufacture, advertising and the built-in obsolescence of commodities.

Money, jobs, refrigerators, defence systems: the triumph of the Free World over the alternatives. A veritable colossus of stability.

As the liberals would have it, the West was witnessing the (welcome) end of ideology, in which revolutionary mass movements would be without foundation, socialist ideology without credibility and class struggle without content. Not only were these developments held to be self-evident, they were held to be desirable. (It was an assumption of these end-of-ideologists that "ideology" described only the idea system of socialists and socialist societies and not, for example, the idea system of North American capitalism.) It was assumed that post-war North American capitalism had succeeded in trans-muting the conflicts, alienations and aberrations of class society into a generalized prosperity and welfarism under a "regime of experts"[7] and technocrats.

In Canada, liberalism assumed the decisive authority of electoral democracy, the political primacy of Parliament, the equitability of free enterprise, the inevitability of social stability and material progress. Damage was infinitely correctable. And the individual, standing "above the state," was autonomous and self-determining. And beyond class. In Canada there were no classes, only hierarchies.

Further, in her international relations Canada, free of the taint of colonialism and imperialism, could be trusted by Third World and Old World alike. To call her relations with the imperial United States "dependent" would be to misconstrue them. They reflected, rather, mutual expediency and benefit. Neighbourly continentals, Canadians and Americans "naturally" saw eye-to-eye on most issues. A Canadian ambassador to the United States: "I regarded the Canadian-United States alliance as our most precious international asset. . . ."[8]

There were, however, ideological and political disjunctions. Note these. In 1954, Alan Freed, Cleveland, Ohio, disc jockey, played to an audience of white teenagers records of what was called "rhythm and blues." Black music. "A sound that told of dirt and fear and pain and lust."[9] Rock and roll ("My baby rocks me with a steady roll") was mesmerically rhythmic and single-minded, over and over the shout of the sexually aroused, street-wise outsider. Neither frothily escapist nor swooningly sentimental, rock 'n' roll rubbed your nose in the sweat of your life. In the dance to Little Richard, Chuck Berry, Buddy Holly and Elvis Presley was the movement toward an alternative unity and community to the classroom and the lonely crowd. In 1956 Jack Kerouac's *The Dharma Bums* was published, one star in a constellation of work by writers such as Lawrence Ferlinghetti, Gary Synder, Allen Ginsberg — the Beats, the Beatific Generation — who repudiated suburbia and the desk job, who got stoned, got drunk, fornicated and intoned the disciplinary measures of Zen and the open road, who against "Moloch whose mind is pure machinery! Moloch whose blood is running money!"[10] postulated jazz, delinquency and the camaraderie of poverty. In 1957, in Murdochville, Quebec, nine hundred miners in the United Steelworkers went out against Gaspé Copper Mines. Seven months later, by the combined force of the company and the Union Nationale provincial government, the strike was smashed — as would the Duplessis government itself be, three years later.

In 1960 the CCF government of Saskatchewan introduced medicare, and in the fight to institute it, the idea of community self-administration was reborn. In 1961 the New Democratic Party, an amalgam of the CCF and organized labour, was founded and two years later had a national membership of 209,034. By this act, the Canadian Labour Congress, unlike its American counterpart, the AFL-CIO, committed itself to political intervention.

At the same time, throughout the Fifties, the American sociologist C. Wright Mills was publishing books critical of the assumption of liberal sociology regarding the structural and functional "inevitablity" of power relations in modern society. Mills denounced ideologies of "political complacency," the "fetishism of empiricism" and the "pretentious methodology"[11] of North American social science. The American writer Paul Goodman was exploring the various absurdities of growing up in America and the utopian alternatives to the technocracy. And in 1961 the first English translation of the early writings of Karl Marx was made available in North America. And here those who read it encountered the Marxist notions of "alienation," atomization and the "division of labour" as cleavages between the human being and the human deed, none of it to be remedied without the "emancipation of society from private property, from servitude," which is to say the "emancipation of the workers."[12]

1954. The French army surrenders its garrison at Dien Bien Phu in Vietnam to the Viet Minh, Vietnamese national liberation army. The Geneva Conference produces an agreement on the cessation of hostilities in Indochina.

1955. Rosa Parks, a black, refuses to give up her bus seat to a white passenger in Montgomery, Alabama.

1956. England, France and Israel invade Suez, the colonialists' last naked waltz in the Middle East. At the twentieth Congress of the Communist party of the Soviet Union, Premier Khrushchev speaks of the crimes of Joseph Stalin. In Poznan, Poland, there are worker uprisings. In Hungary, a completely corrupt Stalinist party collapses; there is no Communist of any popular credibility to step forward. Soviet tanks and troops fill the vacuum in Budapest. Fidel Castro and a handful of guerrillas land in Cuba from the boat, *Granma,* and ascend into the Sierra Maestra. In Montgomery, Alabama, the preacher Martin Luther King organizes a boycott of the segregated bus lines; it will last 381 days.

1957. Federal troops are ordered into Little Rock, Arkansas, to enforce the integration of a high school.

1958. The government of China begins the reorganization of the agricultural communes, further socializing property and accelerating the transition to communism.

1959. Fidel Castro's guerrillas overthrow the U.S.-backed dictator Batista and enter Havana in triumph. Maurice Duplessis, repressive premier of Quebec, dies.

1960. Fifty-six black demonstrators are killed by South

African police in Sharpesville. In South Korea and Turkey student demonstrations provoke the collapse of corrupt and repressive political regimes. President Eisenhower declares economic war on Cuba by slashing the sugar import quota; and the Fair Play for Cuba Committee is founded. Black students in Greensboro, North Carolina, begin lunch counter sit-ins at Woolworth's. The Student Non-Violent Co-ordinating Committee (SNCC) is organized. The birth control pill goes on public sale. In New York the Student League for Industrial Democracy becomes Students for a Democratic Society (SDS). In Quebec Jean Lesage and the Liberals form a government: "la révolution tranquille" begins.

1961. Congolese nationalist leader Patrice Lumumba is killed by Western-supported assassins. The United States breaks diplomatic relations with Cuba and sponsors an invasion at the Bay of Pigs. The invasion is a flop. Chou En-Lai walks out of the Communist World Congress in Moscow. Freedom riders from Washington to New Orleans test the segregation of interstate buses and are beaten and arrested. SNCC begins a voter-registration campaign in Mississippi. President Kennedy announces the formation of the Peace Corps and sends the first combat-level troops to Vietnam. The New Democratic Party, endorsed by the Canadian Labour Congress, is founded in Ottawa.

1962. The Algerian War of Independence successfully ends 132 years of French colonialism. Students participate by the thousands in the civil rights movement; SDS meets at Port Huron, Michigan, and issues a sixty-three-page manifesto. Defence Secretary Robert McNamara confirms that U.S. troops are exchanging fire with the Viet Cong of South Vietnam.

1963. Ngo Dinh Diem, president of South Vietnam, is assassinated. U.S. military "personnel" in that country number 16,800. The U.S. and U.S.S.R. sign a nuclear test ban treaty. In his encyclical, *Pacem in Terris,* Pope John XXIII calls for world peace and church-initiated social reform. Four black girls are killed in the dynamiting of a Birmingham, Alabama, church. Martin Luther King speaks to 250,000 rallying at the Lincoln Memorial at the end of a civil rights march on Washington. "I have a dream." SDS begins its Economic Research and Action Project (ERAP) in poor neighbourhoods of northern cities along the lines of SNCC in the south; ERAP is supported by a grant from the United Auto Workers. President Kennedy is assassinated. Timothy Leary and Richard Alpert are dismissed from Harvard for testing LSD on undergraduates. Bob Dylan writes "Blowin' in the Wind." *The Feminine Mystique* is published. *Canadian Dimension* magazine brings out its first issue. Canada accepts nuclear warheads.

1964. There are 917,000 college or university students in Japan, 455,000 in France, 3.6 million in the U.S.S.R., 5 million in the United States and 158,000 in Canada. In a fifteen-year period, the global student population has increased 2.7 times.

At 22 miles from ground zero of the explosion of a hundred-megaton nuclear bomb, winds of 110 miles per hour blow wood-frame houses apart; at 18 miles, brick houses collapse; within a 39-mile radius, exposed clothing is set aflame: there is no protection from burning of the retina — the radiation hits sooner than the eye can blink. At 8.7 miles you are in the fireball:[13] like the citizen of Hiroshima, you are a shadow baked into the cement of the sidewalk.

The nightmares of a child ten years old in 1955: radiation sifts silently, sightlessly through the air, through the window and door frames of home, onto the food at the supper table where you eat it like a mysterious salt; sirens howl in the dead of night and do not stop; they howl and howl while the glass windows melt; your parents die, their blank, white eyeballs turned up to the searing flash in the sky, and the Russians — big men in long coats — chase you down the alley; faster and faster they chase as your short legs move ponderously to carry you one more yard — oh, this takes forever — to the gate of your house.

Childhood pastiche: the Bomb, the fallout shelter, the school desk you are to crawl under when the siren goes off, Hiroshima and Nagasaki, Strontium 90, cancer, Intercontinental Ballistic Missiles, the death, hurray, of Stalin (on the front page of the newspaper, in headlines) and of George VI (mother is crying).

"Mankind Must Abolish War or War Will Abolish Mankind!" Thousands upon thousands of placards were hoisted at Aldermaston, England, at Easter time in 1958 as men, women and children clogged the streets on their way, grimly, to the nuclear weapons plant. A year later, in Canada, when the Diefenbaker government announced that it was entering into a Defence Production Sharing Agreement with Washington* and would, in place of the scrapped Canadian-built Avro Arrow jet fighter, purchase the American Bomarc B anti-bomber missile, a group of students and professors in Montreal remembered Aldermaston. For the Bomarc B was designed to carry a nuclear warhead.

"Let Canada Lead the Peace Race!" As the Combined Universities Campaign for Nuclear Disarmament (CUCND), the group marched at Christmas 1959, the first student demonstration since the end of the Second World War, and again the next Christmas. They circulated petitions, vigilled, sang out for peace. In 1961, CUCND launched a journal, *Our Generation Against Nuclear War,* to "give a theoretical dimension, an historical dimension, a philosophical dimension, if you will, to the nuclear disarmament movement. We wanted to create a theory of peace."**

For the post-war generation at this point, the "movement" was CUCND. It was the "peace houses" like Humanity House in Saskatoon where CUCNDers lived cooperatively, and Peace House in Toronto where they had meetings, did mailings and strategized by the seat of their pants. It was meeting with

---

*The agreement provided for "long-term equality of defence expenditure" by each country in the other and for access by Canadian defence contractors to the American market. By 1962 American purchases in Canada had reached $254 million, twice what the Canadian government spent in the U.S. that year. By 1966, as the war in Vietnam was escalating, U.S. defence expenditures in Canada reached $317 million.[14]

**Also active in the movement were the Canadian Campaign for Nuclear Disarmament (CCND), Voice of Women, the Peace Research Institute, *Sanity* newspaper, the Canadian Peace Congress and Youth Campaign for Nuclear Disarmament.

the Quakers at Grindstone Island, Ontario, for workshops on non-violence and simulations of attacks on pacifists. It was debates over the value of "positive neutralism" and withdrawal from NATO as foreign policies for Canada, of unilateral disarmament, of direct action, civil disobedience and mass demonstrations (reminiscent of an earlier generation's experience in workers' and socialist movements)[15] that went beyond petitions and resolutions. It was intensely moralistic and obsessed with ethics, as well it may have been in a world seemingly prepared to blow itself, the various political camps included, up. A world of the Cold War and the time of the witch-hunters and red-baiters — people were being taunted and slandered and hounded out of unions, school boards, political parties, government jobs, on suspicion, sometimes evidence, of affiliation to or sympathy with the Communist party.

> I was taking a political philosophy course at the University of Saskatchewan, 1961, and the professor announced he was going to be discussing Marxism. An engineering student at the back of the room got up and said, "There are those of us, Sir, who are mature enough to appreciate that such things must be discussed to gain a better appreciation but there are many young people in this class whose minds have not yet formed and who may be injured by hearing these things." And I would sometimes wear my CUCND button — that was a sign of participation in the movement — when speaking to groups on campus and people would catcall from the audience, "Hey, Commie!"

In San Francisco, in 1960, the House Un-American Activities Committee opened hearings on the alleged subversive influence of "Reds" in the schools and unions of the Bay area. Student demonstrators, yelling "Down with HUAC!" and refusing to disperse, were handed over to the "goon force," the city police, and clubbed to the ground, kicked down the stairs, and smashed by water hoses into the walls. In Canada no such drama took place but there were bravery and superb defiance enough in the students and youth of the peace movements that were organizing in an atmosphere of fearfulness and bad faith throughout North America. In a country where even the CCF-

NDP (the social democratic party in which the peace movement participated) was virulently anti-Communist, at a time when confrontation and armament were the strategies of "peace," it was then with the perhaps lunatic courage of the politically innocent that the movement activist said: Stop. Ban the Bomb, do it unilaterally, repudiate the spurious patriotism of the warlords, turn your swords into ploughshares and go home in peace and fraternity.

In October 1962, photographs taken over Cuba by a U-2 plane revealed the presence of intermediate-range missiles. President Kennedy, grim on the television screen, announced that these missiles endangered the "peace of the world and the security of the United States" and proclaimed "that the forces under my command are ordered . . . to interdict . . . delivery of offensive weapons and associated material in Cuba."[16] Catatonic, North America, and the Canadian peace movement with it, watched the inexorable drift of missile-cargoed Soviet ships towards the American naval blockade in the Caribbean Sea. This was it, then, the end of the world. We were all going to die: the young and the peaceful and the ethical included, under a hail of nuclear hardware. The demonstrations and the resistance, the efforts to force an independent foreign policy, the appeals to the ultimately common interest of human kind, were as chimera compared to this very palpable scenario of a showdown between the super-imperial powers of East and West.

In the spring of 1963, after the federal election, Prime Minister Lester B. Pearson visited President Kennedy at Hyannis Port. On 16 August 1963 an agreement was signed to bring "special ammunition" into Canada. The first nuclear warheads were secretly delivered to La Macaza, Quebec, on New Year's Eve.[17]

If there had been no more content or context for CUCND than ban-the-bomb, it would have gone the way of all middle-class, liberal and pacifist groups of the time: dissolution.* But by 1964 the student "peaceniks" were already extending the issues of war and peace to include questions of the institutions and systems that create them. At this point it became the

---

*By 1965 most of CCND's branches, for instance, were inactive.[18]

Student Union for Peace Action (SUPA) and the first genuinely "new left" formation in Canada.

He comes from a liberal, middle-class family. He is told that the world is a very progressive place where human energy is an irresistible force that overcomes immovable objects. He grows up in absolute bliss — no Red menaces or crises or blockades in *his* world — where a Hungarian refugee is a tourist. He goes to university. He joins a fraternity. He takes history. He meets shaggy-haired kids in turtlenecks who talk about Cuba and Vietnam. They are very "interesting" and he is fascinated. He is thrilled. He never goes back to the fraternity.

She trudges through the snow on her way to classes, *aching* to go to Mississippi, to witness there, to fight and be hurt, give her life over to a *cause*, something that would release her from the deadening little world of Chemistry 30.

He knows the world is in convulsions and he takes a look at Diefenbaker and Pearson and Douglas and he sees the depressing gap between their policies and the revolutionary possibilites. So he dreams of being a revolutionary: in Afghanistan or Cuba or Vietnam or *anywhere* but here.

He decides to take a year off and travel. To Bangkok he goes and sees an old man and his grandson pick food to eat from a garbage heap. To Singapore and the eleven-year-old prostitutes in the marketplace. To Hiroshima and the Peace Museum where he stares in shock at the photograph of a child five minutes before his death. He turns around. A group of Japanese people are staring at him. What's he going to say? I'm a Canadian, I didn't have anything to do with this?

She is eight years old and she likes to look at the titles on all the books on her mother's bookshelves. There is one that fascinates her. It's called *Das Kapital*. She goes into the kitchen and asks her mother: What is this book? This, her mother says, is my Bible.

She goes to a hootenanny in the residence, and a political science student stands up to announce that at lunch hour every Tuesday there's going to be a seminar on non-violence. Curious, she joins the seminar. They are reading Sartre and Camus and Bonhoffer and it's all over her head but she sticks it out because people are talking about things she's never heard in lectures. One day she summons the nerve to ask what "those buttons" are about, those black and white buttons with the semaphore sign, for N and D, and learns that the logical extension of non-violence is the campaign against nuclear weapons. That sounds good to her. She buys a button and wears it to a cocktail party.

Political and ethical formations are idiosyncratic as well as social. One can explain and describe at length the *milieu* in which an individual lives and works and has being. One can account for the historical, socio-economic, political and moral dimensions of that milieu and delineate their tendencies which, in retrospect, are particularly meaningful. One can do all this and still be faced with a mystery: how is it that *this* person here and not *that* one, in 1964, became a radical? Even when the differences of class, sex, region, ethnicity are accounted for, it is the person himself or herself who in the end becomes conscious. In other words, it is perfectly dialectical: biography and society interpenetrate and the radical is made. Timing is all.

In sum: Canada's post-war youth were coming to maturity at the conjuncture of several portentious developments. The gargantuan wealth and influence of multinational, corporate capitalism, the interventionist state, and the ideology of liberalism induced a generalized belief in the "system's" libertarian potentialities and its capacity to produce and distribute prosperity and well-being (in marked contrast to socialism). Youth, the "golden girls and boys," were to inherit a rising standard of living, jobs of their choosing, a variety of *divertissements*, and, more than ever, were to be educated, and liberated from the determinisms of class, race and sex.

Against this full tide of rising expectations, however, other trends were developing, swelling, in contradictory force. Abroad, in the Third World, movements of national liberation confronted neo-colonialist regimes; in Eastern Europe, aspirations for workers' control of industry and for artistic and intellectual freedom of expression shook the Stalinist monolith, the Communist party. In the West, students and intellectuals

assailed the "hypocritical" investment of democracy in armament and paranoia. Nothing, in short, was as hegemonistic as it
seemed.

If there was one moment in which all these deviances came
together, it was that day in 1959 when Fidel Castro, in battle
fatigues and a beard, surrounded by a mass of jubilant
humanity — *compañeros! venceremos!* — entered Havana. He
was this: the man of action; the virile revolutionary riding "the
beast of his revolution," as Norman Mailer put it,[19] scorning
the effete and useless word-mongery of ideology; the humanist-
communist, heretical and compassionate. "Capitalism sacrifices
man," he said. "The Communist state sacrifices man. . . .Our
revolution is not red, but olive green, the colour of the rebel
army that emerged from the heart of the Sierra Maestra."[20] It
was not a Marxist-Leninist vanguard that had scrabbled in the
rocks and bush and graveyards of the Sierra, but the "people,"
the soldiers and the peasants who would come in the dead of
night with fifty pounds of food on their backs for the guerrillas.
It was a seemingly spontaneous act of encouragement to
alleviate those "moments when death was a concept a
thousand times more real, and victory a myth that only a
revolutionary can dream of."[21] Yet they had won and the
boasts of capitalism and Stalinism were vainglorious things.

And in North America — civil rights workers, pacifists,
demonstrators, strikers, peaceniks, beatniks and greasers, all on
their various routes to "that freedom land," which was
manifestly not here and not now.

And in Canada — campuses bulging with students and
construction, a restless faculty and restive administration,
students grieving about their residences, their meals, their
poverty; new organizations — Canadian Union of Students
(CUS), CUCND, Front de Libération du Québec; music, sex
and parties; boys who would not be chartered accountants and
girls who would not be wives.

The NDP was founded in Canada at the same time as the
CUCND was gaining popularity, and indeed the two organizations had close links, mainly through overlapping membership
in New Democratic Youth. For a generation radicalizing itself,
the NDP could not be avoided: it *was* the "left" of Canadian

electoral politics; it was linked to the trade union movement; it had over a million voters and a "respectable record of resistance to the schemes of big business."[22] Far from avoiding the NDP, in fact, hundreds of peace activists were deeply involved in it as the one place in adult Canadian society where they could hope for a sympathetic hearing.

Compared to American radicals, who found sustenance in individualistic heroes, outlaw mythologies and high-minded sentiments (Jeffersonianism, Woody Guthrie and the imperishable folkways of the down-and-out, Billy the Kid), the Canadians took encouragement from a political organization, a political collectivity, and thus were never to be quite so orphaned as the Americans whose continuity with radicalism had been devastated by the Cold War and McCarthyism. It would be the judgement of the Sixties whether the NDP was able to sustain the long haul of revolution but in 1963, poised at the border of a new left, the Canadian radicals had the advantage of one foot in history.

PORTRAITS

Gail Price Douglas, "artist, mother and westerner":

Waspish. Middle-class. This was the neighbourhood and the family she was born into, in 1946. A close family. Dad a manufacturer's agent, a salesman really, mum the ideal mother who stayed at home to raise two children and entertain her husband's clients. Close, and argumentative. Father and son would have a go at each other every Sunday night at the dinner table. Political arguments. It was here the daughter learned to hate politics: from her point of view it generated nothing but tension and stress among people. What did it have to do with the good life? The good life. Needs taken care of — education and travelling — as though this were normal. Some people had more money than her family did and others had less. Normal. It would not be until 1967, and her first trip abroad, that she would ask: Oh my God, where have I been all my life?

She was not, however, to think only of marriage as her future work. She was to have a career. Her father was adamant about this, and because the family was committed to the ethic of service, she was to choose a career in which she would serve others. So much for her girlhood dream of a life as an artist: she would not be able to support herself this way, the family said. She decided to study social work.

Campus life, *circa* 1964. She joined a fraternity, Kappa Alpha Theta, for girls of good family, rah! rah! Fraternity parties, dates, getting drunk on ethanol in the grapefruit juice. But there was something here in the fraternity that would endure. She made friends with women, strong, loyal and unquenchable friendships that would sustain her long after the romances and the fun had dried up and blown away.

The politics of the day passed her by. She would walk past earnest young people passing out pamphlets in the quad and wonder what on earth they were bothered about. (Her brother, in the meantime, had gone off to Berlin and then returned, a Marxist. Marx this, Lenin that. She thought it was a lot of bullshit.) Quite completely unaware of the issues burning up the brains and hearts of some of her fellow students, and not at all curious about them, she was, she says, a good little girl. Her parents' values and her own were identical. There was, however, one moment when they were challenged. She went to a conference on minority groups and was accused there by a black Jamaican of being prejudiced. She was depressed for days afterward by the possibility that this was true.

Then, in 1968, she went to the University of British Columbia to do her master's in social work and walked right into the storm around the issues of student participation in university committees, the relationship of faculty and students, student input into courses and methods. For the first time the fact that a fellow student was a radical impressed her. If this was politics, then she was intrigued.

In the summer of 1969 she was a member of an interdisciplinary group of students who lived together in an old church in the inner city of Vancouver and worked on projects with community self-help groups. They painted up an old bus and drove it around the neighbourhoods. A perambulating drop-in centre. Italian kids. Drop-out kids. Glue-sniffing kids. At night the students would sit together and rap for hours about what was happening out there in the streets, what was happening inside here to their social worker spirits. Once a young man, very excited, rapped enthusiastically about social change and violence, and she, listening, freaked out. She started to cry, she was so scared. What had she got herself into?

Fall of '69 in Vancouver. Kitsilano and Fourth Avenue. The final flourishing of the hippies. She loved them. Loved their style and their sensuality and their humour. In a communal hippie house she learned to relax, to turn on, to make love with abandon and indulgence. Here at last was the break with discipline! duty! guilt! Here at long last was a space in which the long-repressed artist in her unfolded and stretched out. Among the hippies it was "okay" to express her own self. She began to weave. In 1969 Gail Price came into her own.

Lydia Semotuk, "single woman, self-employed researcher on western Canadian populist movements, consultant and lecturer in business administration, a 'seeker' still":

Social Credit Alberta in the Fifties was not the most hospitable environment in which to grow up Ukrainian, left-wing and working-class, but this was precisely the milieu that engendered her. To her chagrin at the time, her father spoke with an accent and was only seasonally employed, as a carpenter, and neither parent was what you could call an intellectual. There was a decidedly pro-Soviet bias in the household. What it came down to for her father was windows and sugar. Before the Bolshevik revolution the Ukrainians didn't have windows in their houses or sugar to eat. After the revolution they had both. At the same time, her parents' message to her was: "We want you to have all the good things this society here has to offer but you must never forget where you came from. You are a Ukrainian." And they bundled her off to the Ukrainian Centre (Communist) for Ukrainian language and music lessons, the textbooks wrapped in cloth so the kids on the bus wouldn't see this "funny" language she was studying. It was okay to be Ukrainian but only among Ukrainians.

In public school it was her great good fortune to have a few teachers who quickly picked up on the fact that she was never in the "in-group," who broke through her lack of self-worth, and who introduced her to music and to politics. They were articulate and unconventional teachers trapped in inner-city, "jock-type" schools. One teacher lent her a portable record-player and the records of Kathleen Ferrier; another brought *Time* magazine to social studies class and made sarcastic references to its contents; yet another stopped her in the corridor one day and said, you know, there is a field of study called political science. And a man from the Ukrainian Centre, who was a humanist and a Communist, told her — it was at the height of the civil rights campaign in the southern United States — that just because some people have black skin doesn't mean they aren't the same as you or I, that they don't hurt or cry, that they smell any different. She had never thought of that before.

In high school, she knocked on doors for the NDP and enjoyed arguing with people while pamphleteering. Her parents were CCF supporters and she herself had a burning conviction that what the party said was right. She called herself a socialist, meaning humanist (people are created equal and have the right to equal justice and protection) and unionist (her father used to say about the old days that if he'd had a union his employers wouldn't have been able to get away with the things they did).

With the execution of convicted murderer Caryl Chessman in California in 1960, a recurring theme is triggered in her life. The world is made up of two classes, those who have power and those who don't. Chessman was a man utterly without power and she was absolutely taken with him — and with Fidel Castro, the man who fought, against formidable odds, on behalf of the poor and weak of his people, and won. Not only that: he'd taken on the United States, and she'd been anti-American since those first lessons about *Time* magazine.

From Day One it was understood that she would go to university. It was a big thing: she would be the first one in her family to go. She loved those first couple of years on campus. Finally she had found her place, where it was acceptable, even encouraged, to be an egghead, to enjoy sitting around talking ideas and politics. It was even better to be a left-winger. And so at last she had friends. (They were mostly men. Women were peripheral. They were introduced as so-and-so's girlfriend.) And a discipline. She studied political science, even though the department chairman tried to convince her that as a woman she would be happier in some other field of study.

In the summer of 1964 she travelled to Europe and discovered that she felt comfortable there, that she could make her way through the wide and lovely world beyond home. And discovered that she was sexual and that it wasn't a bad thing, this being attracted and attractive to men. Her self-confidence soared.

But back at university she began to waffle. Her liberal arts education was having its effect: it was becoming ever more difficult for her to say what was absolutely right and absolutely wrong about anything. She quit the NDP. Drifting into the "movement," feeling strongly committed to the issues of war and peace and justice, she nevertheless was afraid to speak up at meetings. What was happening was this: in her gut she knew the movement spoke to her beliefs, but *intellectually* the system she had in place was falling apart. She could march in an anti-war march but couldn't write a hard-hitting speech or organize. She could be articulate with three friends over dinner and speechless at a strategy session. On the one hand her education was telling her there are no answers. On the other hand the movement was saying there certainly are.

In the middle of this perplexity she met the Toronto student radical Peter Boothroyd. He was a graduate student in sociology, a radical superstar, a keynote speaker for the Student Union for Peace Action across the country. A heavy. And now here he was in Edmonton, organizing the masses. She met him at a political science club meeting, and when he came around asking for names and phone numbers of volunteers for a teach-in, she gave him her first name. But would not give him the second, the Semotuk, the Ukrainian name. No, not to this Anglo superstar. A year later they were living together and this was the most momentous decision thus far in her life. To break strong family ties and the family's morality. To decide, at age twenty-one, without social or sexual experience, to live with a man outside of marriage.

Living with Peter, she had whole worlds of politics open to her. Through her own choice, her self-image, she subordinated herself to him, to his vision, his ego, his society. In the summer of 1967 they moved to Toronto for a few months and there, surrounded by his circle of radical friends, her self-confidence became a puny thing. They intimidated her, these male movement personalities, these friends who took it for granted that her place was to cook and keep the apartment clean and who would not even make eye contact with her in discussions. They helped themselves to her generosity and never said thanks.

By 1970, back at the University of Alberta, she hadn't even done her thesis, so turned off she was by the "liberal arts" approach to political science and by the department's American orientation. In the midst of dramatic events right there on the campus, they were studying voter patterns in Massachusetts! In order to take a course in Marxism, she had to go over to the philosophy department and there, of course, were all the superstars again, so she didn't dare say anything in those classes either. The male radicals were the darlings of the Marxist professors.

If she were to put a label on what she became as a result of these experiences it would be "feminist." Civil rights, Cuba, Vietnam, yes, she had powerful feelings about all these issues, but they were not *her* issues in the end. Neither any longer were the issues of her ethnicity and class origin, for they had ceased to be troubling when first her friends' interest and admiration and later her own reawakened consciousness of her father's history and convictions had made her proud. In their place the woman's pain emerged. Around the issues of birth control and abortion and women in the workplace, she could finally speak, she, Lydia, not the superstar's appendage anymore.

Robin Hunter, "regretfully independent, revolutionary socialist":

He came into the world in 1943, sucking dead air, people trying to blow him apart, in an air raid shelter just outside London. He was born into a working-class family, and when his father joined the Canadian army, for a job, the whole family moved to Canada.

Of course the family was Labour. In high school, when he became aware of the differences among the Canadian political parties, he understood that of course he was CCF-NDP.

A girl in high school, the daughter of the family they were renting rooms from, came home one day with a comic book put out by Swift Packers. It was all about the virtues of the free enterprise system. His dad overheard the conversation, butted in and said, "Oh, that's just capitalist propaganda." That stuck with the boy. Now he had a label for the thing he was opposed to.

At school there were teachers who encouraged his reading (Upton Sinclair, G.B. Shaw) and a gang of bright Jewish kids who challenged him: one kid was reading Freud and another claimed to have read Marx in the original German. In the eleventh grade (enough was enough) he marched down to the CCF offices downtown and announced to those war horses of the party, Nellie Peterson and Bill Irvine, that he was a socialist. They were very nice to him and sent him home with a copy of *Monthly Review*. He took *Das Kapital* out of the library, with his father's encouragement. His dad read four pages of it back in his wild youth.

To be able to get to university, he joined up with the Reserve Officers Training Plan. This quickly became a grotesque contradiction, for he had also just become a member of the Combined Universities Campaign for Nuclear Disarmament. His idea was that if he could make contact with the peace people, he could bring them into the CCF-NDP. Then he read Bertrand Russell's *Common Sense and Nuclear Warfare,* and the peace movement acquired a justification all its own. Russell called Kennedy and Eisenhower swine and murderers and laid on them the responsibility for the fate of the whole human race. Up to then, the nuclear bomb had been, to him, a fact of life. Now it was outrageous.

Now began a lively time. Lots of different political theories, lots of discussion. There was music. Folk songs. From when he had started hanging out with CCF Youth to the time when the Beatles made it big in North America, he never listened to AM radio. No. He was listening to Pete Seeger and the Weavers. And the young Bob Dylan. He went to a student conference in Guelph, singing "Blowin' in the Wind" with great gusto the whole way there.

Summer 1964. He went to Cuba with a number of other young Canadians, and that was the first time he heard anyone talk about dope. And separatism. The separatists from Quebec bloomed in Cuba — the Cubans were very sympathetic to them – and they became more articulate than they had ever been in Canada. It was a separatist who first argued with him that the Labour party road in Britain was not the way to socialism, that the worker in the British factory does not feel any more in control of that factory than does the American worker in his free enterprise factory. He had to admit that was true. And that the NDP did not have the answer to it. A revelation.

Fall 1964. He went to study political science as a graduate student at Indiana University, and, casting about for the campus socialists, joined up with Students for a Democratic Society. SDS would eventually become a mass student movement across the whole of the United States. In 1964 it was coming into being in Indiana over the Vietnam war issue. In fact, its first big anti-war demonstration took place right after the Selma civil rights protests. One right after the other. The slogan was: "Take the Troops from Saigon, Move Them to Selma." It seemed the right slogan at the time. The fraternities mobilized against the demonstration and broke it up. Another revelation.

There were SDSers who were "red diaper" kids, who, like him, had grown up in families and communities sympathetic to socialist and Communist ideas. There were SDSers who were in anguish over what was happening in America and who wanted to relieve that anguish through politics. To them, the "half-way houses" of the traditional socialist parties were too moderate, too circumspect and compromised. They wanted a community of and for themselves. They sought to overcome their alienation through mass actions.

He was much more developed than any of them. He knew he was a socialist and he could argue why. He argued with them. "Yes," he said in SDS, "we're right about the war but we can only achieve our aims if we're socialists as well." That position grew and grew in SDS so that by 1968 SDSers were asking not do we need socialism, but how are we going to get to socialism? what do we have to build? And the answer to that became more and more often: the working class.

There was another strand of radicalism, the "action faction," those early demonstrations against Chase-Manhatten bank for holding shares in South Africa and the "burning, moral" thing about the war, where it was more important to put your body on the line than to get people to join you there. And then there were the spiritual people. Back in 1964, when *Maclean's* interviewed some of the students who had gone to Cuba, a girl had said, "Canada needs a revolution." Hunter was still in the NDP then and he thought that was ridiculous. But by 1968 he understood that she had been talking about the need for a whole turning around in our assessment of each other. And she was right.

Classes, meetings, arguments: they were his whole life. And music. Still he kept himself open to music. In his household there was a bluegrass band, and when he was at home he heard the blues, bluegrass, guitars, banjos, some fine voices. And read poetry — William Blake. And smoked dope. Dropped acid. From inside the maelstrom of a "trip" he began to worry about his cosmic consciousness. A close and unsparing look inside told him he was in danger of dying within. He began to hector his political friends, interfering in their daily business with questions. He'd say to them, "You realize what we're trying to do here. It's going to be a hell of a fight. It's going to tear our souls apart. We've got to be ready. We've got to get in touch with how beautiful the mass movement can be." The drugs had given him clarity, a glimpse into the present, into how things can be *right now* if you want them to be.

He was involved in the anti-war marches to Washington, in Angela Davis and Chicago 7 defence work, in Panther support work. He became aware, along with some other SDSers, that the tremendous talent of the women was not being used, that the men were being developed as leaders, the women as den mothers. The movement was dissipating its energy. Weird relationships, in and out and up and down, lovers going crazy. He married. It seemed iffy. He couldn't relate to this person, his wife; was it something about him? Why couldn't he get along with women? Of course he supported women's liberation but he worried that it wasn't taking place in his own life, in the lives of his women comrades or in those of the men. In 1967, when the SDS women raised the issue, a big Texan got up and drawled, "Well, folks, our gals are pretty liberated. They fuck who they want and nobody gives a damn about it." He was aghast. He knew this wasn't what the women meant.

When SDS fell apart in 1969, the Trotskyists picked him up.

PART I
PEACE AND WAR

I
PEACE NOW!

December 28 [1964]–January 1 [1965] marked the end of Canada's student peace movement known as the Combined Universities Campaign for Nuclear Disarmament. At its annual conference, held for the first time in Regina, the CUCND decided to constitute itself the Student Union for Peace Action . . . .

The conference attracted perhaps the most impressive group of young Canadians that has yet been assembled in any one place. And many of them had their credentials: Howard Adelman, czar of the growing university co-op residences; Richard Guay, vice-president of UGEQ [Union Général des Étudiants du Québec], the powerful runaway French-Canadian student federation; Doug Ward, head of the external affairs department of CUS [Canadian Union of Students], the federation of English-speaking students; Hardial Bains, founder of the dynamic UBC [University of British Columbia] Student Federation; Jim Harding, president of the Saskatchewan NDY [New Democratic Youth]; Dimitri Roussopoulos, editor of *Our Generation Against Nuclear Warfare* [sic]; and of course, Arthur Pape, chairman of CUCND . . . .

But before the conference was one day old, it was clear that they knew nothing about the power structure of this country, how decisions are made and who makes them. And nobody could help them, for the answers to these questions are not found in any textbook or learned treatise. In fact, nobody knows how power works in this country, or even who has power. Observing this conference, I could not help feeling that this is the most challenging task before the peace movement and anyone else who wishes to advance social change.

— *Cy Gonick (from "Students and Peace,"*
published in Canadian Dimension,
January – February 1965)

3

Labour Day weekend, 1964. The Bomarc base in La Macaza, Quebec, was heavy with nuclear warheads. To the base came members of the Combined Universities Campaign for Nuclear Disarmament and the Student Christian Movement (SCM), to juxtapose against these emblems of the strategy of death their strategies of civil disobedience and personal witness. They would sit in at the barbed-wire gates of the base as hostages for the security of "the people."

For forty-eight hours they sat in, with placards and songs, and slept in sleeping bags on the road in the rain; thirty-one times they were removed from the road only to retake their places. When, the demands of gentlemanly conduct having been met, the base commander ordered base traffic to move again, truckloads of guards were brought in. And, kicking at the vigillers, pulling their hair and forcibly dragging them off the road and throwing them into the ditch, the guards cleared the gates.

It was a scenario from the Fifties, a script assembled by an older generation from whom a personal and singular commitment to hold the state accountable in a time of general fear and helplessness was the essence of strategy: anything more aggressive or hostile smacked of violence, authoritarianism and brutishness. To large numbers of CUCNDers, however, the handshakes, prayers and limp bodies had begun, in their dreary repetition, to smack of futility and inadequacy. At best they made the protesters feel better and created something of a nuisance for the authorities, but at worst they deflected into pacifism and non-resistance the best rebellious instincts of the people.

What the Bomb represented was not just megadeath (although this would always and rightly be its most horrific significance) but also society's powerlessness to effect change. And it was precisely here that the student peace movement could begin to move beyond homilies of non-violence and human dignity. To subsume *all* social and political issues within the urgency to ban the Bomb was, CUCND argued, to succumb to mere strategies of survival.[1] The point was to ban the Bomb with the power of the people; to act against, to struggle with and to prevail over the power of the warlords where they held that power — in the "basic structures and attitudes"[2] of society.

For their inspiration CUCNDers took the instructions of the American civil rights movement, the Cuban revolution,* the community and tenant organizing of the American Students for a Democratic Society** and their own experiences in North Bay, Ontario, where they attempted to organize the community to reject the military foundation of the local economy. "Peace" was inseparable from social action, militarism from monopolistic power. If you were to live without war, you must first usurp those at the levers of the war machine.

Accordingly, 150 "peaceniks" assembled in Regina*** in December 1964 — CUCNDers, New Democratic Youth, Quakers, young Communists and unaffiliated youth looking for a base for their yearnings for a commitment — to bring the strands of people's diverse experience together in a coherent statement of radical purpose. In spite of the lack of ideological unanimity on the issues of the priority of disarmament, the efficacy of electoral politics, the role of decentralized organizational structures in "democracy" and the context of peace action, the group did coalesce around the felt need to *act*. To get out into the streets and the neighbourhoods and there to make the connection, in direct action and community organizing and the information of everyday life, between nuclear weapons, technology and powerlessness. As to which actions should be undertaken and for what purpose, it was further agreed that "all social issues were related" and so people with concerns from disarmament to education to psychotherapy "were all shown to be equally working for 'social change.'"[3]

They left Regina, having set up the Student Union for Peace Action. Completely independent of any other radical formation, SUPA grandly, even grandiosely, committed itself to the

---

*In the summer of 1964, forty-five Canadian students travelled to Cuba under the auspices of the Fair Play for Cuba Committee and were deeply impressed by the Cubans' pride of achievement in their anti-colonialist revolution.

**The Economic Research and Action Project (ERAP).

***". . . because it was in the middle of the country and because that's where the Regina Manifesto was written when the CCF was formed. It was an historic site."

panoramic aim of working toward the fundamental changes in institutions and attitudes that would abolish war, racism, poverty, undemocratic political and technological procedures, and bellicose and belligerent values.

> I got interested in SUPA because it was an attempt to change the world. There's no point in putting it narrower than that.

> I wanted the world to be just like SUPA, only bigger. Loving, warm, intelligent, bright, sensitive, non-exploitative, lovely. We were less concerned with the vision of what was going to happen than any other group I know. Which I think is very healthy. People would always say, "What vision of the world do you want? What are you building? Tell me what it is so I'll know if I like it or not." The answer would be, I think quite properly, "Help us build it the way you want it. And as we go along we'll build it."

SUPA was a movement, with all the spontaneity, flexibility and diffuseness that characterize movements and not organizations or parties. It was inevitably a movement: the medley of youth drawn to it, the nature of their commitment, and the principles of their conduct made it so.

There were four "types" of SUPA activist.* The "disillusioned liberals" hoped, through protestant action, to force bourgeois society to realize the liberal rhetoric concerning freedom, justice and equality. The "cultural anarchists" posed the student peace movement as a popular and democratic alternative to the authoritarian, hierarchical and exclusive structures of the rest of society. And the "red diaper babies," the people out of working-class or Communist or CCF backgrounds, familiar with the vocabulary of anti-capitalist perspectives, hoped to hook up the energy and ideas of the pacifist and civil rights mass movements with sympathetic elements in the left-wing parties and in the unions. And there were the scores of drifters, the ones who, profoundly moved by the courage and principled conduct of the ban-the-bombers, the civil rights workers and the

---

*Typology of Daniel Drache, political scientist.

Cuban revolutionaries, knew only that they too wanted to commit their body and their spirit to such honest battle. "We were like secular evangelists, people with commitment, faith, a set of beliefs. We were shock troops, running here, running there, throwing caution to the wind in the name of social change."

There was a glue that held such an ideological hodge-podge together. Called "commitment," "intensity" or "chutzpah," it was the capacity to serve heart and soul in a project: the full-time dedication to the group, the engagement with ideas and principles that changed your life, determining the household you lived in, the people you made love with, the ways in which you used your spare time, not to mention how you dressed, the books you read, the music that moved you. What you believed and how you lived were inseparable. Politics was not just a set of ideas and arguments; it was also a way of being, an instruction in how to live well and an invitation to determine values through action. ". . . many of the values of SUPA can only be validated if people begin to 'live the movement,' 'live their values.' "[4] And the first place in which the movement was to be lived was in SUPA itself.

Because the movement was committed to non-violence, democracy and self-determination, it proposed for itself equality of participation, non-hierarchical structures and open-ended objectives. At one level this meant, for instance, that there never was a formal SUPA membership — it was a mailing list, it was whoever put in some time at the Gestetner or on a project — and there never was more than a shoestring budget, haphazardly administered: staff salaries of twenty-five dollars a week, unpaid telephone bills, people prodded to write something, get it down, run it off, buttons and bumper stickers for sale, ten cents, please, for "Scarce Resources: The Dynamics of American Imperialism" by Heather Deans.*

At another level, SUPA was "lived" in its meetings. "It was a generation that would rather talk than read. Instead of writing things, we discussed them. At meetings, meetings, councils,

---

*SUPA's Research, Information and Publications Project, which put out research papers and reprinted pamphlets, was a major fund raiser.

conferences, meetings." Two principles prevailed: participatory democracy and consensus (adapted from the Quakers' "sense of the meeting" and from the practice of the civil rights movement). These principles allowed participants an *experience* that was the opposite of their experience in the larger society, where they were intimidated and disregarded. Here in the movement meeting they were encouraged to speak openly about feelings as well as ideas. There were no rules of order. Rather than take votes, the group would discuss until there was unanimity or consensus of thought so that a decision taken would reflect the feeling and idea of every person present. There were no designated leaders, for leadership means authority and authority means people with a vested interest in maintaining their power over others. "The notion that any one bunch of people can always have correct ideas is mad. It doesn't happen in real life so why should it have happened in SUPA?"

These were the principles. In practice, however, they were distorted. The rhetoric of absolute equality of participation obscured the fact that some people were more articulate, more self-assertive and more socially adept than others and so were able, through manipulation of group dynamics and through striking political and personal alliances with other "high-powered" members, to assume leadership in all but name. And, of course, because the group was held to be structureless, it became impossible for aggrieved individuals to appeal to any structure or apparatus or office for redress: "There wasn't any place you could go to draw up a resolution, say, to have the rascals thrown out." People would drift away or fall into glum reserve at the point they could see no way to influence the decision of the *de facto* leadership.

As for consensus, this arduous process, requiring great patience and tolerance, of "getting the sense of the meeting" was sometimes bypassed by the "heavies" who would meet at parties, say, come to an agreement among themselves and then later at the meetings "proceed to ram their decisions down everybody else's throats."

The process was not always so abusive, but it was bewildering and hurtful and alienating often enough to undermine in the rank and file of SUPA supporters their faith in the rectitude of movement praxis.

There were tensions, too, among chapters. In spite of the autonomy of SUPA chapters (yet another movement characteristic) there was still a feeling among the Saskatchewan members that Toronto was high-handed and arrogant and full of self-importance ("They'd come out to see us, thinking they would 'organize' us") quite unwarranted by the facts. Relative to its population, Saskatchewan boasted more SUPA adherents than Toronto. Furthermore, because so many of them had come out of CCF or union homes, they saw themselves, in contrast to the Torontonians, as rooted in their community and naturally as continuous with it, and did not see SUPA as a creature of their generation alone. "The Torontonians seemed to be just skilled organizers without a base." The Montrealers, grouped around *Our Generation*, looked askance at the style of the "national office" in Toronto, at the people going off in all directions with no more complex questions to ask than, "Is there energy here? Commitment and intensity?" What the Montrealers asked was, "What is the relationship of one action to another? How is an action chosen? Is it a correct action?" It was, in fact, the combined pressure of the Saskatchewan and Montreal groups, dating back to CUCND, that "decentralized" the movement and enhanced its democratic ethos.[5]

In March 1965 thousands of civil rights demonstrators twice tried to march the fifty-four miles from Selma, Alabama, to the state capital in Montgomery in support of black voting rights. Twice they were turned back; there were some who died, beaten back by the nightsticks and tear gas of the state troopers. Over the next few days hundreds and hundreds more demonstrators rallied in Selma to demand an end to the violence. On March 21 three thousand people marched out again from Selma; accompanied by federal troops, they reached Montgomery four days later, singing "We Shall Overcome."

SUPA, with members of its own who had been in the South with the Student Non-Violent Co-ordinating Committee (SNCC), put out the word in Toronto: the news from Selma is appalling, get down to the U.S. consulate and sit in. And they did, for a week, at first a handful with the press looking on. But when the *Globe and Mail* ran a picture of young protesters being ejected from the consular grounds as they attempted to present a petition, hundreds more demonstrators "started coming out of the woodwork" to sit in too. All kinds of people, but most especially university and high school students, who had, before Selma, never dreamed they would do something like this: sitting on the sidewalk of University Avenue, huddling under blankets, singing their hearts out,* listening raptly to civil rights workers who had been "there," and charging the doors of the U.S. consulate right under the noses of the mounted police. And still more people came. So this was the movement.

The demonstration galvanized SUPA. Suddenly they were responsible for the well-being and the education of a thousand people, and they were scared. How many of these sitters-in, they wondered, had been trained in non-violent civil disobedience? They sat down with them, explained the philosophy, described the tactics; they took them by the carloads to the Student Christian Movement (SCM) office and ran them through a "quick session on how to do a non-violent demonstration," returned them to the sit-in, and picked up another carload.

Back at the SUPA office, a law student was delegated to be the "administration."

It followed as the night the day that there had to be an administrator, and that was me because I was in law. But really I was just hopeless. There I was sitting in the office coordinating phones and food and blankets and donations. People brought in all kinds of stuff; they brought chickens and bought hamburgers for us — it was quite dramatic. It really captured the entire city. I was totally inadequate in the job, and the guy who set up Rochdale College later, Howard Adelman, walked in one day, about the fifth day that I'd been sitting there, struggling out of this mountain of paperwork and junk and empty hamburger packages, and he walked in and said, "Who's the adminis-

*They sang "We Shall Overcome," the anthem of the civil rights movement; some, more leftist than civil libertarian, sang "We Shall Overthrow."

trator?" I said, "I am, who the hell are you?" He said, "I'm Howard Adelman and I'm going to clean this place up." So he walked in and he just took over. He had been an administrator for years; he had run corporations and done all kinds of stuff. Here I am on a mountain of junk with clothing and bedding in one corner and hamburgers in another. It was just pathetic. He sat down and did what I now know an administrator does. He put together a task force of twenty people to clean the office up, which was step one — it was just that basic. Step two was to prepare flow charts and step three was to start delegating.

Some SUPA people were up in Ottawa attempting to lobby the government, put pressure on it to "take a stand"; others were on the phone with SNCC activist Stokely Carmichael, getting from him the stories out of Selma that SUPA then released to the Toronto press where it was picked up by the American press ("There was a blackout of news in the U.S. itself so we felt, in the SUPA office, that we were right there, in the centre of the world"); and others hosted the black kids from the South who came to check things out, Rennie Davis of SDS and people from ERAP of the American north-east.

Right in the heat of the thing Davis came up and gave a talk in our Peace House. It felt like the revolution was finally here, what with all the people out in the street. Davis told everybody to quit school. He said we were just in training for the system, so if we were really serious we should get out of school. A number of people proceeded to renounce school right there on the spot. It was like a conversion experience. . . . The movement fever had caught.

Immediately following upon the sit-in, supporters of SNCC in Toronto (among them were several SUPA people) set up an office and staff right next to the SUPA office and called themselves Canadian Friends of SNCC. They channelled down to SNCC in the South the money that had come in as donations from Canadians; they wrote letters to make contact with any Canadians working in the South and passed their stories on to the press; they sponsored benefit concerts; they put out a newsletter in which they "anthologized" the news

from the civil rights movement and reprinted letters received by
the office from Canadian civil rights workers.

They dispatched Rocky Jones to work among blacks in
Nova Scotia ("We sent him down without any money. I think
he must have eventually given up on us") and sat through
interminable meetings.

> The meetings tended to go on and on and on for hours and
> hours and hours, which was all right for me but a little
> difficult on the people who had to go to work in the
> morning. The theme of these meetings was what to do with
> this tremendous, huge mass of people who had foregathered
> as a result of the Selma sit-in. There were those, who we
> called Trots — this was probably unfair, because our
> definition of Trotskyism was quite sweeping in those days
> — who wanted to recruit these masses of people into union
> work and socialist types of activity. But we thought that the
> purpose of the organization was to support the people in
> the South, period. We thought we were responsible to a
> group of people in Alabama, say, who in fact didn't even
> know we existed.

There was an uneasy tension between the two offices:
SNCC and SUPA. SNCC had all the glory and all the
excitement of Selma attached to it, while SUPA was seen to
be simply plodding along in the unglamorous and, to some,
less-than-radical pursuit of Canadian social issues. What were
data on the lives of native people, stuck away on reservations
far from the gluttonous maw of the media, compared with the
spectacular scenarios of poor blacks set upon by dogs, two feet
from a camera? SNCC people would wander into the SUPA
office, "laying trips of all kinds." "What are you doing at that
desk? You're not really people, you don't have any heart.
You're just typewriters." A year later Stokely Carmichael
assumed chairmanship of SNCC, expelled its white activists,
and in Toronto "radicalism" was once again the charge of
SUPA, for better or worse. The fevered novices would have to
engage themselves with Canada, or not at all.

When SUPA broke with the single-issue campaign for
nuclear disarmament, it had assigned itself the task of looking

into the roots of war, which is to say, had assigned itself social analysis. There was a tendency in the first year of its activity to draw this analysis in very broad strokes, as though SUPA inhabited a meta-society in which the categories of action, violence, class and power applied not to any particular social place but to all places. SUPA was in the world, among people, alongside communities, working for social change. Where? Here. Where is here? Anywhere. SUPA defined the Cold War as the "central problem"[6] of the age and envisioned a Canadian foreign policy of non-alignment. SUPA prescribed vigils, demonstrations, sit-ins and sit-downs as the action of dissidence. SUPA sought new answers for the new age, declaring national loyalties to be outmoded. SUPA called for the creation of "unions of people" as a new form of political grouping. Nevertheless, for all SUPA's gaseous abstractions of "policy" from international economic relations, of the "new age" from anti-colonialist revolution and of the "people' from cleavages of class, sex and race, its vision of harmony, unity and peace did contain an explicit critique of capitalist society and did postulate the means by which this society might be subverted.

According to the social analysis of the movement at mid-decade, post-war technological society has developed along lines of increasingly monolithic structures — the state, the military and police, big business, the university, the unions — that concentrate power and authority and wealth in the hands of an inaccessible elite. This is a dangerous situation. "The threat of World War III cannot be separated from the trend towards centralized undemocratic decision-making, both political and technological, nor from the restrictions imposed on civil and academic freedom, as these are inexorably related to the growth of the war-fare state."[7] The people who pay most heavily for this arrangement are those who can least afford it — the poor, the dispossessed, the helpless — who must pay in the coin of their poverty, their lack of status, their powerlessness.

Electoral politics are an illusion of popular participation in decision making. "Despite all our glorification of democracy in Canada, the real centres of power remain far out of the reach of the electors and remain intact and totally undisturbed by elections no matter who is elected."[8] Liberals and Conservatives come and go but the directors of the Bank of Montreal, the CPR, General Foods and McGill University are with us forever: they cannot be dislodged at the ballot box. Conclusion: a society of materially comfortable, self-determining and fearless people is unrealizable in the present socio-economic and political system. "Therefore SUPA is dedicated to a revolution which would create in Canada a new and self-directing order."[9]

What, then, is to be done? If the "system" is centrist, elitist, inaccessible and violent, then the "revolution" must be populist, democratic, non-violent and inclusive. It must come from the grass roots, that place where the people are; as demoralized, apathetic and despairing as they may be, the extent of their hopelessness is the measure of their dissaffection.

Poor people, Indians, blacks, Doukhobors — these have not been assimilated into the economy or value system of the mainstream society but are, in fact, its detritus, the debris of urbanization, homogenization and industrialization. In their life-styles and values and attitudes and self-images is the crack in the "system" in which the young activists can insert themselves. Chipping away with the tools of participatory democracy, community organizing and non-violent confrontation, activists would eventually widen that crack into a great, gaping hole through which the revolutionary multitude would step, reversing the old order in the path of their forward movement.

It was very much to the point that *students* would undertake this organizing function, for they are critically situated in modern social relations. Economically dependent, patronized by the university administration, passively absorbing the corporatist world view of the intellectual body politic, students, like the dispossessed, lack self-determination. Unlike them, however, they are temporarily members of a critical community wherein they may learn skills of potentially liberating value.[10]

Addressing the question of the relationship between the university and social change, SDS had instructed that a "new left"* must start "controversy across the land."[11] SUPA agreed. From the campus would radiate ideas and proposals critical of social and political "inadequacies."[12] From the campus into the community would come the bearers of perturbing news, and of scenarios of emancipation.

Summer 1965. High on the success of the Selma sit-in, hearts and minds on fire with the idea of democracy and the possibility of community, confidently equipped with the skills of non-violent action and consensus decision making, SUPA prepared to do work in its own backyard.

As to the precisely correct approach to community organizing, this, like so much else in the movement, was up for grabs. The argument went back and forth between those who would limit the approach to "enablingship," to bringing people together without coercion and without interference in their perceptions, and those who called for a more active "leadership," a leading of people up against the power structure with the tools of analysis and agitation. Nor was there anything structurally fixed about the SUPA community-organizing projects. Other than sponsoring them, doing a lot of fund raising and giving moral support, the national office steered clear of any kind of executive direction of the projects. It was up to the field-workers to find their own funds, work out their own methodology, make their own mistakes and score their own successes. It was important that the field-workers not only seem to be but in fact be independent of any bureaucratic control. SUPA activists, it must be clear, were neither missionaries nor social workers.

As for the field-workers, there was no unanimity of values among them either, beyond the agreement that "peace cannot be imposed from the top. That was understood." Further than that was every position from "confronting capitalism" to "equalizing opportunity" to "helping the poor Indians," reflecting the diversity of experience of people in Saskatchewan, say, who had cut their teeth in the co-op or medicare movements and the people of Toronto, say, who had gone straight from their middle-class homes to university to the slums of Kingston.

And so off they went. A bunch, on the Student Neestow Partnership Project in Saskatchewan, to Indian reservations

---

*As far as I can tell, this is the first reference to a "new left" in the literature of the period (1962). It would cease to be a generic term only later as *the* new left.

and Métis settlements, to "do something about" the appalling poverty and demoralization of these communities. Off they went, nine project workers, mainly but not exclusively from Saskatchewan, to live in tents or sleep on floors, wash clothes, milk cows, bake bannock, chop firewood, and blister and fester alongside their constituents; to sit in kitchens drinking tea and waiting for something to happen. What happened was that in the age-old manner of such visitations from white folks, the native people kept their silence. What happened was that field-workers were snared in webs of rumours (that they were secret agents of the welfare department, for instance) and caught in the cross-fire between jealous families or involved in the competition of young native men for the status that accrued in hanging around white women. The native culture they had idealized as a deeply rooted resistance to the barbarity and crassness of their own seemed rather a culture of "passivity," "submissiveness" and "utter impoverishment"; the social action they had dreamed of taking now seemed an unconscionable intrusion into a closed and self-protective community. "All power is white power. What am I doing here with my vocabulary of participation and facilitation? What do I know beyond my outrage and my anguish?" This they did take away with them: an insight into the colonialism of the white bureaucracy enmeshing native lives and an utter contempt of the liberal rhetoric of democracy.

On the Kootenays Project they went, eight of them, driving from Ontario to Castlegar and Krestova and Ootoshenie, to the communities of the Doukhobors, the quintessential pacifists who understood the unity of social action and the inner life. In temporal action, in hospitality, pacifism and communalism, humanity may be rejoined in love. To the Doukhobors they went, hoping to persuade them to see themselves "as agents of social change, as allies of the poor, the Indians, the labour movement, the intellectuals."[13] They vigilled together on Hiroshima Day, ate together, planted gardens together. That was fine as far as it went. But it did not go much further than the old people. Young Doukhobors, the SUPA activists discovered to their chagrin, were educated in public schools and employed at the pulp and paper mills; were taking out loans for a car and getting loaded every second night at the bar, unregretfully discarding Doukhoborism just at the point when the young "Anglos" from outside were picking it up, like the dollar that falls out of somebody's pocket in the parking lot.

"Finally we want to emphasize that it very soon became clear to us that a project of this kind cannot be terminated after a summer."[14] They never went back.

Twelve, mainly from Queen's University, were assigned to Kingston, to the north end among the poor working-class and welfare families. They moved into two big, old houses (our place is at the bottom, as ordinary people in a neighbourhood, eschewing privilege, and clearing out a space where people can take a stand) and knocked on doors: Hello, can I come in? I'm from the Kingston Community Project. At the kitchen table, over cups of coffee, and weaving in and out of chores and squalling children, came the stories: complaints about the housing, grievances against the landlord, fears for their children's safety, worries about the boyfriend, the police, the food budget, the heating bill. Would they come to a meeting? Some would never. Others, visited again and again, the conversation dribbling off into gossip and baby talk, said yes, they might. The meeting: a handful of tenants, a row of SUPA field-workers. SUPA wrote up a petition, SUPA circulated it, SUPA organized a tenants' council, SUPA did all the talking in a confrontation with a landlord (who threatened to evict his tenants unless they apologized).

This was very discouraging. The project workers weren't supposed to be bloody *social* workers, do this, do that, tell me, tell me, they were "enablers," working *alongside* people to collectively, collaboratively, figure out how to fight city hall and the landlord. Gradually it dawned on the project workers that to the residents they looked, acted and sounded like the middle-class interlopers they were ("Maybe we should all have got jobs in the area"), asking a lot of questions — here's another survey, so smart, so confident, they must be in charge.

If only they knew. Back at the houses where the project workers lived there was much confusion and despondency.

We started out with a rule that men couldn't sleep at the women's house or vice versa but that broke down. Then we all began to eat at the one big house. There were twelve people on the project and we had forty dollars a week to feed people. We were really into suffering. We ate incredibly bad meals. We were into some kind of Christian moral fervour although we wouldn't have called it that. Everybody was supposed to have a part-time job and pool all their money, and that was what was going to go to people's tuitions the next year because nobody was going to have a summer job that would earn them enough money for their tuition. All this money was to be pooled and then divided up. So I got a job, this real shit job, working from ten at night to two in the morning in this really, really horrible restaurant and I would work all day on the project and Thursday, Friday, Saturday and Sunday nights at the Tropicana Restaurant. Oh, it was awful. And I pooled all my money. All my tip money, everything. I remember a meeting in which I thought I should be allowed to keep my tip money and was told, "No, it's got to all be pooled." Now some of the people never did get jobs and others never did pool their money. I can remember being really angry because some of the men didn't do any work. Myself and two other women did virtually all the cooking. The men didn't do any of the housework and the place was always a mess. They would come over for dinner and would sometimes do the dishes, but badly. People were getting colds all the time so another woman and I said, "We've got to start putting Javex in the rinse water," and we were accused of being middle class because, after all, poor people had colds all the time.

Ironies in triplicate. Tenants intimidated by the cleverness of the field-workers, the field-workers by the power of their own project "leader," and the project itself by the superiority with which they endowed their model, the SDS ERAP projects. (Fourth irony: ERAP in turn was an adaptation of community-organizing strategies of SNCC in the South.) By the time that the idea of community organizing had arrived in Montreal

Street in Kingston, it had travelled a circuitous, not to say tormented, political and psychological, route indeed.

During the project Tom Hayden came and talked about what ERAP was doing in Newark. Newark was our model, our idea of heaven, of what we could do. We were so caught up in Tom's charisma that it never occurred to us that our situation was different, that there is no "ghetto" in Kingston, that Kingston is not an industrial city, that poverty in Kingston has its own very peculiar generation, that there weren't high-rise tenements in Kingston where rent strikes could be carried off with a lot of punch. We never analysed where we were. Newark was like a grid we laid on top of Kingston's north end and it was supposed to work the same way.

Of course it didn't work. And they paid for it with depression, self-deprecation and guilt; with exhaustion and bewilderment; with a terrible feeling of being torn between listening more closely to what their neighbours had to say (even when it didn't sound very radical) and to the directives of the "leader" who had his own agenda; with the realization that "we were weekend organizers."

The field-workers went back to school. Five full-time organizers (three ex-students and two housewives) took over and "cleaned it up." Months later they pulled off ATAK (Association for Tenants' Action, Kingston) and voted a member onto city council. Weekend organizers they were not.

The summer-project field-workers gathered at St. Calixte, Quebec, for SUPA's Fall Institute. They came bedraggled, exhausted, hungry, bursting with stories and with the need to purge their frustration and sense of failure. But they came high and hearty, too, with every moment that had been comradely and revelatory and creative. "I cannot tell you what kind of an experience it was." And here in their conversations, quiet and confessionlike, extravagant and prolix, in the sunshine by the water and in the basement with beer and instant coffee, in the meetings looking for consensus, crawling hand over foot to an agreement, a myth about SUPA was born. Yes, there had been very bad times in the community projects, but these were washed away by this coming together of comrades to build something out of the beginnings, this finding "in the truly human and basic things a real opening to communication and trust"[15] — ain't gonna let nobody turn me around, turn me around — and so on, ten days of this, "dignity," "human potential," "liberation,""change," "revolution" and so on.

The myth was that SUPA had just begun to construct itself as *the* new left movement of social change and passionate commitment. The fact was that already at St. Calixte, in 1965, were the undercurrents of its collapse a mere two years later.

Present at the meetings were observers from the Company of Young Canadians (CYC), the government-created and government-funded youth corps, who were casting about for a constituency.* "They floated in on the excitement of our meeting. They said that CYC believed in community organizing and had government backing for it. They said we could not afford not to join them." Those SUPA activists who were confident of their ability not only to sustain the enthusiasm and commitment of that summer but to deepen and enrich it repudiated CYC, saying that a government agency could not make the revolution. But others were tempted. CYC had money, it offered salaried jobs and consultants' fees and all the

---

*By an Act of Parliament in 1966, the Company of Young Canadians was established as an independent Crown corporation to be governed by a council of fifteen. Ten of these councillors were to be elected by the volunteer field-workers and the rest appointed by government. In fact, a provisional council, all government appointees, governed the CYC until 1969. In the words from the Speech from the Throne, through the CYC the "energies and talents of youth can be enlisted in projects for economic and social development in Canada and abroad."[16] The example of President Kennedy's Youth Corps was very much in Prime Minister Pearson's mind. Unfortunately, during its first years of operation, the CYC was the subject of numerous disputes regarding the administrative role of the volunteers, the top-heaviness of its bureaucracy, the inaccessibility and irresponsibility of some of its staff, and the fact that in 1967 two CYC volunteers were discovered at an anti-war demonstration! By the early Seventies, several CYC staffers had become civil servants in Health and Welfare, Manpower, Secretary of State, the CBC and Information Canada. In 1975, CYC, along with other community-action projects funded by government, was closed down.

accoutrements of a real office, and it had lots of publicity. When SUPA's report on the summer projects was compiled with CYC money for the CYC, it was the beginning of the end.

Present also were activists who saw in the general euphoria a substitute for analysis, in the niceties of the democratic process an evasion of a critique of the decisions disgorged by that process, and in the fetishism of participatory democracy and consensus a dreamy side-trip away from the hard questions of program.

> I can remember Jim Laxer dropping in and saying, "This is either the greatest thing that ever happened or the biggest crock of shit that ever was." I can remember Dimitri [Roussopoulos] looking over a group of apple-cheeked young idealists and saying, "Let's not forget that the brain is also part of the human anatomy." I can remember somebody-or-other from the U.S. saying, "I would assess, from this meeting, that this outfit has about a year to go."

It was downhill from St. Calixte. As SUPA fell upon hard times, as funding sources for projects dried up, as CYC plucked off its stalwarts one by one, breeding suspicions and paranoia,* and as people cracked under the strain of holding down jobs *and* community organizing, SUPA began to turn around and around and in on itself, looking for the idea that would save it.

Saskatoon conference, December 1965, freezing on the hard, wooden benches in the basement of a Unitarian church. The excitement of the summer dissipated in worry and anxiety and doubt. How can a middle-class kid sink deep enough roots in a community to break through the suspicion and narrow self-interest of Indians, blacks and workers? Maybe community organizing wasn't, after all, supportive of "basic revolutionary change," whatever that was? Why are the projects falling apart? Are they just artless patch-up jobs on situations of gross social dislocation, the proportions of which were beyond the calculations of an "enabler?" What's SUPA

---

*A false rumour that one political "heavy" had taken a CYC job caused *Our Generation* to cancel publication of an article he had written on the CYC called "Cash In or Drop Out."

for anyway? Newsletters, reprints, literature, tables, study sessions. Big deal.

Waterloo conference, December 1966. "Waterloo, like it or not, was an ideological conference."[17] Burned out or stunned or "lost in the field," many felt that community organizing was bankrupt. Reluctant to make yet another leap of faith into mid-air, the rank and file of SUPA activists called for an effort to "clarify ideology, policy, program and structure. That is, where, how and with whom to work in this culture. Leave us not cathart again. Leave us do some work."[18] In the workshop on class analysis: had or had not the labour movement "sold out?" Paul Goodman's session: an impatience with his courteous counter-communities of self-education.* A plenary on organizing the middle class: revolutionary "cadres" should be prepared among students, professionals and white-collar workers. An open caucus: SUPA must outgrow its apolitical approaches.[19]

Gone, the heartfelt themes of non-violence and world peace, the giddy hopefulness of organizing the communities of the dispossessed, the intense scrutiny of procedures. In their place, a Draft Manifesto Committee was charged with coming up with a "statement of aims, to articulate a new left ideology, to offer the youth of this country a political manifesto."[20] It never did get written: there was no "consensus."

Ideology: ideas at the basis of some economic or political theory or system; also "visionary speculation." In both senses, SUPA had an ideology, in spite of the best efforts of some of its members to resist systematizing their ideas, to resist "labels" and to value their practical experience over their ruminations. For all that, everything SUPA people did, from their projects among the dispossessed to sitting in at the American consulate to writing papers on student syndicalism, contained an "implicit definition of reality, a view of human nature and deep convictions of right and wrong."[21] It remained to make them explicit.

"SUPA is at present an ethical movement in search of

---

*Goodman was heard muttering, as he left the conference, that compared to the American movement there was an awful lot of "Marxism" among the Canadians.

analysis."[22] That the search was often halting and fruitless was a measure of the movement's discontinuity with the body of socialist thought of the old left. There were no ideological givens; one began only with the givens of one's political experience and from that extracted an idea of what was going on. Those widely read in socialist literature were exceptional, and those who had grown up in socialist milieux were by no means unaffected by the virulent anti-communism of the Cold War period and by Budapest, 1956, and the revelations of Stalinist horrors. One read *The Communist Manifesto* in an undergraduate political science course but otherwise regarded Marxism as "irrelevant" to the modern world. As too abstract or too theoretical or too programmatic. As austere and anti-people. Rather one read C.Wright Mills, Paul Goodman and George Grant, in whose studies of power, disclosures of social absurdities, and forebodings about the dissolution of the Canadian nation in technological "homogenization," respectively, the movement heard resonances of their own inchoate yearnings and deep dissatisfactions that the vocabulary and categories of Marxism did not evoke. "The word 'radical' meant a great deal to us because it had a kind of generic excellence. It meant we were determined to go to the root of understanding the crisis of our time."

This meant, for instance, that in regard to the revolutionary role of the working class SUPA disregarded the accumulated wisdom on the subject and postulated instead the revolutionary potential of the poor, the coloured, the anti-social. Here with the irremediably alienated an alliance could be struck — and not with a working class that had seemingly assimilated the acquisitive, selfish and licentious values of the middle class.

This meant, too, re-evaluating the role of the CCF-NDP — for, whatever it had been in its glory days of organizing the farmers and "progressives" in resistance to the abuses of capitalism, it was now a bureaucratic and hierarchical party that distributed authority from the top down, shamelessly neglected the grass-roots supporters* and avoided any head-on

---

*The Saskatchewan NDP government lost the 1964 election to the Liberals in part because "many of us had seen the NDP 'sell out' the

challenge to the capitalist *status quo*. How was it possible, asked the new left, that the parliamentary process and welfare statism could ever incite the revolution? How was it possible, as "revolutionaries," not to be down among the people, taking the measure of consciousness and opposition from the data of everyday life? From there one could see their pacification at the hands of social democracy. "If the NDP continues to move toward mainstream politics, as sure as anything the need for a new radical people's party will develop in this country."[23]

And it was precisely in response to this need that some in SUPA, by 1967, impatient with the movement's "looseness," its haphazard program and analysis after the fact, demanded that at the forthcoming conference in Goderich, Ontario, "ideology" be discussed and related to "programmatic activity."[24] To tighten up the slack in new left thinking, a coherent and scientific ideological discipline was required, something like Marxism, for example. "We cannot improve on *The Communist Manifesto* in . . . the economic analysis of our society."[25] They would not yet call themselves Marxists, but they were at least prepared to acknowledge that the hundred-year-old socialist idea could teach them a thing or two about where they lived and how to go forward out of the "realms of necessity."

The Goderich conference, September 1967. It was the last SUPA conference. Where there had been a couple of hundred at earlier conferences, here there were forty; it seemed that those who had joined up with CYC stayed away. And by the end of the week those forty were no longer a union, for peace action or anything else. The glue that had held the disparate elements of SUPA together had dried up and the elements fell away from each other under the pressure of "ideology."

Ideology: was Marx "correct" and should SUPA become a Marxist organization; could one live as a petit bourgeois and be radical; wasn't it time to have a dues-paying membership and a national board answerable to members; was there not a "new working class" taking shape under modern capitalism, and

community clinic movement in its backroom deals with the doctors in the medicare crisis."

could it not be radicalized; how much longer were the women of SUPA expected to tolerate the contradiction between the rhetoric of democracy and equality and their own second-class status in the group? There was no agreement. Here, finally, "consensus" would only have violated the discrepant convictions of movement radicals.*

Those who rejected Marxism and could not live with a SUPA transformed from an informal network into an "organization" quit. Those who could not wait for a male-dominated left to take up women's liberation quit. Of those remaining, twelve were named to the New Left Committee to "engage in ideological communication and other activities designed to further the New Left in Canada"[26] and to report back on what should be done next. The SUPA newsletter became the *New Left Committee Bulletin* for a couple of issues. But the committee itself was not heard from after that. SUPA: December 1964 to September 1967.

> The New Left, and SUPA, has reached the end of a particular phase. It can be described as the phase in which a small part of this generation attempted to break away from the politics it had grown up in; to act out its anger at the complacency and hypocrisy of society; to develop the basis of a politic that would fundamentally transform that society. In large measure, it has failed in this attempt...."[27]

Why, at the same time as the American SDS was consolidating itself as a national radical student organization, did SUPA fall apart? The comparison is not gratuitous — Canadian radicals made it all the time, for better or worse. To some, SUPA had been, unfortunately, the "major instrument for drawing American New Left ideas into Canada,"[28] an instrument, that is, of de-Canadianization. To others, however, these "American" ideas were no more influential than, say, the ideas of syndicalism

---

*"There were a whole lot of splits then. The Trots were getting heavy and there were the Hegelian phenomenologists and the hard-line Marxists. I remember one night at the NDY house when people were screaming, roaring, practically having fist fights over the issue of where we were politically. This was supposed to be a party."

and anarchism that flourished in Montreal, or the social democratic idea in Saskatchewan, or Maoism on the West Coast. Besides, there were SUPA members who were all too aware of the inadequacy of American radicalism. "Were Americans interested in Saskatchewan populism? Nyet. In the Québécois? Nyet. In the Maritimes? Nyet."* American radical analysis did not go very far, the Canadians discovered quickly enough, in explaining the Canadian particularities of Quebec and the native peoples, of regionalism and Prairie socialism. When it came down to confronting these features of their situation, the Canadians were on their own.

And on their own, at the end of 1967, they concluded their movement had largely failed to revolutionize Canadian society. Why? Because, said the New Left Committee which succeeded SUPA briefly, SUPA had failed to develop a coherent analysis of Canadian society. Mere "naive populism" and "radical sentiment" did not begin to get close to the heart of the matter — "the structure of modern capitalism and . . . its specific characteristics in Canada"[29] — with which they had to contend before they could proceed with a truly radical program.

We must, said the radicals, finally deal with who we are. And what we are is cultural amnesiacs, people deprived of a sense of our historical specificity, people incapable of defining Canada as something more than "some sort of" post-industrial society in which poverty and alienation "for some reason" still bedevil us and in which the working class has "somehow" been put out to pasture. "I would add," wrote Dimitri Roussopoulos in the SUPA newsletter at the end of 1966, "that . . . SUPA, for example, is an urban, middle-class youth group in a sophisticated colony, recently referred to as a branch-plant society. . . . We must repeat this description to ourselves until it fully sinks in, and we understand all of its implications."[30]

They had also to deal with the fact that, in rejecting the organized industrial working class as the most promising

*"SDS people used to come up to Toronto to rest. Tom Hayden came up and Carl Oglesby. Tom stayed with Clay [Ruby] a week and didn't say a word. He was overdosed, burned out; he came up to rest and never said one word to us."

agency of social change, SUPA was stuck with a group of social "marginals." Oppressed, these marginals surely were, deprived as they were of education, employment and organization, but they were also, as a result, demoralized, isolated from each other and far removed from any consequential place in the economy. "SUPA relying on the 'oppressed' for a power base was really a bunch of ephemeral petit bourgeois 'good guys' trying to nail Jello to a wall."

In terms of its own internal dynamics, SUPA was too often incapable of handling the psychological "baggage" people brought in with them. The ideal of the group was to put back together what the society had ripped apart: the personal and the political experience. The ideal was to create authentic community; but "to get to the point where one knows how to do this requires experimentation and trust and commitment, and often what happened was that one's initial attempts fell very short of the goal. For a lot of people this meant simple betrayal."

Betrayal. Feelings of hurt, feelings of rejection, feelings of inadequacy. Who am I and what am I doing here and why am I with these people and not those over there? Feeling *déclassé* and that the bridges had been burned on the road to getting back. Yet stuck here too in a morass of rivalry, jealousy, resentment: I feel put-down, I feel dumb, I feel unattractive, compared to so-and-so I'm a real loser. This is politics? "I don't think politics can be a place to do therapy, but we were mixing them up all the time. If you don't come to terms with that, a great deal of political arguments are simply a cover for personal pathology."

But the *coup de grace* was the intervention of CYC. Opacity of motivation, ideology and practice blurred the line between the function of CYC and SUPA, and as SUPA floundered many activists simply went over to CYC, thinking to continue there what SUPA had begun. They argued they would "radicalize" CYC and would put together a network of radicals working in "crucial constituencies" right across the country. Their critics, however, charged them with careerism and compromise. They said CYC's money was tainted and that the state was moving in to social sectors of the oppressed on the backs of movement idealists.

They went over. They became an agency of state. I can remember when CYC came out to Saskatchewan to court us: they picked us up in their big, beautiful van, took us to the hotel, fed us filet mignon and wine and asked us, would you like to work for us, we pay well, and blah, blah. We said, no, this is an attempt to co-opt us, it's crap, it's bullshit.

By the end of 1967, CYC had absorbed most of SUPA's Toronto-based leadership in staff or consultants jobs, had hired half its project workers into its own volunteer groups, and had linked up with most of SUPA's extant projects. By the end of 1967, SUPA was dead and the chance to mature politically was forfeited.

Those SUPA members who had not joined with CYC dispersed into the Canadian Union of Students,* local community organizing, magazine and newsletter publishing, the CBC, graduate school. Through them a radical critique of Canadian capitalist society was in fact disseminated right across the country and around them the new left would be re-formed.

The tasks of this second wave of the new left — the organization of a movement for an independent socialist Canada, and for an independent socialist Quebec — were already on the agenda, as it were. The war in Vietnam had shocked the peace movement out of its woolly aspirations for "international peace" and forced it to come to terms with the operations of American corporate capitalism in Canada as well as abroad.** The growth of nationalist and separatist movements in Quebec had forced a revision of the Canadian new left's historical antipathy to nationalism and the nation-state. ("How could we be nationalists in Quebec and internationalists in English Canada when everywhere was the same enemy?") By 1966 they had discovered the nationalist George Grant and had had a "passion for the nation" awakened; had read a working

---

*CUS was the national umbrella organization of English-Canadian university students' councils.
**See next chapter.

paper on the data of American control of the Canadian economy; and had sat through long, late and soul-searching meetings with the people from Montreal. They came to understand that in Quebec was a "subject people" organizing to take control of their own political, cultural and economic life: had this not been precisely the ideological justification for SUPA's activities, this right of a community to self-determination?

> . . . the anti-authoritarian current in the peace movement was one of its ways of finding its way to the Québécois, I think. . . . The capitalist world's youth, in Berkeley and Berlin wanted to wear shaggy clothes, smoke forbidden substances, eat natural food. They wanted these things because they wanted *to be themselves.* Well, the Québécois were also trying *to be themselves.*[31]

But first the new left would regroup on the campuses of the universities, refer again to the constituency from which it had extended itself, tendril-like, into the scattered communities of the dispossessed, and propose for itself the project it had assigned to those communities: power, its theory and its strategies.

"Even when we ourselves would be forced to call ourselves 'liberal,' we have retained a peculiar, almost unshakable will to be radical, not to compromise with power,"[32] For all of SUPA's inadequacies and failures and ill-conceived strategy and ill-fated programs, it had been a cathartic experience for its adherents, purging as it did the politics of the Cold War and the ideological hegemony of capitalism in North America. It was the beginning of the renewed debate in Canada on the nature of capitalism and imperialism, and never again would the social critics on the left be so politically and intellectually artless as they had been when they first, in indignation and in sorrow, walked back and forth in silent accusation at the gates of the warmongers' enterprises.

Nor would they ever be so exquisitely tenderhearted again. There was a period when, in their anxiety for rigour and discipline, they excoriated themselves for the liberalism and sentimentality of their first protest, but they need not have been so stern. In the morality of outrage and bearing witness, in the oaths of commitment, in the exuberance and excitement of conviction that this was a new age, that the ancient, abusive and ignominious order of illegitimate power was vulnerable,* in the candid need for a community, a place to feel at home with the first brothers and sisters of one's life, were some of the new left's finest moments. They need not have been ashamed for such passions.

"Actually," says a former SUPA activist, "we were a prophetic minority trying to call into being a mass movement." Until such time as the movement of the masses would roll over the landscape, crushing inequity, malfeasance and despair, the determination of a handful that life could be otherwise would be a reminder: where there's smoke, there's fire. Next time.

---

*"There was a very real feeling that something was going to happen. Any day. It felt as if one would be a fool to assume that nothing was going to happen. Nobody would have considered taking a five-year subscription to a magazine. It was pointless. You wouldn't get full value, you wouldn't get all your issues. We all lived very marginally because we expected society to change. We didn't save money or think about our futures very much and when we did we felt badly about it. Because it represented faintheartedness."

II

WAR IS GOOD BUSINESS, INVEST YOUR SON

This is the war story of a boy who grew up in Calgary, the toughest guy in his high school. Not that he'd been born that way. Time was he'd get his ass kicked by the bigger guys. Then he put a punching bag in the basement of his parents' house, went down there every night for two months, beating the hell out of that bag, freaking out his mother, but building up his body into a fighting machine. Proud of it he was, emerged proud and without fear, cleaned up his tormentors, went to California and two months later was a Screaming Eagle in the 101st Airborne in Fort Campbell, Kentucky. He had enlisted. Then he volunteered for Vietnam.

We had films and classes. They showed us a map of Vietnam, said Americans were there to stop Communist infiltration from the North and that the South had asked for help. There was a treaty the U.S. had signed — they were obliged to help. That's it.

Out of the 140 guys that went over [in 1966] two came back. I'll tell you how we were wasted. Dak To, for instance. We were coming down a ridge line and we ran into what we thought was a point. Just three or four guys. Our point ran into theirs. So we thought, okay, the thing to do is flank out and hit them from the sides and take them. We did that but the trouble was it was their point all right but behind them was a battalion, 640 or more of those guys and 140 of us. We locked horns. It was eight o'clock in the morning and we fought until eleven o'clock that night. I was a machine gunner and I melted three barrels on my machine gun that day. Literally dripped off. Got another barrel, screwed it on. I was crying, I couldn't even see who I was shooting. I just kept saying, "I don't want to die, I don't want to fucking die," and I'd start shooting again. I was pissed off. "You bastards, you're not taking me." We were surrounded. You couldn't run. All you could do was fight.

One of the things that always boosted our morale was knowing that if you ever got hit, you were going to get the hell out of there, the Angels of Mercy would come get you and you could count on going home.*

I helped put the wounded on the choppers. One was a friend of mine. We're throwing him into the chopper and he says, "Where's my boots?" I says, "Shit, don't worry about your boots, you're going home." He says, "I want my boots. Goddamn it, Craig," he says, "give me my fucking boots!" His legs had been blown off at the knees and I couldn't see why he was worrying about his boots. He says, "Goddamn it, my *feet* are still in them!" His feet were still in his boots and that's what he cared about. A hundred yards away, his useless, bloody feet.

I saw napalm used, gelatin gas. It was delivered by aircraft and dropped in a bomb. They'd bomb the area and it would spread out like a blanket. And everything it landed on went up in flames. Sometimes they'd spray it and it would adhere to everything. If it hit you your whole body would be blanketed with this jelly and just like that go up in flames.

We used white phosphorus, "whiskey papa," as a marking device. It was packed into big bullets and wherever they hit the ground they would burn, immensely burn, and send up clouds of white smoke. That stuff was deadly. Where it lands it consumes whatever is in its way. If you got a piece on your leg, it would eat the bone out without destroying the outside of the leg. But the bone will just melt away.

At first, the way I looked at what I was doing was that I was on a hunt. I did a lot of hunting when I was a kid and now I was finally tracking a prey that was worth something. The only thing I really worried about was I didn't want to die with my face in the mud. You can't imagine how muddy it was sometimes. In the Mekong Delta, in the rice

*Angels of Mercy: medical evacuation helicopters.

paddies, you'd be walking up to your waist in water and the mud would be past your knees. It was the river silt. It was pretty hard fighting in stuff like that.

There was grass that grew eight feet tall. We called it elephant grass. It grew wild in the meadows and the clearings and was very sharp. If you grabbed at it, it would cut your hand open. Ants were a real menace. They'd make their nests over the jungle trails. So you'd be walking through the jungle and all of a sudden, thirty, forty of these things would drop down on your back. They called it the three-minute strip. You had all this stuff on you, this backpack and your pistol belt and your harness that you held your backpack on with, and in three minutes you'd have it all off because in no time they could take chunks of meat right out of your body. That was the worst. Fire ants I hated the worst. A lot of the guys couldn't stand leeches. You got them when you waded through the rice paddies or waded across the rivers. Guys would pass out before they made it from one side to the other because they lost so much blood, if you can believe that.

We went into a village once and it seemed that it was deserted. But looking around we thought there's something wrong here. We looked a bit further and saw ants gathered in patches on the ground and you wonder what they're eating. You kind of know but you don't want to know. You look a little bit more and it was blood patches, dried blood, that the ants were eating. We thought, well, something took place here. We could see that a scuffle had taken place. It was maybe a village of thirty families, maybe forty, it's hard to tell. Thirty hooches, they call them, grass huts. We checked around some more. Finally one guy went over to the well. You don't usually drink out of the well because a lot of times they'll poison it before they pull out. This guy was just going to wash his face. He lowered the bucket and brought it up and it was red with blood. He said, "Come here you guys, I think I'm on to something." We took a hook, a meat hook almost, which was sometimes used for dragging the dead off the battlefield. You'd put a meat hook in their shoulder and then you could drag them a lot better to the chopper. So we put the meat hook on the well rope and sent it down there and pulled it up — part of a lady's body, arms cut off, legs cut off, head cut off. Her tits were cut off. We just kept digging around in the well and we pulled out half a dozen kids, half a dozen women and then we just threw them all back in. There were no men in that well. We guessed what had happened.

When I first went over, keeping alive was the most important thing. I didn't have any *feelings* one way or the other about fighting. I'd kill somebody because I was trained to kill. I don't know if you can understand that. Keeping alive was the most important thing. But after a couple of months I saw that my buddies were being wasted, I saw what was happening in the villages, and I started to hate. I *hated* the enemy. They were just like dogs, and I'd just as soon kill one of them as look at him. I killed and mutilated. I'd cut off their ears and wear them around my neck along with my dog tags.

Then one night something happened. We came upon three North Vietnamese sitting around a campfire getting stoned. They smoke a lot, those Vietnamese. They were sitting around a campfire and we killed all three of them before they even knew what hit them. They were just sitting there, these guys in the firelight, they're sitting around laughing and talking and *they were people* all of a sudden. They weren't just dogs anymore. That's when I started thinking, shit, just what the hell am I doing?

The thing that made it worse still was the attitude of the officers. Straight out of officer candidates' school. Really gung-ho. They're going to get a bunch of medals and make a lot of brownie points. You try to tell them, "Look, we're here to do a job and stay alive too and we know some things about that they don't teach you in school." But you're just a grunt, a private, and they're officers, and they don't go for it. One particular NCO, a sergeant, a coloured guy, was a real asshole. He was really bad. Getting a lot of guys killed is what he was doing. He was sending guys out when there was no need to send guys out ahead. He'd tell guys to move, when he knew that it was impossible, just to create a movement, just to get the enemy going so that he could see where they were at. He'd sacrifice guys' lives. Everybody talked about it and said we've got to get rid of him. So back in base camp, somebody wired a grenade to the guy's bunk, underneath his bed. You know how a bunk sags when you sit on it. The grenade was taped to one side and a wire was tightened across it and taped to the other side. The idea was when the sergeant sat down on the bunk, this would pull the pin out of the grenade and that would be it. The handle flies off and boom! Well, what happened was the guy he was rooming with went to mail call, picked up his mail from home, came back to the hooch — we slept in "hooches" — which we weren't expecting and instead of sitting down on his own bed sat on the sergeant's bed to read his letter. It was sickening. We wasted the wrong guy. There was an investigation but it was thought he did himself in. A lot of soldiers shot themselves so they could get sent home. Some even pulled the plug on themselves because they couldn't handle it anymore.

It got to the point where I didn't know what I was there for or why. I saw what the "dollar" was doing to the South Vietnamese — never mind what the Communists were doing. We were messing up that country for a dollar.

One day I'm in the jungle, the next day I'm in San Francisco. Out of the plane, onto the street. There was no parade for us. Just a couple of shrinks in white coats asking, "Did it bother you? Would you like to talk about it?" No, I didn't want to talk about it. I agreed with the anti-war demonstrators. All these kids saying they didn't want to go. I was right behind them. "Right on. Don't go." What had I accomplished in Vietnam? Not a goddamn thing. All the guys that had died over there had died for nothing.

Some vets joined the marches. Suddenly we weren't the army anymore. We were "the people" and the police and the National Guard were kicking us in the face. They had billy clubs and were beating us up. One day we were marching with candles, we were singing, "Give peace a chance," and they turned the firehoses on us — said we were a fire hazard — and sent us flying ten feet down the concrete.

There came a time I figured I had been fighting the wrong war. I came back to Canada. It was that, or buy an M-16 and hit up the police, one by one.

Not since Auschwitz had the word "genocide" resonated so expressively in North America. A whole people were the target of a total war as the American government and American army boasted of "bombing Vietnam back to the Stone Age." There were no half measures in this. On the one side were industrial and technological development, massively destructive weapons, and a society permanently riven with the antagonistic need for economic and ideological supremacy. On the other side was an entire population mobilized to fight a "people's war"; a whole society supported strategically and tactically the manoeuvres of the guerrillas, for the struggle was for the life of the nation itself. The only response possible to this militant unity of Vietnamese men, women and children was the liquidation of the people *in toto*. Genocide. "When a peasant falls in his rice paddy," spoke Jean-Paul Sartre to the International War Crimes Tribunal in 1967, "mowed down by a machine gun, every one of us is hit. The Vietnamese fight for all men and the American forces against all."[1]

The very concrete possibility that a people could be utterly devastated by the American war machine focussed the peace activists' heretofore generalized horror of war on the specific history of the Indochinese War. "War" now had a chronology, a place of operations, statistics, and its victims had a name. Canadian students began to familiarize themselves with Vietnam. They were to learn by heart.

With the decisive defeat of the French by the Viet Minh guerrillas at the garrison of Dien Bien Phu in 1954, and with the convening of a cease-fire conference in Geneva, it seemed that the last of the colonialists had been driven from Vietnam and the task of reuniting the northern and southern territories into a nation could be undertaken. The most important of the Geneva Agreements provided for the military withdrawal of the French to the south of, and the Viet Minh to the north of, the seventeenth parallel, for elections to be held within two years for a national government, and for the establishment of an International Control Commission (made up of India, Poland and Canada) that would supervise the implementation of the agreements. It was widely assumed that because the Viet Minh, at cease-fire, controlled half the country and more than 60 percent of the population, its representatives would win the forthcoming election. The United States, it was to be noted, did not sign the agreements.

That same year the provisional government of Ngo Dinh Diem, with U.S. backing, was installed in Saigon. In 1955 Diem proclaimed a republic in South Vietnam. From this point the great unravelling of peace began.

In 1956 Diem unilaterally renounced the Geneva provision for elections and reunification. He issued an ordinance providing for "all persons considered dangerous to national defence or collective security"[2] to be interned in concentration camps, and he set up kangaroo courts that summarily handed out death sentences for every manner of opposition. Fatefully, he replaced with his own appointees the elected local village chiefs and village councils. And, although he expropriated over a million acres of privately owned land, less than half was ever redistributed among the peasants. The rest was held by the government and sold to the highest bidder: 45 percent of the land remained in the hands of 2 percent of the landowners. Feared, hated, isolated from the 80 percent of the population that lived in the villages, the Diem regime spawned its own assassins.

In 1960 the South Vietnam Veterans of the Resistance Association* and a group of Buddhist and Catholic leaders called for resistance to the Diem regime. Guerrillas, chiefly ex-Viet Minh cadres, more or less systematically kidnapped and killed Diem's village officials. In December 1960 the National Liberation Front (NLF) of South Vietnam was proclaimed and its military arm, the Viet Cong, organized. The Vietnamese were at war again.

---

*Veterans of the anti-colonial wars against the French and Japanese.

It was about 1963 that the war in Vietnam sank into the consciousness of Canadian radicals. The escalation of U.S. military personnel (16,800 "advisors" in 1963), the suicidal protests of Buddhists (*monks,* for God's sake, setting themselves aflame), the "pacification" of NLF-controlled areas by the rounding up of peasants (*farmers,* imagine it, their pots and pans on their backs, ducks waddling at their feet) into fenced-in "strategic hamlets," guerrillas who struck without warning and disappeared facelessly back into the jungle (and for every thousand who were killed or captured, a thousand were recruited), finally the assassination of the tyrant Diem: there were instructions here in the nature of American power and the system that buttressed it. At home, against the righteous uprising of the blacks, squads of police and mobs of segregationists; in Vietnam, against the freedom-thirsty guerrillas and peasants, the U.S. Army.

If at first this was merely disturbing to the Canadian onlooker, it quickly became appalling. Between 1963 and 1968 civilian casualties approached 150,000 a year, American troops had increased to 464,000 and their dead to 19,670. The U.S. government was spending $4.2 billion and detonating 700,000 tons of explosives a month. And the only declaration of war that Congress had made was to ratify the Gulf of Tonkin Resolution.*

"It changed my life." For the twenty-year-old, with liberal fantasies of state-sponsored reform already dead in the dust of Dallas and the Bomarc missile base, Vietnam was a radicalizing rebirth. In magazine and newspaper articles, in television news reports, in pamphlets and speeches, the grievous catalogue of American infamy was a daily event. "Oh, my heart was hardened." And, later, the mind enflamed when it was understood that this was not so much America as imperialism letting loose its dogs of war.

---

*The resolution was declared in 1964 when two U.S. destroyers, ostensibly on intelligence patrol, were allegedly attacked without provocation. The facts that they were inside North Vietnamese territorial waters at the time and that the CIA had already made clandestine attacks on the North only came out much later.[3]

The war in Vietnam inspired fear, loathing and contempt. The president of the United States, who once had said he would not send "American boys" to do the dirty work of "Asian boys," now proclaimed his people would not be defeated, would not tire, would not withdraw. Against a Viet Cong commissar, who had come out of the peasantry, spoke their dialect and confronted their exploiters, the government of Saigon sent officers trained by the French, who spoke French, who during the first Indochinese war of liberation had stood on their aristocratic balconies watching the Viet Minh take on the French army. Small wonder the troops of the ARVN (Army of the Republic of South Vietnam) deserted (in 1965, 93,000 out of 600,000), refused commands and to the consternation of their American "advisors" left great gaping loopholes in battle through which the Viet Cong made their escape. Later, of course, at the press conferences, the American officers would claim "a great victory." "We have them in a trap and we're about to spring it," they said, while the Viet Cong were long gone and the ARVN were killing their own men by blind shelling.[4]

Inside the wire fence, the "pacified" village. Immediately outside its perimeters, a battalion of Viet Cong, cutting roads, ambushing convoys, overrunning outposts. In 1967, in national elections in South Vietnam, the government won an abysmal one-third of the vote, this in spite of having jailed or otherwise disbarred its opponents. Graft and bribery were widespread: the going rate for appointment to the police force was $250 and for an import-export license, 8¢ for every dollar of imports.[5] By 1964, 74 percent of South Vietnamese districts were delinquent in delivering their taxes to Saigon:[6] either they were not being collected, period, or they were disappearing into the maw of officials on the take.

The troops were not home by Christmas 1965, as every American had believed in that first optimistic glow, thinking Vietnam was a skirmish, easily and tidily wrapped up, the sort of thing the American army was good at, nor by Christmas 1966 — no, not for a decade of Christmases. Simply, the Vietnamese were indomitable. If the B-52 bombing raids did not wipe them out, then surely the napalm would, and then the flamethrower tanks, and the machine guns and grenades, and if the Viet Cong still survived, hiding perhaps in their underground burrows in the jungle, or just melting away into that thick and dark foliage, why then the army would simply bring in bulldozers and plow the whole thing down, scrape the earth clean of its jungle, and the VC would just have to find another hiding place. Which they did.

For the American soldier it quickly became a question of not going raving mad — forget the heroics — in this jungle war; of hanging on to even a shred of morale when it was clear the VC knew the territory and you did not, the VC planted the mines and you stepped on them, the VC picked the ambush and you walked into it.

You had to find your way of coping. There were those who mentally resigned from the army and signed up for their own war where you look after "your own ass first, then your buddy and fuck the mission,"[7] or who, blood-crazy and pressed against their breaking point, would not stop killing until the body count equalled the population count. Some learned how to "detach" themselves emotionally, to find a cool place in themselves from which they gave themselves orders and into which no grief or rage could enter. Some joined the anti-war movement in sympathy, wearing the black armbands of solidarity while on patrol or declaring their own private cease-fire with the enemy or signing a petition as did sixty-five men of Bravo Company, First Battalion, Twelfth Cavalry, First Cavalry Division, declaring they would not go out on suicidal night ambushes, orders or no orders.[8]

You had to cope too with being wounded, with that conviction that no wound was worse than yours, not even that "slab of meat" in the next bed, its arms and legs blown off by a booby trap, wildly thrashing its bleeding stumps and shrieking for help.[9] One way out of here was in the rubber bag to Saigon and, finally, home. "Be the first in your block," sang Country Joe, "to bring your boy home in a box."

But at home it was the pictures. On the quad, in the lobby, some group or other had a table, a booth, and there, fluttering in the breeze of passersby, were the colour photographs of war. The dead soldiers in long-shot, monstrously littering the plains of battle, devastated landscapes, the close-ups of GI's eyes, even in the shadow of their helmets drilling you with their terror — these images, as dreadful as they were, one had seen before from other wars. It was the children of Vietnam who blasted the parameters of sympathy.

They are skinny and barely clothed. They stand behind barbed wire, holding their baby brothers and sisters. They are orphans, asleep in the squalor of a camp. Their slender, perfect limbs have been shattered and blown off, their flesh gouged with shrapnel, their faces pitted, torn at, burned away, infested. In the hospitals, on muddy mats, they lie in their own blood, a hole as big as a fist in the back, a broken bottle shoved up the vagina, the hand melting away from the burning phosphorus, and die, their malnourished bodies incapable of resistance. They are weeping, they are staring into space, they are, unaccountably, even trying to smile.

Through to the mid-Sixties, the war in Vietnam was understood to be an American event, indeed, a quintessentially American event, the representation in bloody 3-D of the American character and American way-of-life. Vietnam was the Western movie writ large, the last frontier extended one more kilometer, production and consumerism played out in the most insatiable market of them all: war. Canadians clucked their tongues and shook their heads and wished Americans could be more reasonable in their politics, perhaps take a lesson or two from the Canadians, but, in the end, it was *their* problem.

Peace activists knew better. Analysing the root causes of war and researching the institutional basis of poverty, exploitation and social unrest, first as ban-the-bombers and then as community organizers, they had already understood how deeply implicated the Canadian state was in militarism and the war industries. Their reading had turned up a twenty-year-old record of Canadian-American collaboration in defence systems, from the Joint Board of Defence in 1947 to expenditures on the Pinetree and Dewline radar systems, the relinquishing of an independent foreign policy in favour of the "block politics" of NATO, the setting up of an integrated North American Air Defence system (NORAD) in the Fifties and the signing of the

Defence Sharing Agreement of 1959. This latter agreement was to figure sharply in the debates about the war in Vietnam for it provided for equal defence expenditures by each country in the other and for the dropping of "Buy American" requirements for American contractors. "For all purposes Canadian industry would be regarded as an extension of American, the logical accompaniment of a foreign policy which was but an extension of the American. The Department of Defence Production could set to work drumming up competitive bids by Canadian business, using the Canadian Commercial Corporation, a crown corporation dating back to 1946, as the go-between between the Pentagon and Canadian contributors."[10]

There's no business like war and the Canadian contractors cleaned up. The figures started to come out in 1966. Canadian Industries: exported to the U.S. small arms, rocket and cannon propellants, plastics and other explosives; Cyanamid Canada: artillery propellants for the U.S.; Dorothea Knitting Mills: green berets for the Special Forces in Vietnam; de Havilland Aircraft of Canada: the U.S. Army Caribou and Buffalo aircraft.[11] In 1967 Litton Systems (Canada) was awarded a six-million-dollar contract for weapons equipment for the F4 fighter aircraft, used extensively in Vietnam; Valcartier Industries, a three-million-dollar contract for ammunition; Canadian Acme Screw and Gear, a three-million-dollar contract for parts for 4.2-inch shells.[12] *Our Generation* reported that by 1966 U.S. defence expenditure in Canada amounted to $317 million, up from a paltry $25 million in 1964, contracted out to over six hundred Canadian (and Canadian subsidiary) companies.[13]

The "dirty little war" was ours too. We supplied it and we propped it up at home. In 1965 Prime Minister Pearson, in a speech at Temple University in Philadelphia, reassured his audience that "the government and great majority of the people of my country have supported whole-heartedly U.S. peace-keeping and peace-making policies in Vietnam,"[14] whatever those might be. In 1966 he agreed with the American position that Hanoi had been "unresponsive" to the idea of negotiations, dismissing the fact that the U.S. refused to negotiate with the NLF.[15] In 1967 Justice Minister Pierre Trudeau was convinced that "the imposition of an embargo on the export of military equipment to the U.S. [as had advised a group of University of Toronto professors]. . . would have far-reaching consequences that no Canadian government would contemplate with equanimity."[16] As indeed they did not.

Student newspapers uncovered the relationship between the Defence Research Board (an agency of the Department of National Defence) and the universities. Research funds from the DRB were channelled, in 1967, through 385 projects in forty universities across Canada. Among these projects was one to "investigate the influence of genetic change on the stability of airborne microbes," a problem in the functioning of biological weaponry, and another developed a more effective and powerful nerve gas than CS, which was already being used by the ton in Vietnam.[17]

But it was the revelations concerning the part Canada played on the International Control Commission that confirmed our government's duplicitous posture vis-à-vis the people of Vietnam. (Incredibly, in the midst of the military mayhem, the ICC was still charged with its function of supervising the implementation of the Geneva Agreements.) The *Montreal Star* charged the ICC's Canadian officers with "acting as informants for U.S. intelligence agencies," and the CBC claimed that an officer had passed along to the Americans valuable photographs of a bombing raid on the oil storage dumps near Hanoi.[18] In 1965 Hugh Campbell, who served on the ICC from 1961–63, admitted in a political science forum at the University of Victoria that he had received orders from his political superiors to "ignore" the delivery of aircraft and other war material to Saigon from the U.S., a flagrant violation of the Geneva Agreements.[19]

In 1964, U.S. Secretary of State Dean Rusk visited Ottawa. Ottawa agreed that its ICC delegate, Blair Seaborn, should "plan to spend much more time in Hanoi than have his predecessors," and in due course Seaborn went to Hanoi, bearing instructions from the Americans that an intransigent North Vietnam could expect only destruction. "At that point Seaborn had ceased to be a dispassionate intermediary. . . and had become a virtual spokeman for the American policy."[20] It was as much as Hanoi expected. "The Vietnamese people know that the Canadian government has always supported and tolerated the intensification of the armed aggression of the United States."[21]

O Canada. How was one to live within her? Like the young man in the David Lewis Stein story, lying on his bed and covering his face with a blanket, we tried at first to keep the "little brown men" of Vietnam at bay by pleading that there was nothing we could do for them, absolutely nothing.[22] Yet, like the narrator of Dennis Lee's *Civil Elegies,* we knew that "yank and gook and hogtown" were "linked in guilty genesis," we knew — it was in the newspapers — that we were fashioning "other men's napalm," we were "burning kids by proxy," we were abominable.[23] Like the American refugee worker in Ian Adams's article from Vietnam, the "good guy" in a tea shop watching a shuffling, horrid parade of mutilated women, children and old men outside the window, we also were surrounded by the silence of staring, accusing Vietnamese.[24]

There were two solutions. One was to attempt to exculpate the nation through personally assumed guilt, to breast-beat and pay penance in the coin of depression, self-disgust and nightmare. The other was to accept responsibility and fashion that into the tool of consciousness, analysis and resistance with the thousands of others who would just as soon hit the streets as sit in front of the television, weeping.

In 1965 seventy thousand people marched in Washington in an SDS rally against the war. Later, twelve thousand people participated in a Berkeley teach-in organized by the Vietnam Day Committee, and in front of the Pentagon, three Quaker pacifists burned themselves to death in symbolic solidarity with the immolated Vietnamese.

In 1966 three soldiers in Fort Hood, Texas, refused orders to ship out to Vietnam. SNCC denounced the war and gave encouragement to those who would resist the draft. Students began sit-ins at local draft boards, and the first conviction for draft-card burning was secured.

In 1967 the Spring Mobilization Against the War culminated in a 200,000-strong march in New York, a vigil at the Pentagon ended in violence, tear gas and arrests. Men and women stormed Selective Service offices, destroying records, refused to pay income tax and attacked politicians with balloons filled with blood and urine.

In 1968 Chicago police and National Guardsmen brutalized thousands in demonstrations organized by the National Mobilization Committee to End the War. Draft deferments for university graduate students were abolished. And veterans of the war in Vietnam held a peace march in San Francisco.

From the beginning, the concern of the Canadian anti-war movement was *to make the connection* between Canadian citizenship and the suffering of victims of war. In this global village of a world, no one was non-partisan, no one could climb down off the hook. As the delegates of the Voice of Women said to the leaders of the Canadian political parties:

> The Canadian government and people must accept the full implications of their claim to be a peace-making nation — an independent nation — and express openly their disapproval of the United States' actions in Vietnam. . . which are causing unimaginable suffering as well as violating the principles of the United Nations and the right of all peoples to self-determination.[25]

It was in this spirit that SUPA organized a protest vigil at the University of Toronto in the late spring of 1965, a silent ring of students and professors, staring sternly at Adlai Stevenson on his way to Convocation Hall to pick up an honorary degree. (Adlai Stevenson! erstwhile liberal, U.S. spokesman at the UN, apologist for the Bay of Pigs and for bombs over Hanoi!) Rather more aggressively, it was again SUPA that set up on campuses the tables layered with pamphlets and photographs documenting Vietnam (let no student later say s/he "didn't know" about the war) and ignored, in an act of "civil disobedience," the ban at the University of Alberta on "political booths."[26] In November SUPA arranged bus transportation down to Washington ("As citizens of the vast American economic and cultural Empire. . . we must travel to the heart of that Empire and we must protest")[27] for peace activists wishing to join the multitudes organized by SDS and the National Committee for a Sane Nuclear Policy. In Toronto, in Ottawa and in Regina, on Remembrance Day, SUPA members "vigilled" at the cenotaphs. Again that silent, accusing posture before the dead, for the benefit of the living.

But these events, as symbolically important as they were, were feeble in comparison with the coup that was the International Teach-In at the University of Toronto in October 1965. Backed by the university administration (indeed, President Claude Bissell was honorary chairman), faculty and student council, the guts of the thing were the organizing committee of professors and students who first met in June. (Among them were SUPA activists.) And while it was the consensus of the committee that a teach-in "might make possible a confrontation between speakers who would not meet together under any other auspices,"[28] it was also the hope and ambition of SUPA that it would be the place where the peace movement and the university would coalesce. For the teach-in was to be called "Revolution and Response," and in 1965 that meant only one thing to the peace activists: Vietnamese social revolution and American military response.

It was a phenomenon, this teach-in. Held at the university ice rink, it drew 4,000 students, 120 journalists and, by radio hook-up, an additional one million listeners; it went on for three days with seventeen speakers and cost $35,000.[29] It was the intention of the liberal members of the organizing committee that a teach-in be a debate, a presentation of conflicting "philosophies and policies," a means to "focus concern, expand understanding and stimulate constructive, realistic thought and action,"[30] — *not*, perforce, a demonstration or rally. And so it was that the students listened to both Robert Scalapino, chairman of the Department of Political Science at Berkeley, and Phuong Margain, secretary general of the cabinet of Cambodia. Thus:

> *Scalapino:* There can be no question that large-scale guerrilla activities in the South were started on a signal from the North, and in accordance with a revolutionary strategy that stems from Chinese communist teachings and has been attempted in many areas of Asia.[31]

Margain: Whatever this participation of the Democratic Republic of Vietnam in the war effort of the NLF be, it is far from attaining the gigantic dimensions of the American military investment in South Vietnam. It is this investment which constitutes the *only true foreign intervention.*[32]

Heady stuff for a student mass up to then educated on the subject by *Time* magazine and press releases from the Department of External Affairs. And indeed there were SUPA members who were pleased, even elated, by the educational achievement of the teach-in.

It was international news. It was a huge political event at the university. People came with banners, they came with literature and slogans, classes were cancelled. I mean it was *huge.* Sure, the organizers brought in some big Yanks but they also brought George Grant, the Red Tory, who talked about nationalism and technological empires and multiversities and dehumanization and manipulation by the social sciences. This was the first time those issues were brought back home; we returned to our roots there. Isn't that interesting? Vietnam forced us back to ourselves and opened us up to the ordinary people at the university who were being politicized for the first time. This was their point of conversion, this was the moment they came into the left.

But, according to other student critics, the teach-in had also made serious errors. When the aforementioned Scalapino refused to appear on the same platform with Michael Myerson, a Berkeley graduate student who had recently visited Hanoi and was to speak for its policy, the organizing committee dropped Myerson. (Angry students created disturbances during Scalapino's speech as a result.) Similarly the committee made no effort to protest or even publicly discuss the fact that the Canadian government would not issue visas to representatives of the NLF unless the committee also invited representatives of the Saigon government. (In the end the NLF did not participate.) Hard on the heels of the teach-in and inspired and instructed by it, SUPA pressed the issue of Canadian responsibility towards and complicity in the Vietnam war. That winter of

1965–66, following the membership conference in Saskatoon, SUPA proposed an Ottawa/Vietnam Action for the spring. Originally envisioned in very grand terms — busloads, train-loads of Canadians, Americans, even Mexicans — this action ultimately consisted of an "open letter" to the House of Commons, a two-day teach-in at the University of Ottawa, and civil disobedience on Parliament Hill.

The fruits of the preceding several months of discussion between SUPA and the Red Tory nationalist, Professor George Grant, were delivered during these days of the Vietnam action. In their open letter, SUPA not only enumerated the data of complicity (armament sales, performance on the ICC, et cetera) but situated them *historically* in the colonial relations between Canada and the United States, arguing that in the "basic structure and fabric of Canadian society," in economic dependency, in the enlistment into the priorities of another nation, in fear of reprisal, we are condemned "to complicity in this cruel war."[33]

As for the civil disobedience, there was an anguished debate about how it should be done. (People sit in on the roadway to the Houses of Parliament to block traffic; the RCMP drags their limp bodies six, seven times off the road; an officer, in exasperation, yells, "Arrest them," and so they arrest sixty-one of them, dragging their limp bodies to a paddy wagon.)[34] On the one hand were the so-called "politicos" in favour of a well-planned and well-disciplined action, and on the other the "personalists" more interested in an action that would develop as it went along.[35] In the end it seemed to be a bit of both. One enthusiastic participant felt that the action had demonstrated that "SUPA is one of the very few organizations whose members possess the level of analysis and degree of commitment" necessary to spearhead a "mass all-inclusive citizens' movement" against the war;[36]* *Our Generation* announced that the trial of the sixty-one arrestees (they had all pleaded not

---

*More immediately, the aim of the sit-in had been to persuade the House to debate "the Vietnam issue." The only response they got was a donation of coffee from Tommy Douglas.

guilty to charges of obstruction) "will be an important political trial in the history of this country."[37]*

Anti-Vietnam war actions erupted across the country in the next two years, 1966–68, as often as not initiated by university students with sometimes only a casual affiliation with SUPA. At the University of British Columbia (UBC), the Internationalists, a hodge-podge of new and old leftists who had been meeting together since 1961, often were the instigators of the marches into downtown Vancouver that brought all kinds of anti-war elements together, from members of the Communist party to members of the Unitarian church, to make speeches, do some singing and get shoved around.

In Winnipeg, Young Socialists (Trotskyist) were active and effective in the Vietnam Mobilization Committee: they organized marches and burned the American flag.

In Montreal, in 1967, eighteen hundred students were demonstrating in front of the U.S. consulate when they were forcibly broken up by mounted police; forty-eight were arrested and charged with unlawful assembly.

> In Calgary, twice a year, once in the spring, once in the fall, we took to the streets and had a very pleasant march downtown. The authorities invariably obliged by calling out mounted forces. But no one was hurt. It was great fun, actually. It was always against the war in Vietnam that we marched. For one thing, we could get more people out for that than anything else. It was all very well for us students to sit around living rooms and talk forever about American penetration of Canada's oil industry, blah, blah, blah. But you couldn't organize a march around that. We made the connection anyway. We were reading [Harry] Magdoff** and knew that what the U.S. was doing in Vietnam was practising imperialism.

Toronto, 1968. Pickets demonstrated at the offices of

---

*A majority were found guilty and took a short jail sentence.
**Well-known Marxist economist associated with *Monthly Review* journal.

Hawker-Siddeley and of Litton Industries. The Ontario October 21 Mobilization to End the War in Vietnam called a mass rally at Queen's Park. "Speak up if you value your life. Silence is approval." In 1969 the Welcoming Committee for the NLF sponsored a meeting in Massey Hall where they hosted two NLF representatives. "It is not only by your blows against the enemy," the Vietnamese visitors had said earlier in Montreal, "but by your heartbeat that we will win."

And in the heart of the Canadian student, the will that the Vietnamese should win was strengthened and renewed again and again by the Dow Chemical issue. Dow Chemical of Canada supplied polystyrene to the napalm plants of California, and once you had seen that photograph of the Vietnamese youth, victim of napalm, his chest a mass of open flesh, his mouth and chin melting down grotesquely into his neck, his eyes and nose black craters — and yet he was still alive — you had no choice but to interfere with Dow Chemical and all its works.

Between 1963 and 1968 the U.S. air force dumped more than 100,000 tons of napalm on Vietnam. In 1966, the year the tonnage jumped from 17,659 to 54,620, a new, hotter compound, Napalm B, had been developed. It burned at 2060^0 Fahrenheit, was impossible to scrape off and could melt hands.

The Save Lives in Vietnam Committee in Toronto and Voice of Women nationally mounted a campaign to boycott Dow Chemical products: Saran Wrap and Handi-Wrap. At the University of Toronto in November 1967, the student paper *Varsity* publicized the Vietnam-related activities of companies including Dow Chemical, that recruited students into professions, and in response students sat in on the porch of the old house on campus that was used as the job-recruitment centre. The man from Dow was inside, barricaded, and there he stayed for several hours while the students talked and heard speeches. That same week students at the University of Waterloo leafleted their recruitment centre, UBC students blocked the doorway of their centre and in Winnipeg, they were outrageous.

It was the only demonstration at a Canadian university that actually forced Dow off the campus — opposed to having a sit-in and getting nowhere. Here we used our brains and we pulled off a number. We had seventeen people at the demonstration initially, which is not a hell of a lot. Dow was using the Canada Manpower Centre at the university; so we went by to case the joint and we noticed these two outward handles on the door. I said, "What would happen if we wrapped a chain around them and locked the fuckers in?" So we went out and we bought a two-inch chain, the heaviest chain we could get, and a big padlock. I went inside and said, "Hi, I'm from the demonstration and I want to talk to the guy from Dow." They said, "He doesn't want to talk to you." "Look, if you let me talk to him, we'll be gone in five minutes." So they let me talk to him. The guy was just perfect. He was like a cartoon character of what an imperialist warmonger should look like. A big, tall guy with an eye patch and a straight-out chin and high cheekbones. He looked like a member of the SS. We couldn't have asked for a better character. So I did the very liberal routine. I said, "Listen, there's seventeen people out there, all we want to do is read you a statement and then we're going to go away. So why don't you step outside?" So he steps outside and we read him our statement: "You fucking imperialist warmonger, you get the fuck out of our campus! That's our statement." The guy was shocked. I had set him up. He stood there for a minute, you could see the blood draining from his face, it was great. He turned around and walked back inside. Out came the chain and the padlock, "click" on the doors and the shit hit the fan. It was marvellous. First of all, the Commerce and the Engineering students came down to fight with us. We had fist fights. Really heavy duty fist fights right in the hallway. Hundreds of people came to support us and hundreds of people came to oppose us. So that the whole foyer of this building was like one gigantic cacophony. Arguments and fights. People getting into shouting matches and punching each other out. The administration chickened out and ordered Dow off campus. That night we had a debate with about three thousand people in the student building. An active debate which we won. Our opponents tried to make the argument: Do you have the right to interfere with our personal lives if we want to go to work for Dow? We smashed them in the debate.

By 1968 Canadians were marching in front of the U.S. consulate in Toronto, bearing the flag of North Vietnam and shouting, "Victory to the NLF!" They had come a long way from guilt.

Where had this nerve, this courage and commitment in the Canadian middle-class students of the anti-war brigades come from? And why this passion in defence of the Vietnamese (a race and culture of strangers) and in horror of the Americans (a nation of cousins) in those whose emotional and political geography heretofore had mapped out only the names and places of cozy home and family?

The answers are first of all in the Vietnamese and the Americans themselves. As the anti-war movement, internationally, spawned literature and spokespersons and disseminated the point of view of the Vietnamese, Canadian protesters were able to make that very important intellectual and emotional shift out from under the prevailing ideological perspectives of their society to see the war from the point of view of the Vietnamese. And so they understood that, for the NLF and for the North Vietnamese, Communist ideology, of all ideologies, was anti-imperialist and committed to the liberation of oppressed colonialized peoples; and that, armed with it, these people were simply carrying on, by an intensified means, an ancient struggle.

Even if we are to carry out the struggle for ten, twenty years or longer, and have to suffer greater difficulties and hardships, we are prepared and resolved to fight and fight to the end until not a single U.S. soldier is seen in our country.... The people and liberation armed forces of South Vietnam have written a golden page in the glorious history of their people.[38]

From the program of the NLF the Canadian radicals learned that in contrast to the Diems and General Kys of the Saigon government, the liberation front was committed to a "national democratic coalition government," to a thorough land redistribution, to a foreign policy of neutrality, to the reunification of the nation. From observers who travelled in Vietnam, they became aware that the resistance of the Vietnamese was profoundly self-motivated. It was the South Vietnamese themselves, not the Northerners or the Chinese or the Russians, who first took up the arms of revolution against the hated Diem administration. It was the 230,000-strong Viet Cong (compared with 50,000 North Vietnamese regulars in the South) who suffered 100,000 dead and 182,000 wounded by 1967.[39] It was with the sustained American bombing of the North that the war in the two halves of Vietnam became a single war. From the French journalist Bernard Fall's sequence of books, they became convinced that the NLF, contrary to American claims, was an indigenous force, which could not be "simply blasted off the surface to the earth with B-52 saturation raids, or told to pack up and go into exile in North Vietnam."[40] From Pham Van Dong, the prime minister of North Vietnam, who was interviewed in Hanoi by the American anti-war activists Herbert Aptheker, Staughton Lynd and Tom Hayden, they heard:

> There is no hatred between our peoples — we have no ill will toward American people.... Please, if you should see President Johnson, ask him why is he bombing my country? Let him explain exactly how the Democratic Republic of Vietnam is threatening the United States of America?[41]

Confronting a people such as these — resolute, heroic, popular freedom fighters — were the Americans, the bureaucracy, the military, the multinational corporations, who represented violence, aggrandizement and falsehood, for whom "peace" meant the "elimination of nationalist and socialist threats to the established order" and "freedom" meant the "maintenance of 'liberal' governments offering no opposition to the large-scale investment of American capital. . . . "[42]

America, profit-obsessed, war-hungry, hate-ridden, draining its blood into the machines of death, "screaming ceilings of Soap Opera/thick dead Lifes, slick Advertisements/for Gubernatorial big guns/burping Napalm on palm rice tropic greenery."[43] America. There was no choice. "The rising cry for justice would pierce Heaven itself."[44]

> From the American anti-war movement we began to discover things about our own community and actions we could take right here. Like the Safeway store. All my life this was a place at the end of the street where I bought Coke and doughnuts and now suddenly it wasn't just Safeway anymore but Tenneco Industries and Tenneco was an investor in Southeast Asia. It was a moment of being confronted with the untruths of our dreamy lives. The war in Vietnam was a series of moments where you either turned your back on the truth or you went with it and doing that you could never go back to where you had been.

To the protests of the American movement, Canadians added their own, demanding the accountability of our own institutions, denouncing the duplicity of our own politicians, exposing the Achilles heel of our economic subordination. Ourselves as deputy war-traders.

The war in Vietnam "discredited the ideology of the *status quo,* the complacent tone of affluent capitalism. The conventional wisdom is no longer trusted; it has brought too much evil into the world, and Vietnam is its great abomination."[45] The war. Against the American capitalist monolith, the Communist cell organization and the guerrilla in sandals. The war. Suddenly we were vulnerable to Asian peasants who told us we had had our hour in history and now was the time of the little brown people who would seize from us the time.

"The people of Vietnam changed my life."

III

HELL NO, WE WON'T GO

Q. Well, suppose we close with what seems to be the important question. The man in the United States who is drafted and is unwilling to serve — what are his alternatives?

A. The alternatives for a person who conscientiously opposes the war in Vietnam are few. If, as with most people, he is unable to obtain the status of a conscientious objector, then he is faced with making one of the following choices. He can either violate his own conscience and go to Vietnam, committing in his own mind immoral and despicable acts of murder; or else he is faced with the alternatives of refusing to fight and being sentenced to about five years in prison, as is now the common procedure. What we wish is to provide Americans with a third legal alternative, and that is the possibility of immigrating to Canada. But it should not be considered that this is necessarily an easy alternative, and I think Canadians should think back to their own parents and grandparents. We live in a nation which was founded and developed primarily by immigrants, and we should be able to realize that immigration — leaving one's family, friends, familiar surroundings and the security of a home — is a difficult choice. . . . It is not to be undertaken lightly, and in this regard it is a complete misconception to use the term "draft-dodger." . . . My contact with the persons who have come to Canada convinces me that this is an extremely difficult choice and that it is being taken on the basis of a profound conviction of the immorality of the war in Vietnam and a dedication to one's own moral scruples.[1]

— Morton Brown (from the interview "Vietnam, Professors and Draftdodgers," published in Student Advocate, *Simon Fraser University)*

For all the pain and outrage that the war in Vietnam inspired in Canadians, there was one horror we did not have to face: a boy we knew going to war, a boyfriend, a lover, a member of the family become killer, a boy we knew dying. We did not have dead to bury.

What we did have were young Americans arriving among us to stay alive. This we could do: open up social space for refugees, people who had quit their country and now, homeless, needed some new place in which to begin again the labour of citizenship.

Who, after hearing their stories, would not let them in? These were tales of desperados, men living underground, identities discarded at the first whiff of the police closing in, men brutalizing their bodies — starving themselves, chopping off their own fingers or dropping rocks on their toes, contracting diseases — and men choosing the stockade before they'd choose boot camp. Men and women of the anti-war movement, to whom it had become clear that America was going to kill them. . . .

It was October 1966, and I was at a demonstration at the Oakland army induction centre. We were there to stop that induction process for a day. It was melodramatic. It was scary. It was still dark when we moved over to Oakland. Thousands and thousands of us, you could hardly move, sitting down and singing in the dark. Cops were arriving by the busload, the tactical squads from all eleven towns in the Bay Area and the California State Highway Patrol and the total Oakland police force and Berkeley police force. Then when dawn came, I'll never forget it, there we were, sitting on the ground, waiting for the sun to light us up as targets.

The cops were walking from one end of the street to the other, wave after wave of them, they had batons — it was the first time I'd ever seen a three-foot lead-weighted stick. It was clear they wanted to break people's heads. It sounds like a watermelon sounds when it hits the pavement when those things take people's skulls and crack them. It just goes *thwok*. Rose and fell and rose and fell, sounding like a

watermelon somebody dropped, fell again. You'd see
them hit somebody's head and it would be like ripples
going away like the lines on a map and then the blood
would start to come up four inches from where the stick
had landed on their head. People couldn't leave because
they couldn't see because they had both hands over their
face. I found myself standing on top of a car screaming
"Sieg heil!" at the cops.

Riots, tear gas from helicopters, Black Panthers busted, shot
up and busted again, the Fourth of July and more riots,
National Guardsmen on your block, streets cordoned off with
rolls of barbed wire, bayonets. There must be some way out of
here.

Men and women in the Peace Corps, realizing "we were
instruments of American foreign policy," were humiliated and
ashamed by that realization. Stricken by the contradiction
between official history and what they witnessed in the Third
World of the effects of the intrusion of American dollars,
military personnel and the CIA, they too stopped wanting to be
American.

There were as many women war-resisters among the
immigrants as men. Sometimes they left by themselves, having
come to the end of their own rope, their own moment of nausea
when not a single more American event could be tolerated, and
sometimes they left with refugee mates. In either case, each
woman had to sit down in self-examination, review her needs
and her motivations, assess her relationships, analyse her
politics and determine her own reasons for staying or leaving.
What a choice. To stay in America and fight, in demonstrations,
marches and rallies, and to pay the penalty of loneliness and
getting hurt, or to leave with the loved one, give and receive
support and consolation, and pay the penalty of irrelevance to
the struggle.

War-resisters came to Canada because it was English-speaking,
because they didn't need a passport, because they had visited it
as children on holidays to Montreal or to the mountains, and
had found it pleasing. They came to Canada because they

believed they would not be hassled here: Canada was so "liberal," what with its friendlier relations with Cuba and China, its peace-keeping role in the United Nations and Suez, its "British" sense of fair play. They came blind, on buses with a few hundred dollars in their pockets, a bus to anywhere, a bus to get across the border; they came well-rehearsed, in Volks-wagons stuffed with clothes and books and a job already lined up; they came by plane, "just to have a look around."

They left with their parents' disappointment and chagrin still ringing in their ears (" 'Don't make waves,' they told me, 'go into the army, it's the right thing to do, you'll be an officer, they'll keep you in an office with a typewriter, a boy like you' ") and the knowledge that they would never be coming back. This emigration was irreversible.

> As soon as I crossed the border, I was considered to have evaded the draft. That's a five-year felony. I'd crossed an international border to avoid prosecution, that's another five years. I'd left the country without permission of my draft board, that's a third offence. I'd failed to notify my board of my change of address — fourth offence. I wouldn't be going home for a visit.

They had done the unimaginable: "Americans do not really see the rest of the world as habitable." All those years and years of earning their "Americanship," the books and papers they sweated over, the examinations on history, government, the constitution and the Supreme Court — years of this — the patriotic speeches and songs, flags and oaths, learning to be this precious thing — an American — and now they were telling their family, their friends, their community, "I'm leaving."

They called themselves anti-imperialists, critics of American culture, pacifists and, as such, the only authentic repository of American ideals: all those who would consent to fight the war had corrupted the content of democracy and freedom and betrayed the revolutionary inheritance. In Canada the war-resisters would find for their American idealism a second lease on life.

Officially, the Canadian government regarded the draft-resisters as immigrants like any others (offences against the

American Selective Service laws were not extraditable offences). In this one respect at least, in its refusal to treat draftable American males as criminals, the government of Canada could be seen to pursue a policy independent of Washington's interests. On the other hand, because no special case was ever made of any of the American draft-resisters, the government could not be accused of sheltering "undesirables" and "law-breakers." Prime Minister Pearson: "I am sure . . . each individual application [for landed immigrant status] has to be considered on its own merits and all the factors. . . will have to be taken into consideration."[2]

It was this ambiguity in policy that provided the loophole through which the middle-class, educated American immigrant entered Canada and, once here, established him/herself in a manner to which s/he was accustomed. A job in a bookstore, a teaching position, acceptance into a graduate program, placement at a social work agency. Some, desperate for immediate security and funds, vulnerable to exploitation, took jobs at minimum wages from employers who "specialized" in immigrant labour. But not for long. These Americans, too, quickly settled into mainstream Canadian life, not ostentatiously by any means, but comfortably, with a widening circle of friends, a growing library of Canadian magazines and books, and a blossoming sense of commitment to their new community: starting up a photography workshop, joining with neighbours to fight an "urban renewal" project, organizing an alternate school. The good life, in peaceable, laid-back, old-fashioned Canada. The good life, among progressive and enlightened Canadians. "When we got to Vancouver a provincial election campaign was winding up. People were saying the NDP had a good chance of winning. Oh my God, a socialist government, this must be Nirvana!"

But it was terribly lonely, especially for the women. The men submerged their sadness in the adrenalin rush of sheer relief at having made good the getaway and by work, which they were required to get to keep their status secure. He would go off to work in the mornings, and she, in their basement apartment, the flat, grey light of interminable winter at the windows, would go through the classified ads of the local newspaper for something, anything, she might do that would let her meet people. Her father had quit talking to her, and the letters from her friends, who thought that what she had done was "weird," grew thinner and more infrequent. She had begun to notice that, in company, people didn't really see or hear her, as if she had come up to Canada as part of the man's baggage: she was as interesting to them as that. Like the generations of pioneer women before her in Canada, she longed for a female friend. "There was a big, empty feeling. There was nothing to fill up the space of what I'd left behind."

Impressed by the Americans' courage in fleeing the "world's number one police state" and their commitment to non-violence, touched by their vulnerability as rootless strangers stripped of friends and family, invigorated by their tales of the movement and the resistance, Canadian sympathizers gladly and generously made room for them. Let's show our stuff, they said to each other. Each war-resister we welcome and take home is one less soldier for that infamous war, one more comradely link with the international uprising against American imperialism.

In 1966, in Toronto, SUPA set up an office next to its own to house an anti-draft program that would aid and abet draft-resisters and deserters in their desire to immigrate to Canada. According to Clayton Ruby, who was involved in the program throughout its existence, the notion to set it up came from SUPA's reading of the escalation of the war and the inevitability that "the American government would start drafting students on a large scale, and we had to be prepared to smuggle people out of the U.S. on a large scale." SUPA established a telephone roster and a counselling service, and temporarily housed resisters with sympathetic families in the city.

> We smuggled tens of thousands of people into this country. Sometimes we dressed ourselves up as priests and nuns or used real priests and nuns, and we'd drive over the border and back with no hassles. Or we'd use the *Maid of the Mist* boat at Niagara Falls. We'd have someone get on from the American side and someone from the

Canadian side. In those days you were issued a different-coloured ticket depending on which side you got on, and they'd only let you off on the side you got on. We'd simply have our person switch tickets with the American. Easy.

As this kind of work became more important and more in demand (in 1966, 2,447 draft-age Americans were landed; by 1969, 4,405),[3] the program required more than SUPA resources could handle. They "farmed" it out to American immigrants themselves and to the scores of volunteers who were coming forward to lend a hand, from draft and employment counsellors to lawyers and doctors, from church groups to university teachers. At this point SUPA's anti-draft program became the Toronto Anti-Draft Programme and among its most successful operations was the publication of the *Manual for Draft-Age Immigrants to Canada,* an exhaustive book on immigration procedures. Its first edition in 1968 sold 5,000 copies in two months; its second edition sold out at 20,000 copies, and sales kept doubling until 1970 when it had sold a total of 65,000 copies.[4]

Across the country aid groups sprang up wherever American immigration warranted a support structure. (By 1970 there were thirty-two such groups.)[5] In Vancouver the Committee to Aid American War Objectors operated out of an old warehouse near Chinatown. Through its services — a job and housing bulletin board, a mailbox system, magazine and newspaper subscriptions, fund raising, as well as the usual counselling[6] — it was a place in which to ease the culture shock of immigration and on which to call for help.

> Young dodgers would arrive with no idea of where to go for help, with no money or anything else. I'd put them in touch with appropriate organizations, I'd board them, get them jobs, arrange a taxi license for them or whatever. Get them welfare. Legal counsel when they were stupid enough to get caught smoking marijuana. I did all this because I thought an American boy in Vancouver is one less gun in somebody's back in Vietnam.

The Alexander Ross Society in Edmonton provided immigration counselling* and sometimes escorted Americans across the border into Alberta. In Regina the Committee to Aid American War Immigrants raised money for the operations of a local American Deserters' Committee and its two hostels. In Winnipeg the Committee to Assist War Objectors rented an office in the CRYPT building (Committee Representing Youth Problems Today) for one dollar a month and employed a former youth organizer for the NDP as a counsellor. "Yankee Dodgers and Deserters, Welcome to Canada — Don't crash at office, see someone at desk. You'd better dig it here, you're stuck!"[7] In Ottawa the United church operated a drop-in centre and coffee-house for exiles and refugees, and in Montreal the Council to Aid Resisters provided counselling and a battery of legal, social work and psychiatric services. The Union Général des Étudiants du Québec provided, rent-free, office space to the local Deserters' Committee and offered to hide deserters and war-resisters in the woods.[8]

And Americans themselves set up organizations of self-help: in Toronto, in 1968, the Union of American Exiles (its newsletter eventually became the independent magazine *AMEX: The American Expatriate in Canada*); in Montreal and Vancouver as well as Toronto, American Deserters' Committees; in Toronto, in 1970, the Committee to Aid Refugees from Militarism and Red, White and Black. (*"It can't happen here — without help*. Like, Help! Wanted! at the RW&B office: typists, artists, decorators, chauffeurs, typists, envelope stuffers, phone answerers, typists, writers, a bookkeeper, typists, publicists, — oh yes, typists!")[9]

> I was editing a community newspaper in Ottawa called the *Centre Town News,* a four-page tabloid. We'd hire dodgers and deserters to distribute it door to door. Guys from Tennessee and Florida in skimpy leather shoes and threadbare jackets out in the Ottawa snow, delivering papers. We paid them a cent a copy and gave them a bowl

---

*I was told that one of its members, an NDP activist and wife of a professor, had even collected blankets and socks for the "refugees."

of soup. They were living three, four to a one-bedroom apartment, they were homesick as hell. It made me very sad. That's why I agreed to drive one of them across the border back into the U.S. so he could turn around and apply at the Canadian border for status — he was in Canada only as a visitor and was wanted by the FBI for desertion. He'd only been through Grade Ten and had a job offer as a night cleaner, but there are lots of people who will work as night cleaners and it's not a hell of a skilled position. So he didn't have enough points; they wouldn't give him status. I had to leave him in the States.

In 1967 new immigration regulations went into effect designed ostensibly to "achieve universality and objectivity in the selection process."[10] There were nine factors of immigration suitability and units of assessment for each factor — 20 units maximum for "education and training," 15 for "occupational demand," 15 for "personal assessment" and so on — to be assigned at the time of application for landed immigrant status, usually at the border. To qualify for such status, the applicant would have to have a minimum of 50 out of 100 assessment units.

While the regulations did eliminate the arbitrariness of the individual immigration officer's assessment, they functioned in fact to institutionalize the biases and prejudices of the officer (and by extension, of Canadian society) in regard to the characteristics of the "suitable" immigrant, and reinforced at the level of policy what was *de facto* the procedure anyway. Clearly, the university-educated, highly skilled, neat and attractive-looking, bankrolled, married, bilingual (or at least English-speaking) applicant would amass an impressive number of points and would be landed without difficulty. By contrast, a working-class applicant typically had 10 points for age, 5 for speaking English, 10 to 12 for high school education, 5 for willingness to settle in smaller centres, and 5 to 10 points for his occupation. This meant that the remaining 15 points that would qualify him for his landed status had to be earned from the highly subjective "personal assessment." Canada's immigration regulations quite neatly replicated the class and race biases of the United States' draft laws.

The middle-class (and, almost invariably, white) student with his draft deferment came in contact with the anti-war movement while at the university. Refusing to be inducted into military service, he crossed the border to Canada, received a healthy number of points, and entered middle-class Canadian society with relative ease. The working-class (very often black or brown) youth, on the other hand, "who filled the local draft board quotas"[11] and learned about the nature of war in training and in combat, deserted, and, at the border or subsequently, discovered that he did not have enough points to qualify for landed status. (He was poorly educated, un- or semi-skilled, impoverished, "unreputable.") At this point he became a fugitive, a man underground, haphazardly employed, fearful and desperate. In a word, vulnerable.

In Vancouver the RCMP raided five, six times the American Deserters' Committee home, ransacking files and copying down names.[12] At Simon Fraser University, anti-draft activists discovered that

> the University was being dishonest in the way it was dealing with applicants who were war-resisters or deserters. We were demanding greater accessibility for them but the university was lying by saying that there were no openings and even failing to forward their applications to the department involved. They were just sitting on them. We discovered the RCMP would look through student applications from time to time.

In spite of the fact that by 1968–69 the influx of deserters was reaching crisis proportions for the exile community (they were being picked up by the police for drug-dealing, vagrancy and shoplifting; they were "starving in the streets"; they were committing suicide),[13] the government passed the buck of responsibility to the individual immigration officers, instructing them to decide at their own discretion the admissibility of a deserter.[14] Finally, in 1969, five students from Glendon College, posing as deserters, presented themselves at five different border-crossing points and applied for landed immigrant status. Not only were they all rejected, two were handed over to American authorities by the Canadian officers.[15] The resulting hue and cry in Canada, raising the question of Canadian bureaucratic collusion with American authorities, the question of the right of the Canadian government to penalize "political refugees who have rightly or wrongly been repelled by the American military and the war it is fighting,"[16] the question of the Canadian people's right to policies determined independently of American pressure, the government buckled under and announced that as of 22 May 1969, "if a serviceman from another country meets our immigration criteria, he will not be turned down because he is still in the active service of his country." The law could not turn the deserter into a middle-class kid, but at least he would not be hounded.

The underside of the solidarity between the Canadian anti-war movement and the draft-resisters was that "it was easy to impress Canadians. All you had to do was say you had lived in New York and everybody gasped in admiration." Which is to say that Canadians trivialized their own experience. It was all very well to be, say, a student at the University of Toronto (the country's largest) and a participant in the Vietnam Mobilization Committee there, but this was small potatoes compared to Berkeley and the SDS; it was one thing to take pride in one's "Canadian" liberalism and pacifism and another to be voluntarily *affected* by the Americans' "aggressiveness," their assertiveness, their pride and anger, in the conviction that "Canada would be greatly improved by this influx of Americans because we were getting the best of them"; it was one thing to make them welcome, another to be persuaded that

> the draft-dodgers represented a new way of looking at things, new ideas and a new style. They were people who were interested in issues, in the arts, in experimenting with relationships. They took more risks. I associated all this with being American.

Even the more politicized Canadians, the ones who were active in aid programs, for instance, found the war-resisters romantic and larger-than-life, and were reluctant to be politically critical of them because after all, "it was *they,* not I, who had had to make such a heavy decision. I was in awe of them. In awe of the fact that they were here among us at all."

Therefore, the political relationship between the American war-resister in exile and the Canadian radical was, to say the least, problematic. There was the initial period of "shaking down," when the Canadian struck an alliance that was based in part on a romanticization of the American — so courageous, so principled, so sexy! — and in part on an acceptance of the American movement's priority of halting the war in Vietnam. Then a period when, contrary to some Canadian fantasies, the draft-resister turned out to be not an ultra-militant, superlunary being but a deeply offended middle-class moralist, just like them. A period when the American, exhausted, released from the dreadful pressure of anxiety and paranoia, withdrew in relief from "politics" altogether — or was strongly advised to by the community — and went about the business of setting up a new life. Or, still "hooked," tried heroically to keep up with the news "back home," reading every American publication s/he could get hold of, utterly absorbed by the data of the war in Vietnam (pressing the war on the heart, the brain, so as never to forget the cataclysm that had forced this trial-by-exile). A period when the ego of the American grew expansive under the admiring approval of "socialite leftists" who liked to invite "draft-dodgers" to their parties and hear stories of cops-and-dodgers derring-do.

But this period passed, and the question of the integration of the Americans into Canadian radical political activity was confronted. Under pressure from anti-war groups in the United States to continue to serve, however they might, the struggle "at home," some resisters confirmed that their first responsibility was to "war-resisters in the army, potential deserters and to the men and women of Indochina,"[17] rather than to Canadianization and accommodation. Apparently oblivious to the absurdity of trying to be a combatant *in absentia* and the insensitivity of their image of Canada as an undifferentiated, impassive holding tank for American revolutionaries, they would speak of schemes to keep in touch with the "mother culture," the womb of all consciousness, and would agree with Tom Hayden, the SDS activist, that to be "politicized" in Canada is to "insist publicly that all political exiles should be allowed to come home, that you intend to return by whatever means necessary."[18] Others, rather more oriented to the fact that they lived among Canadians, spoke grandiosely of the possibility that ". . . as the U.S. is the oldest and closest enemy of Canada, perhaps it is our role to lead the fight, physically, against the U.S. from our exile,"[19] or even, as in the case of a group of immigrant yogis, to "help Canada into the Aquarian Age."[20]

It was these kinds of postures that drove some Canadian radicals mad and others to serious reconsideration of the politics of the American exile. Mere "libertarians" the Canadians could deal with — the draft-evader who emigrated from a sense of having been personally interfered with by the U.S. military — and the "middle-class shits who didn't give a goddamn about Vietnam or anything else" except to carry on in Canada where they'd left off in America, in a career and life-style into which they vanished unremarked. No, the problem was with the putative *comrades,* the brothers and sisters of the resistance, for whom the place called Canada was ephemeral, impalpable, a mere shadow cast across the north of a continent pre-empted by the beast America, a refuge and sanctuary (thanks very much, folks!) in which to reconstitute the battered troops for the decisive struggle back in the belly of the beast (y'all come and see us, y'hear!), for there is no place as real, as awesome, as prodigious, even in its depravity, as America.

At a time when Canadian new leftists were in a struggle of their own to take their history and their being seriously, to raise the fundamental issues of social power and economic control of the society, to extrapolate from the war in Vietnam the broad outlines of American imperialism and lay them across the grid of Canada, such an attitude on the part of the American exiles was not helpful. In fact, it was labelled, by a Toronto anti-draft program activist, as "American imperialism of the left," this "look[ing] at the struggle in Canada as inconsequential,"[21] this blinkered vision of the scenario of anti-imperialism. If the American truly wanted to engage with imperialism, well, then let them look under their feet. They were standing on the soil of the colony *par excellence.* Let them embrace Canada with the righteousness they now sent in the mails to the "motherland" and take on the beast where it was most sly and meretricious.

From under the weight of the Americans, their war, their resistance, the Canadian new left struggled for the project that was its own.

PART II
STUDENT POWER

I
KNOWLEDGE FOR WHOM?

In science young people learn to do research that will make a bigger profit for the bosses. If young people learn social sciences like psychology, sociology and political science, they are taught to be spies for the bosses. Sociologists and psychologists and political scientists are always studying the workers and especially the poor and the native people and asking them questions. And when they find out things about the people, the social scientists go to the bosses with the information. The social scientists never study the bosses and give the information to the people. And the bosses are always using the information they get about the workers and the poor and the farmers and the native people to come up with new ways to shove the people around.

— from a manifesto of Students for a Democratic University, University of Alberta (Gateway, 19 September 1969)

Although it would be a couple of years in the gestation, the idea that students *as students* were an oppositional force to reckon with had already been evoked by 1964. In that year a CUCND pamphlet, "The University and Social Action in the Nuclear Age," decried the university as a place that merely trained personnel for industrial society, as though students needn't concern themselves further than acquiring the tools of employment and salary. At the same time, the president of the University of California at Berkeley, Clark Kerr, wrote a book that was widely circulated and discussed. In *The Uses of the University* he noted that a modern university had been produced by the intervention of the state,* by the preponderant

---

*The state intervened with grants, subsidies and, as anti-war activists had uncovered, research contracts.

prestige of scientists over humanists, by the enormous growth of the university administration and by the great increase in classroom size which frustrated the personal contact of teacher and student. In short, "the university has become a prime instrument of national purpose"[1] basic to which was the expansion of the "knowledge industry." But: "the process cannot be stopped. The results cannot be foreseen. It remains to adapt."[2]

Student activists would have none of that. That same year, in 1964, at Kerr's own campus the Free Speech Movement (FSM) clashed head-on with the machinery of the "knowledge industry"; the malaise of the university of the Fifties, the "notorious 'inner emigration' " of students to a "place of commitment to business-as-usual, getting ahead, playing it cool," as the SDS Port Huron Statement had it,[3] was overcome. In September 1964 Berkeley students who had spent the summer in the South, on freedom rides and voter registration drives in the civil rights movement, set up tables in the open campus mall to distribute literature and to solicit donations for the movement's projects. The university administration countered with a ban on the use of the university grounds for political activities. On October 1, a student collecting money for the Congress of Racial Equality, who had refused to fold up his table and go, was carried limp-bodied to a police car. The Free Speech Movement began at that moment when a noisy student crowd surrounded the police car and would not let it move for thirty-two hours.

Three months followed of assemblies, vigils and marches. Joan Baez and her "freedom songs." Five thousand picketers: "A Question of Dignity!" "Welcome to Mississippi!" Speeches about the inhuman machinations of the system in the South and the system at the university. Blacks and students: fodder for the machine. "I am a UC student. Do not fold, bend or mutilate." As it was necessary to the machine-system that blacks be enfeebled and exploited, so it was necessary that students be regulated and depersonalized. As blacks had resisted, so must students. So said Mario Savio, an FSM activist who had been in the South.

There is a time when the operation of the machine becomes so odious, makes you sick at heart, that you can't take part, you can't even tacitly take part, and you've got to put your bodies on the gears and upon the wheels, upon the levers, upon all the apparatus and you've got to indicate to the people who run it, to the peo¬le who own it, that unless you're free, the machine will be prevented from working at all.[4]

A sit-in. Eight hundred arrested. A strike. "Shut This Factory Down!" The relationship of the student to this intellectual production was analogous, said FSM, to the relationship of the worker to the assembly line. FSM demanded "meaning" in their education, the "right to know" about world-scale realities, the right to political self-expression and the right to assume the consequences of their speech. Activists were serving notice to the bureaucrats of the university, as they had done earlier to the southern racists, that they would just as soon die* as be "standardized, replaceable and irrelevant."[5] And the militant who would just as soon die is fanatical with impenitence.

Quebec, 1964. The labour unions were being "deconfessionalized" from the Catholic church, and the first operatives of the Front de Libération du Québec (FLQ) were in jail, the explosions of their Molotov cocktails and their slogans, *Students, workers, peasants, form your clandestine groups against Anglo-American colonialism!,* still ringing in the ears of the Québécois. The provincial Parent Royal Commission on Education issued its report and recommended that the old system of elitist, church-administered, classical colleges be dismantled and a new public system of pre-university colleges be put in place. (They were to be called Colleges d'Enseignement Général et Professionel or CEGEPs.) In November, having split from that "bi-national" organization the National Federation of Canadian University Students, Québécois university students set up the Union Générale des Étudiants du Québec (UGEQ) along syndicalist principles. Québécois students had

---

*This was no mere metaphor. Several civil rights workers, among them students, were murdered in the South.

been deeply influenced by the concept of student syndicalism in France, and UGEQ accepted the syndicalist charter of Grenoble University as its charter. Resolved:

> that syndicalism is characterized equally by its recognition of the fact that student problems, in particular problems of education, have their origins in the socio-economic structures, and consequently their solution lies in the recasting of these same structures.[6]

It followed, then, that UGEQ would involve itself as a pressure group and as a negotiating body for students in the massive public debates concerning the proposed reforms of the educational system.

In March 1965 students at the École des Beaux Arts in Montreal, fed up with lack of materials, with the hazardous environment of the very old building in which they studied, and with the antiquarian modes of teaching arts, went on strike. Delegates to a special UGEQ congress empowered the executive to call a general strike of all students in Quebec if the provincial government did not respond to the arts students' demands for reform. Three days later the government began negotiations with the strikers.

In November 1966 a group of radicals within the students' union of Strasbourg University in France ran off, using union funds, 10,000 copies of a pamphlet, *On the Poverty of Student Life,* and distributed them at an official university function. Three weeks later the students' union was closed down by court order, the judge citing the "eminently noxious" character of the ideas expressed within the pamphlet. The pamphlet became very famous.

> The student, if he rebels at all, must first rebel against his studies. . . . At the same time, since the student is a product of modern society just like Godard or Coca-Cola, his extreme alienation can only be fought through the struggle against this whole society. . . . The revolt of youth against an imposed and "given" way of life is the first sign of a total subversion. It is the prelude to a period of revolt — the revolt of those who can no longer *live* in our society.[7]

Between 1964 and 1967 students and police rioted in Argentina, Bolivia, Panama, Venezuela, Japan, Italy and West Germany. The issues were, variously, university autonomy, relations with the United States, government repression, land reform, solidarity with striking workers, sexual freedom, police brutality, the war in Vietnam and the lack of democracy in university government. In China the Red Guard movement had been launched to challenge the bourgeois character of education and the alienation of the intellectual from the manual workers.

In June 1967 a SUPA member attended the annual convention of SDS and later reported that an ideological debate was taking shape between "proponents of two views of the nature of fundamental internal contradictions of American capitalism." One camp argued the classically Marxist position that the industrial proletariat, because of its centrality in the economy, will be the vanguard of the revolution. The other argued, still tentatively, that there is a "new" working class taking shape in modern capitalism — white-collar, intellectual and cultural workers — as alienated, exploited and dispossessed as the proletariat and numerically preponderant.* "This is, of course," wrote the SUPA observer, "a very fundamental question — the most fundamental one, I think, for U.S. socialists (and probably Canadian socialists too). . . . "[8]

In the ashes of the peace movement's projects among the powerless lay the regenerate core of its vitality: youth's refusal to accept the necessity of unfreedom. From the university campuses they had originally carried the message of their resistance to the measures of war; beyond the campuses they had learned of the universality of these measures; back to the campuses they would go, for it was true that, just as the warmongers were everywhere, so the struggle against them

*Already by 1960 only 23.4 percent of wage-earning Canadians were employed in manufacturing jobs compared to 26 percent in service jobs. The vast number of jobs that had opened up in the post-war economy had been the professional, managerial and clerical jobs, while the blue-collar sector had been stable since 1941. In fact, between 1951 and 1961, "professional" jobs (including teachers, nurses, engineers, technicians) had grown by 64.5 percent.

could be waged anywhere, and one might as well take it up with the given of one's life: the university.

In this they were supported and driven on by the international uprising of students against the state and its institutions of war and learning, by the extraordinary nationalist agitation in Quebec with its evocations of the national liberation struggles in Cuba and Algeria, by public outrage at the sickening collaboration of the Canadian state and business in the American war in Vietnam, and by the grass-roots experimentation throughout the Western world with alternative lifestyles. The singular and consistent presence of *students* in all these phenomena pointed to their revolutionary potential, not as surrogates of other more "strategic" classes, not as mere harbingers of others' upheavals, not as vanguards or animators of other social forces, but as who they were, a social formation all their own, a mass of self-conscious and alienated young people collected at a very sensitive point in the web of capitalist relations, the university-factory. From the detours through the missile sites, Selma, the Indian reservations, the proletarian neighbourhoods and the Dow Chemical offices, the radicals were brought back to where they had started: to the university, and to the power that could be mobilized there for its own sake. If the SUPA phase had taught the activists anything it was this: that it is all right to fight in your own interests.*

Their interests were concrete and the fight for them unanswerable. Just as the universities were becoming mass institutions under pressure to rationalize and "industrialize" like any other large capitalist enterprise, so too were students, under the same pressures, becoming a social mass who "in absolute terms have come to constitute an autonomous social force."[9] (It was projected that by 1970 there would be one hundred thousand full-time university students and tens of thousands more in the community colleges of Ontario alone. The 1969–70 budget of the Ontario Department of University Affairs was

---

*SUPA, in fact, had never really left the university. Students were its project personnel, money was raised from among them and literature sold there. CYC, on the other hand, transformed students into civil servants.

close to $500 million.)* These developments were not to be wondered at. New industries and technologies and the swelling bureaucracies of enterprises and the state require for their functioning a new "working class" of intellectual labourers. (As earlier, industrialization had required a proletariat for the mines and mills.) It is the university's job to incubate and hatch this new class: members of an intelligentsia that would forget they had once been self-disposing professionals, an intelligentsia that would relinquish control over the content and development of their work and submit uncomplainingly to specialization and fragmentation. Worse, to only a privileged few would it be given to have, even within these parameters, "meaningful work." Everyone else at the university was destined for salaried or waged work as technicians, clerics, low-level administrators. Like the "old" working class, the new one experiences the dreadful separation of the person from his/her labour and sees the products of that labour snatched by the employers and squandered in the marketplace. "There is an unwillingness to understand," said the Marxist economist Ernest Mandel, "that man's chief productive force will be his creative intellectual power. This intellectual power is only potentially productive today because capitalist society beats it down and stamps it out pitilessly as it beats down the personality and creative impulse of the manual workers."[10]

Within the institutions of education, grievances multiplied. At many campuses, a snobbish and conformist fraternity elite continued their stultifying domination over the student body politic. Campus security personnel seized leaflets that demanded lower residence rates so as to alter the university's

---

*As impressive as this development was, however, it still touched only on an elite. A survey undertaken by the Canadian Union of Students in 1965–66 showed that only 35 percent of the undergraduate population came from the working class.[11] The implications of this statistic were drawn by the sociologist John Porter in his massive study of Canadian social stratifications, *The Vertical Mosaic,* which was being read at the time: the university was the instrument with which the upper and middle classes placed their children in the governing echelons of society and the working class thwarted from so doing.[12] The regulatory mechanism of this placement was student fees. And so it was to become a demand of student radicals that universities be universally accessible. *Abolish fees!*

status as a "preserve for the rich," and administrations accumulated "secret" files on the trouble-makers among students and faculty. Faculty were segregated from students in their own lounges and clubs,* not to mention washrooms. Herded into vast lecture halls of stupefyingly tasteless design, students were "lobotomized" by mechanical lectures, an inflexible examination system and the abiding fear of failure. They were systematically excluded from the planning and operation of the institution, never consulted in the drawing up of curricula, and obfuscated by the separation of data from theory about "why things are the way they are." Economically dependent, the student was confirmed in his/her dependency and "infantilization" in the classroom.

Finally, the elitism and authoritarianism of the university were endemic to the institution. If the university was indeed an "instrument of national purpose," then the soulless bureaucracy and the competitive values of that purpose operated as much on campus as outside it. Here students were trained, by the content and methodology of liberal education, to accept the goals of their society and their role within it. Here were prepared the grey-flannelled cadres of the legions of technocrats, bureaucrats and hacks. And here were linked the interests of the "business-administrative clique" as represented by the composition of the university boards of governors (or trustees or regents).

With some simple research, students discovered that the twenty-seven members of the Board of Governors of the University of Toronto, for instance, represented sixty-seven international corporations (thirty-one American, twenty Canadian, fifteen British and one Dutch), among them Honeywell (with its unsavoury connection with the Vietnam war industry), Argus, and Allied Chemical;[13] or discovered that there wasn't a university worth its name that did not solicit funds from corporations and institutions with investments in South Africa, Iran and Brazil. It took no extravagant leap of

---

*At the University of Alberta in the mid-Sixties, radical faculty disdained the plush Faculty Club for the steamy and clamorous Hot Caf [Cafe] where Arts students hung out.

analysis to draw the conclusions from the evidence that on the one hand a university was funded in part by a corporation with interests in Vietnam, and on the other the same university's administration denied tenure to faculty involved in anti-war work. It was important to understand, as Clark Kerr did, the integration of the university into the military-industrial complex and the state bureaucracies, but beyond that, it was also important to contest this integration, to undermine the ideological underpinnings of the process and to mobilize its casualties.

> If we look out across the world each morning and think honestly about what we see; spend our day in persistent and radical activity to gain freedoms in our local situation; and keep working to relate the two, the human community we all require will grow out of our common action.[14]

The struggle for control over education was no petty struggle. The demand of the student power movement for student control of curriculum and course content, for instance, was the result of a critique of that curriculum in which the connection between "knowledge" and the objectives of that knowledge was made explicit. The academic disciplines of the "educational plant" were in the service of the system: "consultation for the American war machine, apologia for Canadian junior partnership, counter-insurgency studies of dissenters, schemes for pulverizing social conflict, research for corporations."[15] Clearly, by such learning students were being prepared, "softened up," for their roles as intellectual managers of society. "Student power" was a way to throw a wrench into this process by redirecting the aims of education from repression to emancipation, first of the students themselves and then of the society as a whole. Because students are not "outside" society, said the student power activists, because they are in fact embedded in society as the transmitters of the values and idea-systems which permeate every social cell, their refusal to play that transmitting role would have repercussions throughout society. Student power was no simple self-contained appeal for special privileges or exemptions; it was one front, among many, in the broad opposition to the impoverishment of daily life.

Finally, with its strategy of democratically conducted direct action "from below," the student power movement contained the promise of overcoming the "natural order of things" — alienation, insularity, despair and cynicism — by furnishing a *praxis*. Power is recovered in the unity of theory and practice. And where more decisively and significantly than here among the young intellectual labourers who, with their skills and scholarship, understood the nature of the forces arrayed "behind the facts" and the depth of their insidious intrusions into social life? Because they were knowledgeable, because they were insightful, because they were visionary, the students were precisely those, as Marcuse said of them, who "no longer wish to contain the revolution within the framework of the given reality."[16] They demanded, in the name of imagination, the transcendence of that reality in the integration of "eros, poetry and politics"[17] in the here-and-now of dissentient, graceful and loving action.

The movement did not foresee the uses to which its rhetoric would be put by those who were in revolt simply to recover the privileges lost to them in the transformation of the university from a "guild" to a "factory"; and by those who aspired to be the managers and technical experts of the future socialist society, as happy to substitute, in the new regime as in the old, their own emancipated activity for *social* emancipation.[18] Most importantly, in the excitement and melodrama and brouhaha of its most violent moments of confrontation, the student power movement dreamed it had become "the revolution," forgetting the more modest claims of its own theory of student power as *an* instance of contradiction in the system. But what the hell. The dream was just the icing on the cake.

11
BE REALISTIC,
DEMAND THE IMPOSSIBLE

Experience on campuses all across the continent in
the past five years clearly points to one fact: this
system and those who run it cannot tolerate any
legitimate opposition, that is, any attempt to transform this pattern into one which shifts control over
economy and society — including education — to
the level of each and every one of us. And the
opposition to these attempts to de-bureaucratize,
de-centralize and humanize is fierce! What is
happening at the University of Alberta is one blatant
expression of this opposition; like a dying dinosaur
whose time has come, thrashing about against the
smaller but more evolved creatures who will one
day dominate.

— from a manifesto of Students
for a Democratic University, University
of Alberta (Gateway, 26 March 1969)

The era of the student power campaigns in Canada — through
1967 to the end of 1969 — was a period of extraordinarily
imaginative and vigorous youth revolt around the world: the
convulsions on Canadian university campuses may be seen as
part of an international phenomenon of youth's refusal to take
its appointed place in the great machine of capitalist enterprise
and organization. This accounts for the very high degree of
identification there was among all the national youth and
student groups and movements. The excitement and pride with
which news was received about the Zengakuren in Japan, say,
who took on the police in hand-to-hand combat with helmets,
shields and javelins. Or about the students choking the streets
of Poland to publicize their slogan, "Without Freedom, No
Bread!" It accounts for the grief and rage expressed at the news
of the murder of Che Guevara in the mountains of Bolivia at the

hands of fascist police (Che! the prototype, the new man, the socialist as impelled by love as by hate), and the murder of three black students in Orangeburg, South Carolina, one of them shot in the back with a shotgun shell, as they gathered to march in protest against the firing of faculty members.

But the student power movement was not only *in* Canada (and in Japan and France and Mexico, et cetera), it was also Canadian. It was as much engendered by Canadian society as by international developments, and it generated indigenous structures of resistance. Two such recur throughout the events of the period: the Canadian Union of Students and Students for a Democratic University (SDU). In 1966, at its fall congress in Halifax and following upon its survey of fees and accessibility, delegates had impassionately debated the future direction of CUS: as the "dance committee for the dance committees" or as the spearhead of student engagement in social issues. Proponents of the former position argued that a students' union has no "authority" to speak on any issues but those which strictly concern students (that is, the quality of student life). Proponents of the latter had asked: Where does a student issue end and a social one begin? "The issue of residence fees gets you into the cost of building residences, into the cost of money, into inflation, into the dependency of the Canadian economy on the American economy, into inflation rates in the U.S., into Vietnam." When, a few months later, CUS issued a Declaration of the Canadian Student ("The Canadian student has the right and duty to improve himself as a social being and to contribute to the development of society"), the University of Alberta students' union had already pulled out of CUS. Its president, Branny Shepanovich, accused it of being "Communist tinged,"[1] and the fight for the life of CUS was on.

SDU, or Students for a Democratic University, was not a national organization. There were, however, at several campuses across the country, groups that identified themselves as SDU, but were "affiliated" with each other only by a certain style and by the similarity of their campaigns. Much more than SUPA (upon whose demise SDU groups sprang up) and CUS, SDU was influenced by certain Americanisms of the international student power movement, notably "yippie!ism" (Youth International Party) with its emphasis on the politics of outrageous life-style and extravagant gesture. SDU generated "personalities" rather than "leaders." It had no fixed membership (people came in and went out of SDU depending on the campaign of the moment) and frequently overlapped with the membership of New Democratic Youth and Student Christian Movement groups. It included in its ranks advocates of the priority of alliance with the working class, of women's liberation, of Third World struggles, of "touchy-feelyism," of revolutionary culture; published manifestos rather than programs; and adopted a strategy of confrontation through mass meetings, rallies and marches rather than of party politics — "all kinds of sympathizers came out of the woodwork, counterculture people, foreign students, draft-dodgers, radical faculty, just because we were *not* involved in party politics." In short, it took the theatricality of protest as seriously as its rhetoric. SDU could be ferociously entertaining.

Spring 1967. Perched on top of a mountain in working-class Burnaby, British Columbia, the architecturally magical and structurally experimental campus of Simon Fraser University has been attracting left-wing faculty, politically seasoned graduate students, and drop-outs. "It was one big happy family, compared to other universities where your friend could become your enemy on a throw of the Bell curve."

Five teaching assistants from SFU circulate an open letter condemning the attack on the right of free speech of a Vancouver high school student who has been suspended for writing a poem critical of his teacher. When they join in a protest at the high school, one of them, Martin Loney, is arrested and the board of governors of SFU, without so much as a hearing, fires all five. The students' council issues a letter to SFU president, MacTaggart-Cowan, informing the board of governors that should it fail to reinstate the five "the student society would call for immediate strike action by all students, graduate and undergraduate, all teaching assistants, all faculty assistants and all faculty members."[2] After an all-night emergency meeting (to get in and out of the meeting, board members must step across the bodies of hundreds of students camped outside the doors), the board of governors backs down.

October 1967. "Stop Press Bulletin: Premier Thatcher [of Saskatchewan] intends to assume direct budgeting control of the university. . . . Our education will be subject to financial censorship. This is a frontal assault on the university. . . . The faculty must take a stand and consider such actions as mass resignations. The students' union must take a firm leadership stand, explain to the students the implications of this action and consider class boycotts and demonstrations." A mass meeting of students at the University of Regina moves that Thatcher retract his proposal for control. "Autonomy, Not Autocracy!"

3 November 1967. The *McGill Daily* reprints from the American satirical paper the *Realist* a piece by Paul Krassner, "The Parts That Were Left Out of the Kennedy Book." The *Daily*'s editor and two journalists are hauled before the Senate Disciplinary Committee on charges of "committing obscene libel."* The SDU, which has been involved in campaigns for course reform, for open university government meetings and for student representation on departmental committees, organizes a rally in defence of the *Daily*'s action ("Students have the right to publish a newspaper without administration control") that terminates with the occupation of all six floors of the administration building. The campus is in an uproar. SDU heats up the protest with a call for a general strike and some of the sitters-in occupy the principal's office. The police are summoned. Nightsticks flying, they arrest and knock unconscious Stan Gray, SDU chairman, and injure several others.

January 1968. SDU organizes at SFU. Over the semester it raises the issues of openness of university government, adminis-

---

*The offending portion:

That man [Lyndon Johnson] was crouching over the corpse [of President Kennedy], no longer chuckling but breathing hard and moving his body rhythmically. At first I thought he must be performing some mysterious symbolic rite he'd learned from Mexicans or Indians as a boy. And then I realized — there is only one way to say this — he was literally fucking my husband in the throat. In the bullet wound in the front of his throat. He reached a climax and dismounted. I froze. The next thing I remember he was being sworn in as the new President.[3]

tration interference in student affairs, alternatives to elitist student government (mass meetings and sit-ins), and senate complicity in smears against left-wing professors in the Political Science, Sociology and Anthropology (PSA) Department.

> We fought against the grading system, we fought for more open courses, we fought for students' rights in the classroom, we fought for better food in the cafeteria. We walked in and took over the Faculty Club, removed its dividing curtain and "integrated" it, forcing the faculty to look for a secret club. We were so politicized we had militants register in the courses of professors who had a rotten line on race or on women and engaged in classroom struggle sessions with them.

23 April 1968. Students at Columbia University in New York begin a sit-in at the first of five university buildings they will eventually seize and occupy and maintain as "communes" until April 30. They are there because Martin Luther King has just been murdered and his memory demeaned by a university administration that refuses to pay a living wage to Puerto Rican support staff; because the university has grabbed Harlem land for a student gym, offering blacks literally a back door into a portion of the facilities; because the university has expanded over the years by summary eviction of black people from their houses; because the university fired workers who tried to form a union; and because the university, with connections with the CIA and with the Reserve Officer Training Corps (ROTC), has implicated itself in genocide.[4] They demand that the construction of the gym cease and the university break its tie with the CIA. Everywhere are red banners and the slogans of the resistance: "Create Two, Three, Many Columbias!" "All Power to the Communes!" and "Up Against the Wall, Motherfucker!"

24 April 1968. Occupiers break into the office of the president and seize it. The image of the young ruffian, feet up on the polished desk of Mr. President, at once a contemptuous and hilarious gesture, sends *frissons* of indignation through America.

30 April 1968. New York City police break into the occupied buildings and arrest 712 people. One hundred and forty-eight are injured in the process, assailed with clubs, billyjacks, sticks and even fenceposts.

3 May 1968. Students at Sorbonne University in Paris meet in the campus courtyard in a show of solidarity with students of Nanterre University who have been demonstrating against campus conditions. Police charge in and arrest several hundred, dragging them off in police vans. Infuriated, students attack the police and the riot spills out into the streets of the Latin Quarter.

6–10 May 1968. Students strike, demanding full political and trade union rights for students. Enormous processions surge along the Champs-Elysées; they are bearing red banners and singing, until their throats are hoarse and raw, the "Internationale"; at night there are bloody and desperate battles in the street between students at their barricades and police with their riot gear and tear gas (residents sympathetic with the students provide them with food and shelter and give them their cars for the barricades); and all of this is apparently coordinated and refined with no visible "leadership" or program or bureaucracy.

> All we knew was that we had to defend ourselves where we stood; we split into small groups, so that the police services were unable to launch a single, directed attack. Every barricade became a centre of action and of discussion, every group of demonstrators a squad acting on its own initiative. Barricades sprang up everywhere; no one felt the lack of a general in charge of overall strategy; messengers kept everyone informed of what was happening on the other barricades and passed on collective decisions for discussion. In our new-found solidarity our spirits began to soar. For the first time in living memory, young workers, young students, apprentices, and high school pupils were acting in unison. We could not guess what turn the events were going to take, but that did not bother us — all that mattered was that, at long last, we were all united in action.[5]

14–27 May 1968. Inspired by the revolutionary elan and audacity and the politically libertarian atmosphere of the student rebellion, workers occupy their factories, at Sud-Aviation, at Renault, at Citroen; strike committees take over the administration of whole towns and control prices and the distribution of food and gasoline; schoolchildren and teachers take over schools; printers refuse to print the "lies" of their bosses; waitresses, taxi-drivers, soccer players, bank clerks, all strike. Students (but *not* the union functionaries) join the strike committees and together with the strikers call for the expropriation of the factories by the workers in the name of a new society. *Power to the workers' councils / Abolish the class society / Abolish alienation / Humanity will not be happy till the last bureaucrat is hanged from the entrails of the last capitalist.*

27 May 1968. The Communist-controlled union leadership signs an agreement to accept the arbitration of the Gaullist minister of labour. ". . . while the workers as a whole have decided to take over their own factories and to expropriate the owners," wrote a student occupier, "the Communist union has decided for the workers that the expropriated factories are to be returned to their owners in exchange for higher wages."[6]

June 1968. It takes three weeks for the Communist union functionaries to tame "their" workers to the point they finally all go back to work. At an open assembly at the Sorbonne, students publicize their theses: "We must make the revolution. It will be long and hard. We must not allow ourselves to be duped."[7]

June 1968. Two hundred delegates attend the annual CUS seminar in Winnipeg. Excitement at the events in Paris is palpable: at a demonstration attacking the campaign platforms of Conservative leader Robert Stanfield and Prime Minister Pierre Trudeau (both men are in town for rallies), a placard exuberantly summons "One, Two, Three More Sorbonnes!" and, at the seminar itself, well over half the delegates press for free-wheeling discussion about the role of a student movement in revolutionary change in Canada, about spontaneity versus discipline, grass-roots activity versus centralization, the relationship of theory to practice, the function of the multiversity in preparing the "new working class" and so on.[8] Electrified by the news from France, the delegates confront the staggering implications of an insurrectionary working class (so much for its co-optation and complacency) and of the detonating dreams students have of free and joyous activity in the democratic collectivity of the barricades; of self-directed action by the masses (bye-bye vanguard parties!) and of the coming together of the campus and the factory (*real* factories!); and of Daniel Cohn-Bendit's exhilarating exclamation: "There is only one reason for being a revolutionary — because it is the best way to live."[9] Here, surely, in the facts of May–June is the confirmation of the new left project.

> The spectacle of a momentarily insurgent working class apparently sparked into motion by student upheaval — this popularized the notion that the student movement was not just ancillary but was of strategic importance. The March 22 Movement of Nanterre seemed to demonstrate that you could unleash a revolutionary-looking train of events simply by challenging curfew regulations! The student project was thus validated quite independently of any links with the working class.

Summer 1968. Spurred on by the events in France, SDU at SFU runs a student power slate of radical candidates for student council, and wins ten of thirteen seats. SDU pushes for abolition of grades and for making the connections between university democracy, continentalism, imperialism and the national liberation of Canada; and from within it emerges the women's caucus that "raises political issues relevant to the experience of females in this society."[10]

20 August 1968. Czechoslovakia is invaded by troops of the Warsaw Pact nations, and its head of state, Alexander Dubcek, is arrested. "The force that sends young Poles and Russians, Germans and Hungarians into Czechoslovakia is the same force that sends young Americans into Vietnam, that beats up young people in the streets of Paris, Madrid, Chicago, Berkeley and Rome."[11] The invasion is the boot grinding the human face into the ground; it is an iniquitous and gloomy event and haunts the daydreams of the radicals in the West who had rejoiced along with the youth of Eastern Europe when the "Prague spring" only a few months earlier had signalled the revival of the country's political life. The Stalinist political and ideological monolith had begun to crumble under the pressure of hundreds of thousands of rank-and-file socialists who demanded that socialist democracy fulfill itself. The Czech Youth Federation had demanded representation in all state bodies and the right to criticize party policy, and mass meetings of young people had denounced censorship and the monopoly of power and information and demanded the "thorough-going democratization of public life." And now it had all come down to this: clandestine meetings once more (workers standing guard at the doors), sabotage, and students burning themselves to death in the track of the Soviet tanks.

25 August 1968. About ten thousand demonstrators are in Chicago to support the call of the National Mobilization Committee to End the War in Vietnam for anti-war manifestations and to celebrate a yippie Festival of Light alongside the morbid proceedings of the Democratic party and its convention. They are here to remind this bloated bulk of a party that the war it is pursuing in Vietnam will bring its own house down. They are in the parks, dancing and chanting, defying curfews, defying 12,000 cops, 6,000 National Guardsmen, 6,000 army troops, bazookas, flamethrowers, jeeps entwined with barbed wire, tanks, and Mayor Daley's order that looters will be shot on sight. On this Monday night the cops chase the kids out of Lincoln Park with tear gas, and others wait for them as they careen through the side-streets trying to get away, wait for them with billyclubs, not arresting them but clubbing their skulls open; cops are pulling people out of cars, breaking into bars and restaurants and throwing patrons out into the street where more cops are waiting for them, bursting into houses to drag out the occupants for a beating. It is a total, complete police riot.[12]

27 August 1968. The demonstrators are pursued to the Hilton Hotel, where women are hurled through the plate glass windows and the cops go berserk in the lobby, smashing anyone who looks "funny," while the peach-fuzz carpet soaks up blood and people kneel in prayer. "We were absolutely gripped by what was going on in Chicago. Here was a sophisticated political movement mounting massive demonstrations in a direct political engagement with the American state. We were very impressed."

September 1968. The annual congress of CUS takes place in Guelph. In spite of a number of withdrawals of small campuses from the organization, delegates endorse several controversial resolutions, including one from the University of Toronto that "Canadian society is not self-determined; our cultural, political and economic lives are dominated by giant American corporations." Resolutions from the Education Commission blast the Canadian university as an "imperialist institution" and demand that universities refuse money intended for military research, turn curriculum control over to students and faculty, and abolish the practice of tenure, which is a "guild professionalist concept." They pass a resolution that the citizens of the "sovereign nation" of Quebec be permitted to decide whether or not to establish a "bi-national" government with English Canada.

On the second day of the congress a plenary session is interrupted by a file of militants.* Bearing the red flag of socialism and the black flag of anarchism, to the tune of "Solidarity Forever," they hang a portrait of Ho Chi Minh, the Vietnamese Communist leader, over that of Queen Elizabeth and address the crowd. "We've come four thousand miles to this congress to discuss what is happening in the world," says Martin Loney from SFU. "We want to discuss how this affects students. Just look at Czechoslovakia and Chicago and tell me you can't be concerned. . . . CUS exists as a national voice, a place for discussion, a forum, a place to mobilize students." A few days later, Loney is president-elect of CUS and delegates vote three-to-one to support the National Liberation Front of South Vietnam.

Fall 1968. After four years of an intense public debate on education reforms, the CEGEPs are set up throughout Quebec. They are, it turns out, too little too late.

---

*"Some of those calling themselves radicals had long hair. A number wore khaki jackets not unlike those worn in the armed services of countries. Others wore sandals with no socks. None looked like an average Canadian university student whom they insist they represent. Still fewer spoke like the student seen every day on the Canadian campus." (*Gateway,* 11 September 1968)

By the time the reforms are applied, the "Quiet Revolution" has collapsed, the provincial government is in a state of financial crisis and the application is anarchic. The old buildings are simply turned over to the new system with the same old administration, no money comes in for new structures or libraries or labs. The illusions turn into bitterness.

The syndicalist illusions — that the interests of student-workers coincide with those of the progressive Ministry of Education* in the need to modernize and corporatize education for the up-and-coming professional classes — crumble in the face of the actual situation of students. The system continues to stall working-class youth in the CEGEPs, and both openings in the universities and jobs upon graduation are denied them. Under the "tremendous influence" of the May–June events in Paris, of the developing national movement in Quebec, of a series of strikes by bus drivers and teachers, and of UGEQ's leadership of mass demonstrations against the war in Vietnam (*"Québec aux Québécois! Vietnam aux Vietnamiens!"*), the students of the CEGEPs sit in and occupy their colleges. They demand job guarantees, teacher and student control, increased access to the universities. They demand that the bursary and loan system be scrapped and students be paid a salary. But the occupations are first of all an explosion of anger, anger at the way they have been shoved around and cheated and duped by the state, anger at the betrayal of their expectation that they would be able to propel themselves out of the dead ends of Québécois society. *"S'instruire c'est s'enricher,"* said the slogan, but it wasn't true: the state could not deliver; the security of the students *was not theirs to control.* The occupations last a week and a half and are followed by mass student and teacher expulsions and a regulation banning political rallies and leafleting in the majority of CEGEPs.[13]

October 1968. When Pierre Trudeau comes to Regina to unveil a statue of Louis Riel, twelve hundred students demon-

---

*There had never been a Ministry of Education in Quebec before 1964.

strate, demanding that student loans be made available to all academically qualified students. Trudeau tells them they are "selfish."

October 1968. At the University of Waterloo students occupy the students' centre and intend to stay until they secure legal control of the building: "We regard the board of governors as an illegitimate authority." At the University of Calgary SDU activists reject a proposal that the students' union building be run by the administration, the faculty and the students jointly: "It's *our* building," they say, "we paid for it, we'll run it ourselves."

October 1968. Wearing gas masks and yelling "Thought police! Thought police!" members of SDU invade and disrupt the Faculty Club at the University of Alberta. At UBC, two thousand chortling students, one squealing pig and Jerry Rubin, American yippie, crash the "faculty only" restaurant and bar.

Fall–winter 1968. CUS is in a national struggle with campuses that are holding referenda on whether or not to stay within the organization. Field-workers fan out across the country, making contact with sympathetic students — SDUs, university newspaper staffs, co-op groups — and agitating at assemblies, workshops, debates, in the cafeterias: "We'd stand up on a table with a bullhorn and start talking." They point out what the student gets for the sixty-five-cent CUS dues: a travel plan, regional exchange scholarships, publications, research. But more: discussions situate the university in the political economy of Canada. "Increasingly there is the feeling that we will have an anti-capitalist, anti-imperialist university or no university at all." The university is inseparable from the undemocratic structures of the economy *and* from the international struggles for national liberation: "Our feeling was that CUS wasn't worth preserving as just a dance committee, even a social democratic dance committee, if it wasn't anti-imperialist." The university and society overlap: "Looking at the university is another way of looking at society." A student cannot ask that her/his union be in the one and outside the other. *There is no such thing as a student problem.*

November 1968. Student research at SFU turns up the (not unrelated) facts that only 17 percent of SFU's student population comes from the working class and that sitting on the SFU senate are, among others, W.M. Hamilton, president of the Employers' Council of British Columbia; Cyrus McLean, chairman of B.C. Telephone; Mark Collins, a director of MacMillan-Bloedel; and Jack Diamond, co-operator of the B.C. Jockey Club. There are on the senate and board of governors no representatives from labour, nor from the native community, the teachers' organizations, and tenants and welfare organizations. Research also indicates that students who are turned away from SFU go to the community colleges where they accumulate credits that are in turn "disqualified" by SFU. Thus is the working class streamed into the two-year colleges and away from SFU.

There is a hue and cry among students demanding an "open admissions" policy to SFU from the colleges. The demand is formulated as a motion to the senate (there are three student representatives to the senate), where it is defeated. Immediately, more than a hundred students occupy the administration building and for three days and nights sit in,* eating peanut-butter sandwiches, watching Mickey Mouse cartoons, singing and arguing. They rifle through administration files where they discover and disclose that the RCMP is operating in considerable force on campus as plainclothesmen and has been given by the university administration some six hundred files on students and faculty, including draft-resisters. The demand continues: public negotiations with President Strand for open admissions.

At 2:15 A.M. of the fourth day of the occupation, 150 RCMP men hit the campus, which is deserted except for the occupiers and some "crazies" from the drama department who are rehearsing *Coriolanus.* President Strand is shouting through a bullhorn, "The university will not tolerate any longer any interference with the use of its property. There are two options: each of you may leave the building or the RCMP will remove

---

*Earlier in the fall, the Marxist philosopher Herbert Marcuse had spoken to some three thousand students. "We loved it. It was very inspiring. He lectured on the Great No, the negation, the Great Refusal; the logic of his position was, resist! fight!"

you. The decision is yours." Sixty students leave voluntarily. The 114 remaining decide to be arrested and are led out one by one through a cordon of police who are holding back a crowd that has by now gathered. The crowd is shouting, "Keep the faith, baby!" and the occupiers are singing "Gimme that Old Time Religion," and, over the public address system, which the crazies from *Coriolanus* have installed on a roof, comes the "Horst Wessel Song" and "The Party's Over," over and over again. The 114 are charged with the felony of "mischief: the unlawful and willful obstruction of the lawful use of private property," which carries a penalty of up to seven years imprisonment. "The experience was very humbling: you challenge the university with what seems a very simple issue; you just give it a little tap on the shoulder to see how it'll react and *wham!* Imagine what it'd do over a *big* issue."

December 1968. Seven hundred students at an Arts teach-in at the University of Alberta give a rousing ovation of approval to a philosophy professor who urges them to organize an Arts union to function independently of the administration and the students' union. "Nobody is going to emancipate you. You've got to emancipate yourselves." One hundred and fifty students forthwith march over to the Sociology Department and demand it answer their concerns about the "suppression of democracy" in the department at the hands of a five-man faculty "junta."

February 1969. More than one thousand students boycott classes at the University of Regina in order to attend a teach-in on the interrelated problems of students and the community. Representatives from the labour unions, from faculty, CUS and the NDP observe the meeting. One motion supports the university's employees' union in its contract negotiations with the board of governors, and another calls for the abolition of tuition fees.

February–March 1969. Two politically active, Marxist sociology professors at the University of Alberta, Don Whiteside and Seth Fisher, are denied tenure. The department chairman admits they are being dropped not as bad teachers or researchers but as elements who are not "capable of working effectively as a member of this department and of the university." Student supporters translate this to mean that Fisher and Whiteside are being penalized for their "minority views," and a campaign by an SDU student defence committee starts up, charging the university with authoritarianism, rigid conservatism, secrecy and abuse of due process.

28 March 1969. Fifteen thousand demonstrators are outside the gates of McGill University chanting, *"McGill français! McGill aux Québécois!"* while police, helicopters, riot trucks and cruisers seal them off from a handful of students within singing "God Save the Queen." The demonstration is the culmination of a first wave of protest against the Union Nationale government's Bill 63 which proposes to institution-alize English-language education "where there is a need for it." Arrayed against the bill are the Mouvement pour l'Intégration Scolaire (which demands French unilingualism in education), the Front de Libération Populaire (an above-ground version of the clandestine FLQ), the Comité Indépendance-Socialisme, the Montreal Central Council of the Confederation of National Trade Unions (CNTU), CEGEP students and a number of McGill students who denounce the privileges of McGill.* McGill's SDU exposes the university as an institution of anglophone privilege guilty of helping sustain "more than two hundred years of economic exploitation and national oppression" in Quebec.[14]

Spring 1969. At the convention of UGEQ, neither the "left" tendency of political unionism nor the "right" tendency of business unionism commands a clear majority of delegates. UGEQ collapses and the left tendency becomes the *"mouvement syndicale politique"* and heads for the streets.

Spring 1969. Karl Dietrich Wolff, of the German new leftists' SDS, visits Canada. In his many interviews, from Montreal to Vancouver, he reiterates the themes of the international new left: that radicals must understand the structures of their own society as continuous with imperialist

---

*The 17 percent of the population of Quebec that is anglophone occupies 42 percent of all university places, one-third of government grants goes to English-language institutions of higher education and less than 5 percent of McGill's population is francophone.

structures ("Vietnam is not a mistake"), that people must be mobilized to struggle *at the place* where they live and work, on issues of local control, and that such struggle must be decentralized because "that is the only way to keep in touch with the spontaneity of the masses."

A week after Wolff's visit in Toronto, Clark Kerr comes to speak to education administrators. The Toronto Student Movement,* a group of Marxist-oriented students' union activists at the University of Toronto, decides to stage a contestation on the occasion of this visit: "Stop the spectacle!" Kerr, after all, is not only the theorist of the "multiversity"; he is an advisor on industrial relations to U.S. presidents and a proponent of the "post-conflict" industrial society. Together with students from Glendon College and York University, TSM members stage a psychodrama in the hall where Kerr is speaking.

> In the middle of his speech we stage a silent replay of an incident in Berkeley during the Free Speech Movement days. Kerr had come out to address the students; Mario Savio came forward to rebut him and was seized by security personnel before he could speak. This is what we replay in front of Kerr. In the middle of it we ourselves are seized by security guards! Pandemonium breaks out.

Summer 1969. TSM splits, between Maoist "workerists" and neo-Marxist "student powerists." The latter reconstitute themselves as the New Left Caucus and commit themselves to the development of a "mass revolutionary student movement" responsive to the industrialization and proletarianization of the student, the massive disaffection of youth from middle-class values and life-style, and the international momentum to stop the war in Vietnam. Inspired by the anti-Stalinist resistance in socialist societies such as Czechoslovakia, the NLC rejects centralism and party discipline. Inspired by the student-worker alliances in France a year earlier, the NLC begins

---

*Not to be confused with the Maoist Canadian Student Movement groups that were being organized on campuses, the TSM in fact "preempted" the Maoists when it took that name for itself.

reading about the history of the Canadian working class, and opens up again the pages of the Regina Manifesto.

August–September 1969. The thirty-third annual congress of CUS meets in Port Arthur, Ontario. With only eight student councils committed to CUS membership for the coming year, the organization's finances are thin indeed and its credibility as a national union stretched to the snapping point. Politically too, CUS is shaky: there is no ideological consensus. It does manage to pass a motion in opposition to Americanization of Canadian universities (but rejects the idea of a quota system to regulate the number of Americans teaching here); a resolution denouncing the authoritarianism in the classroom that "prepares the student to fit uncritically into the corporate capitalist structure"; and a recommendation that campus bookstores, libraries and food services be reorganized as co-ops.

But the organization is under attack right and left. From one wing come charges that it is impossible to implement the radical policies of CUS among the mass of "unconscious" students. From another comes the charge that it is not policies but structures that must be re-examined, that CUS's base must be shifted from "elitist" students' councils to a voluntary, radical, grass-roots membership. From yet another comes the recommendation that CUS once again organize students around "student" issues, like housing and employment. And, finally, from the University of Waterloo, comes a proposal that CUS affiliate with the International Workers of the World (a radical syndicalist union effectively smashed in the Twenties but carrying on with a handful of sympathizers). Because of the irreconcilability of these critiques, the congress shuts down with a third of its agenda unpresented. Delegates leave to fight the critical referendum campaigns at Carleton University and the University of Toronto.

At the University of Toronto the New Left Caucus engages in classroom provocations, challenging the ideological direction of some social science courses, and resisting the "professionalization" of graduate studies (that is, the speed-up of Ph.D. "production," rigidity of deadlines and the introduction of comprehensives). Having developed a critique of "spectacular radicalism" (by which radicals provide "entertainment" while the university proceeds with its business as usual) and counter-proposals for disruption of and intervention into the "processes of reproduction of the industrial forms of higher education,"* the NLC decides to test these ideas at Fall Commencement ceremonies at the University of Toronto. At University College, authority figures at the high table address platitudes about education to the serried ranks of passive students down below the long tables. "You, the graduands of this estimable university are about to take up the tasks to which the society of free men calls you. . . . " In the midst of these perorations the NLC begins to heckle, students pick it up, others begin to counter-heckle, and the ceremonies conclude in confusion. NLC repeats the intervention at Victoria College, but here the administration knows they are coming and invites them to speak. A member does so, and talks of sexual repression and the female orgasm. NLC, as a result, grows rapidly: more than a hundred people show up at its next meeting and leave, wearing an NLC button, "Bring U of T to a Climax."

Fall 1969. Panicked, the University of Toronto administration calls for a hardening of university disciplinary procedures and warns that any further disruptions, in or out of classes, will result in expulsion. At the same time, the disciplinary code is being rewritten and the old Disciplinary Committee has been replaced by a provisional committee on which students' council representatives sit. These representatives happen also to be NLC members; they show up at the next committee meetings in red armbands and announce they are withdrawing. Through them the NLC demands that the administration's threats of expulsion be rescinded. Wanting neither an occupa-

---

*The idea was that the "spectacle" of university processes must be ruptured and discredited if a climate for serious ideological struggle with the institution is ever to take place. Students must be won from the mesmerizing spectacle. "This was a vulgarization of the notion of 'contestation' but not quite as vulgar as the American idea of confrontation. The American idea was to do something so terrible that the agents of the state — the police — would be brought in; the violence at the hands of the police that people would experience would finally disabuse them of their liberal illusions about the nature of the state."

tion of Simcoe Hall nor to call in the police as a result, the administration relents and a liberal disciplinary code wins the day.

At the University of Alberta a united front of SDU, SCM, the Maoists and assorted free-lance leftists decides to resist the implementation of a Law and Order Committee charged with revising the disciplinary code of the university. Taking the position that the very existence of such a committee is offensive, the front arrives at a public meeting of the committee and, at a pregnant moment in the proceedings, unfurls onstage a bedsheet painted with an enormous swastika. "People went mad."

September 1969. Tuition fees go up yet again, and at the University of Regina the Students' Representative Council calls on all students to withhold their fees until further notice.

24 September 1969. Teachers and students in the Political Science, Sociology and Anthropology (PSA) Department at SFU go on strike. "The Focus of the strike," reads the Statement of Strike Principles, "is not to stop others, outside PSA, from going on with a bureaucratic education. Rather by developing active and relevant learning and research, as 'counter-courses,' we can begin an alternative to Strand's university."[15] And indeed they do, in discussions on women's liberation, communes, critical social science, sexuality, the colonization of Canada, at the "Louis Riel U."

The strike culminates a process of rupture in the corporate-liberal consensus of the university, a process that goes back to the bust of the 114 and proceeds through administrative interference in PSA when the department was placed, in July, under "trusteeship" because of its alleged "administrative inefficiency."

The fact is — and this is what brings the students out on strike along with the faculty — the administration can no longer tolerate the functioning, radical democracy of PSA. Responding to the clamours of students and faculty for self-government and participation, PSA for several months up to the imposition of the trusteeship had instituted: faculty-elected committees and chairman; a student plenum with elected committees parallel to those of the faculty and with equal powers to initiate meetings and to veto policy (in fact, every decision of the one plenum had to be ratified by the other); open files and records of meetings.* "Parity came from a belief held by large numbers of students and PSA faculty that, despite differences in knowledge and experience, teaching and learning are best accomplished as a two-way process requiring discussion and argument rather than coercion and obedience."[16] Here in PSA, students are experiencing real collectivity, the give-and-take of intellectual and political partnership, the excitement of explosive ideas being nurtured and cultivated,**and the realization, in the concretions of democratic committees and radical analysis in the classroom and everyday involvement in the processes of government, of their struggle as students.

The four demands of the strikers are: an end to the trusteeship and the reinstatement of its elected chairman; acceptance of the recommendations of the PSA tenure committees (faculty and student); reinstatement of four professors whose contracts have not been renewed, contrary to the wishes of the PSA committees; and fundamental recognition of PSA's experimental practices in organization and educational procedures.

24 September–3 October 1969. The strike is on. Students boycott classes and form picket lines outside the classrooms; mass assemblies of hundreds meet every day to discuss the execution of the strike; strikers sell T-shirts emblazoned with a drawing of "The Little Man," Karl Marx, who gets his ass kicked at "Seven Flavour University," and propaganda is produced and distributed in town.

People want to control how they work, when they work,

---

*When the trusteeship was imposed, PSA was also at the point of involving secretarial staff in departmental discussions and policy decisions.

**"We brought in Marcuse and the students brought him flowers and a big kiss, we brought in Ernest Mandel, and D.F. Fleming who'd written the first revisionist history of American foreign policy. He came up from Tennessee in his 1941 Chevrolet. It wasn't an easy thing, you know, to get the hippies, with their dope and spouting revolution, together with an eminent old man."

the conditions in which they work — not just the wage-packet for which they work. Students too are no longer willing to be bought off with a degree-packet. They want to control how they work, when they work, the conditions in which they work. And the administrators and the boards of governors, the same as the owners and managers, oppose it. . . . This is your struggle too.

3 October 1969. The administration of SFU suspends eight of the striking faculty, relieves them of all teaching and committee duties, withdraws their voting privileges, and moves to obtain an injunction against the strikers. The non-striking (minority) PSA faculty elect a new chairman and adopt a new constitution for the department, eliminating all student parity arrangements. The strike has been decisively extinguished.

23 October 1969. The students of the University of Toronto vote in a referendum to withdraw from CUS. Its financial base shattered, CUS dissolves.

The post-mortems are replete with recrimination. The national office failed to act on its own resolutions, they say, neglecting follow-up work on the resolution of support for the Vietnamese NLF, for instance. Harassed by right and left, it drained out its precious energy in referendum battles rather than fulfilling its policies from campus to campus. While the union was rhetorically anti-capitalist and anti-imperialist (especially during the term of the second-to-last president, Pete Warrian), calling on student unionists to become a "national liberation front" for Canada in solidarity with other national liberation struggles, the majority of rank-and-file members manifestly were not. "The Canadian student in his or her broad general context did not want the revolution. They went to university to get an education and a job. In three years, in dropping in on CUS seminars and congresses once or twice, you don't necessarily come out an anti-imperialist revolutionary." The revolution is not something that is accomplished by fiat after a conference of "heavies." It is painstakingly cultivated at the base, at the "indigenous" level of the campus, program by program, action by action, until the mass of students "organically" confronts authority with the will to stop the machine.

CUS turned up its nose at the student issues of travel, exchanges, discounts, bus fares, all those things every human being has at least some passing need for. At the same time they were romantic and adventurist. Typical meetings were euphoric with delegates passing motions to smash the bourgeoisie or whatever, radical measures that would require socialism tomorrow to implement. But the leadership didn't have to go back to the individual campus to explain such policies and fight for them.

They particularly did not have to go back to the "regions," to Brandon, Calgary, Wolfville, Port Arthur, beyond the support system of the national office (located in Ottawa), beyond the heady abstractions of anti-capitalist rhetoric to the concrete details of a particular situation in a *locale* where specifics of class and ethnicity and region militated against the adoption holus-bolus of CUS policy. "Delegates knew all the answers when they were sitting at the conventions, listening to the arguments back and forth. But that didn't mean they could defend at home on their own their vote for victory for the NLF."

Still there is much mourning at the demise of CUS. Gone the one forum where students could communicate as a national body and experience the solidarity of resistance expressed en masse. Enter the fragmentation of the collective refusal. "The forces of repressive reaction have won a major battle."

29 October 1969. Thirty thousand people march in the streets of Montreal against Bill 63. In spite of this, in spite of a strike in half the post-elementary schools in Montreal, in spite of the protest of delegates to the general councils of the QFL and the CNTU, in spite of the "total social and political effervescence" these protests signal, the bill is passed.

"Students cannot make a socialist revolution. Students cannot even establish a red base on campus without considerable support from the surrounding population. . . . The role of the student movement in Europe has been primarily as a catalyst. Its effect has been by example. Its tactics call to mind the early militancy of the working class. Its cultural concerns find a response in the crushed conditions of life and work of members of the new working class. Where social contradictions are acute the student movement can act as a spark." So wrote the New Left Caucus in Toronto in 1969. So it wrote, still hopeful, still purposeful, still mindful of its assignment. And even when the social tensions are not "acute" enough to shoot off sparks, there is still this for the student movement to do: "To grow, to expose, to contest. In some cases even to inspire." For, just as the activists themselves had been inspired by the revolutions and liberations that had preceded them, who was to say that they in turn would not inspire some wave of students yet to come? Battles may have been lost in 1969 but the war was still theirs to win.

PART III
COUNTER-CULTURE

I

BACK TO THE GARDEN

Between October 1967 and May 1968 the *Georgia Straight*, underground newspaper in Vancouver, printed the following items: interviews with Mick Jagger ("Do you feel different from other people in any way?"), Jimi Hendrix and Eric Burdon; news about the provincial government's probe into narcotics use, about the biggest bust in the city's history (fifteen drug squads versus fifty denizens of "hippie haunts" and "skid-road drug hangouts"), and about the bust of seventeen "loiterers" at the courthouse fountain; "Imaginary Space" columns by poet Gerry Gilbert, and columns by socialist alderman Harry Rankin — for example, "The Tenant as Nigger"; articles about the June War in the Middle East, about the "unified life" by Mishra, and "God's Secret Agent .005" by Timothy Leary; and an obituary for Martin Luther King.

First there was the music. The great waves and rolling of it, smashing to smithereens the decorous cadences of the life of a middle-class teen-aged girl, her drudgery over textbooks, the constant supervision of her life, calf-length skirts, and blouses buttoned up to her neck, *no jeans allowed!* sit straight, knees together, smile, use deodorant, shave your legs, *watch your language young lady!* the benumbing fear of bad boys, blood and *going too far;* nothing else was ever going to happen: being a nice girl, a good girl, doing her duty, forever and ever plain, shy and afraid just like this; and then came the music, *circa* 1958.

One o'clock two o'clock three o'clock *rock rock rock,* the saxophone shouts *woo wah woo wah;* the throaty catch and quiver in the baritone of Buddy Holly's voice breaks your heart, pretty pretty pretty pretty Peggy Sue he sings over a thrumming drum roll and electric guitar that, twenty years later, is still unbearably erotic; "I feel like I could die," aching and yearning with the straining melancholy of the harmonies of the Everly Brothers, *thump, thump, thump,* the risk and thrill of daydreams of falling in love with these boys who were not nice, boys with slick, thick pompadours and tight pants and black leather jackets and accents from the wrong side of the tracks. Elvis straddles the microphone and grinds his hips, take me, take me, and all of this is pale-faced romance compared to the roller coaster rock 'n' roll of Chuck Berry and Little Richard.

It was the music of rhythm and blues, the pain and the humiliation of the Mississippi dirt farm merged with the sexual arrogance, the outrageousness, the shout of independence from the city ghetto. But with the mass production of the phonograph, the phonograph record, the transistor radio and the jukebox, it was consumed en masse. And everywhere. It meant get up there and *dance!* Shake and roll and jump and slide and kick, stroke and clutch and swoon, in a ritualized pre-sexual play at the beach, in creaky ballrooms and community halls that had just been emptied of their bingo games, in waxy gymnasiums and in the rumpus room where, oh boy, you necked in the dark corners. It was intensely communal, bodies packed to the four walls, and exclusive of grown-ups. And in its defiance of class and racial conventions it was, this eruption of rock 'n' roll in the schools of the Fifties, the first sign of the appetite of the emergent *déclassé* for the material of the life of the forgotten and the oppressed.

29 December 1963: the CJCA Radio 93 Fabulous Forty Survey listed songs by Bobby Curtola, Molly Bee, Roy Orbison, the Singing Nun and Bobby Rydell in the Top Five. So much, by 1963, for rock 'n' roll. But the generation was in university now, or would be in another year or two, and its concerns had matured past those of the lovelorn, acned punk snarling at his parents. For the first time, one had an intellectual life and, through the news of the civil rights movements in the United States, a quickening of political interest. And here one's life intersected again with music.

Baez, our lady of the ministrations; Angelina, the sky's on fire and with it her voice, its timbres shaking her body as she stood up for all of us and addressed public men and their deeds and informed them they had miscalculated; for here she was, and all of us in ranks behind her, to show they would have to march over our bodies if they would advance to the war. She enspirited our virtue; how could we fail her?

With his plain, rhetorical guitar, Donovan evoked freedom fighters and the seas of blood and bones in which they wallowed, the universal soldier and the sacrifice of his body, and more tenderly, the lover surprised by his love, the hash smokers on sunny Goodge Street and that recurring male archetype that was finally to estrange women, the ramblin' boy, collar up to the wind, thumb out on the highway. Babe, I gotta be free but, babe, don't you ever forget me. *And the war drags on.*

Ian and Sylvia: the lady in the velvet dress from the manse in Southern Ontario and her consort, the dude in a cow-roper's jacket from the ranch in Alberta. It was passion that mated them and passion that drove them back and forth across the country, spinning their songs — *our* songs — of the lay of this land. It was splendid when people around the world sang "Four Strong Winds": we knew the sensation of those winds.

Folk music, handed down from one voice to another, embellished by each personality that took up the song, replenished by the new singer-songwriters, re-created by whatever instrument or skill lay at hand, was a protest against commercialism, mass culture and the cynical relations of the marketplace. In its recitation of disasters, calamities, deaths and burials, it would not let us forget the catastrophes of the weak and the exploited. In its naming of towns and valleys and the heroes of the folk, it rescued our collective past and our landscape from anonymity. In its anecdotes of the workplace and in its celebration of poor people's tenacity and their coming together, from fragmentation and loneliness, for one more family reunion, it reminded us that in community there could be goodness. Folk music was the wailing wall at which we made atonement for the historical culpability of our class and our race.

1965: the "folkie" Bob Dylan picked up an electric guitar at the Newport Folk Festival, the Byrds electrified "Mr. Tambourine Man" (Dylan's acoustic ballad), the Grateful Dead and Big Brother and the Holding Company were formed in California and Buffalo Springfield — rockers all — sang, I think it's time we *stop*, children, what's that sound, everybody look what's goin' down. Another intersection: rock 'n' roll takes up the modes of contestation.

Tough guys, born in Chicago, lean up against the peeling wall of a storefront and pick their teeth: Paul Butterfield and his blues band. The violence of the city, dead friends splayed in the street, the rules for survival ("Shake your money maker" and "Get a gun") are matched by the aggressiveness of the amplified harmonica, the ricochets of the drums, the guitar licks that are like a punch to the side of the head. This is blues shoved through a tunnel of wire.

In the songs of the Rolling Stones is the apotheosis of the male ego in its resentful solitariness, its bloody-minded sexuality, its disposable commitments and its clamorous demands for satisfaction. But in their picking up where Chuck Berry had left off, in smashing the limits to what a rock 'n' roll band could muster in power and propulsion, all else was disregarded as we danced exultantly to their anthems of aggrandizement.

"The rock 'n' roll that came out of Liverpool wasn't telling us to organize; it was telling us, twist and shout!" But then came *Revolver* and where were the loveable moptops in the songs of lonely people, all the speakers without an audience, all the dead without mourners? With George Harrison's admonishment that you don't "hang a sign" on him and in John Lennon's droning seducements to surrender to the shining void, the Beatles had become the great wizards, conjuring up the yellow submarine in which we could cruise in ease and plenitude below the worldly waves of disturbance.

About Bob Dylan. With him, many went to the limits of their speech and their emotions. In his acceptance of the chaos of language *and* being that was roaring at the boundaries of "logic and proportion," in his apocalyptic vision of a world depleted of order, habit and convention,* in his proposition of the ascendancy of personality over society, he claimed for subjectivity a power and authority counterpoised with those of the "real" world.

On our own and homeless, street-wise and street-used, invisible, our secrets stolen long ago, oh yes, we knew how it *feels* to

---

*"As far as I'm concerned," he once said, "I don't consider myself outside of anything, I just consider myself *not around*."[1]

be a rolling stone, foreclosed on our psychic debts, stuck in the ditch of the killing ground of Highway 61, chilled to the bone in the rain of Juarez; yes, this is all true, this is as it is. It was late afternoon, I was drying dishes, and from the radio came a song, a song by Bob Dylan, and I stood transfixed, hand with plate poised mid-air, as the light went out of the room and, yes, I said, the war, the naked, the dead and the dying, the lies and the treachery and the filth heaping up in the streets around my room, yes, we are targets of the riot squad and ambulances of Desolation Row, we are the rearranged faces and assumed names of Desolaton Row. Yes, we accept this grotesque and suffering self these songs make us an offering of. And all the rest of my life I will know I had this hour.

In its celebration of the self over institutions, its adventures along irrational routes to freedom, its release of repressed behaviour even at the cost of disrupting social codes and arrangements, its resolute rejection of prettiness, niceness, good taste and subtlety, rock was thoroughly and viscerally anti-bourgeois. "Erotic politicians, that's what we are," said Jim Morrison, "we're interested in anything about revolt, disorder, chaos, and activity that appears to have no meaning."[2] You can take your middle class and shove it.

As much as it was an anti-social phenomenon, it was also, in its best moments, an attempt to regroup into community. It was the music that drew young people in their masses into the halls and stadiums and fields, there to take note of each other and to share in dancing, embracing and getting stoned. It was music that played to their little circles in the parks, their parties in their hippie pads, their fairs and festivals and carnivals. And it was music that provided the anthems, the chants and the shouts ("Give me an F! Give me a U!" et cetera) of many of their political assemblies. To this day there isn't one of us who cannot hear "C'mon People Get Together" or "Mr. Tambourine Man" or "With a Little Help from My Friends" without reliving in perfect clarity the moment when the song first sank into our consciousness, and we are there again, with the friends and comrades with whom we first broke bread.

From its very beginnings, rock 'n' roll was inextricably associated with sex. As adolescents we used the music and the dance to circumvent the strictures on sexual expression. In our twenties, we used them to elaborate our sexuality. For in the Sixties men and women had become historically new sexual partners (the contraceptive pill and the explosion of student populations meant that for the first time ever women were in some control of their destiny) and the new ideological climate of liberalism generated what was reasonably termed a sexual revolution.

Taboos against pre-marital sex were devastated and the institution of marriage subverted every time young people made love outside the relations of property. Taboos were broken against sexual display and the erotic deployment of the body. "The young are trying to eroticize the world around them, to make it into an organic or whole experience,"[3] as indeed they were, with their pleasures of textures of skin and velvet, of the self-expressive dance, of sensual contact through embrace, of sensual smells and tastes.

If there were an ideology to this "revolution," it was this: if personal freedoms and self-determination of the personality are good things, then, inasmuch as sexuality is inextricable from the personality, a person has the inalienable right to sexual self-expression and self-creation. Furthermore: a person's sexuality belongs, not to society and its marriage-brokers, but to that person.

In their devaluation of monogamy and their refutation of the sexual double standard (by which male sexual anarchy was tolerated, even encouraged, and female sexuality confined to marriage), these new values opened a space in social behaviour in which women could act independently of the hierarchical and dominant-submissive relations of the patriarchal family. "We believed that the traditional practice of taking one lover for life was ridiculous, that sex was as nice and necessary as breathing fresh air, that bodies are beautiful and that a woman should be able to be sexually aggressive and orgasmic and not be put down for it." It was as an extension of this celebration of the beauty and worth of everyone's sexuality that the jubilant dancing and so much of the rock music, its alternately mesmeric and convulsive rhythms and its lyrical and elaborately symbolic *and* straightforwardly erotic verse, were performed.

However, it was the women's liberation movement of some years later that would expose the operations of much of the sexual revolution for what they were: fraudulent. Double standards prevailed in the vocabulary of sexual put-down, responsibility was evaded in the rhetoric of non-possessiveness, and the insistence on the personal construction of sexuality foreshadowed the propaganda that would take the legitimate demands of people for self-determination and hand them back as pornography.

Again, it was the women's liberation movement that would fully make the connections between this false consciousness of sexual liberation and the content of much of the counterculture's music. It was a primordial feminism, I suppose, that made women self-protectively blank out the words to "Under My Thumb" or "American Woman" or "So Long Marianne," or, failing that, to pretend that we were men. Anything to keep on dancing.

If love making was the sensual concomitant of music, dope was its spiritual accompaniment. A group of friends smoking grass together while the Beatles on the record-player sang "Lucy in the Sky with Diamonds" was, arguably, the archetypical counterculture moment. If rock 'n' roll was the propaganda of resistance to bourgeois culture, getting stoned was its exercise.

When Dr. Timothy Leary was dismissed from Harvard University in 1963 for administering the hallucinogenic LSD-25 (lysergic acid diethylamide) to students, he went on the road as a kind of circuit preacher, sermonizing on the miracles of "acid," in particular, and of the consciousness-altering drugs in general. Through these drugs, he said, the modern person could replicate the visionary experiences of the ancients and in this way release the ages-old wisdom of oneness with God (or with the Godhead or the ground-of-being or Nature), a wisdom disparaged and despoiled by monocular, one-dimensional and atomized Western civilization.

Naturally, bourgeois society and its custodians would be afraid of these visions and would seek to inhibit, if not prohibit them. (Leary himself was arrested numerous times and prosecuted.) For the nature of the experience was the shutting down of rational, logical and mechanistic modes of thought, the abandoning of ego-awareness and the loss of delusion regarding the seriousness and portent of the everyday "games" of life, from love affairs to education to politics. The shutting down, in other words, of the very mental processes required by our civilization for its perpetuation. In its frantic attempts to stop these defections from its territory, bourgeois society would distortedly characterize the altered consciousness as "psychotic," would penalize its practitioners and ridicule its pretensions; but, Leary said, these attempts were the hysterical rearguard actions of a disintegrating world order that was doomed by the wretched excess of its own violence, materialism and cerebration.

A Canadian writer, Robert Hunter, in noting that the experience of altered consciousness breaks the mind and the imagination out of the narrow confines of "Aristotelian logic, Christian dualism and the concept of length,"⁴ perceived in this new mode of consciousness the means by which we may avoid the world-wide destruction that the "old," aggressive, fear-ridden and ignorant consciousness is surely visiting upon us. In seeing the interrelatedness of all life and behaviour — no *act* is without consequence and effect — the new or "ecological" consciousness "confronts the penultimate question of how man must order his existence in relation to his planet. It sees *over* the mountain-sized garbage heap and treasure pile of human history and begins to perceive the world again, its view no longer walled in by what has been wrought in the last few thousand years."⁵ The new consciousness must prepare to do battle with the old for the life of the planet.

For all these reasons, the act of getting stoned was to be performed with a solemnity and a ceremony appropriate to the gravity of its implications. Ideally, in the presence of a guide who had already undertaken "trips," the subject of the experience would arrange for sensuous and tranquillizing surroundings, devotional objects of contemplation, agreeable music, simple refreshments, and texts that might be consulted for clues to the meaning of the astonishing sensations, visions and intuitions provoked by the drug.

Such careful preparations were particularly important for the ingestion of the hallucinogens, LSD, mescaline, peyote.* Marijuana and hashish could be smoked more playfully. In point of fact, it was difficult to get high on smoke and not fall into hilarity. But even here there were rituals of conduct: friends would assemble in a circle on the floor, a reverent hush would descend as the bag of dope was opened and the joints rolled in Zig-Zag or fruit-flavoured papers and passed around as an offering to everyone present (it was considered bad taste to "hog" the joint). Candles and incense were lit, a strobe light turned on, the music turned up (Bob Dylan, the Moody Blues, Iron Butterfly, the Doors) and everyone lay back to savour private and idiosyncratic perceptions and sensations or to share an unverbalized moment of oneness with a friend. (It was not acceptable to talk too much or to power-trip on anyone.) It was a ritual of fellowship and concord, all the more piquant for the shared risk in practising this form of civil disobedience, the use of an illegal drug. "He gave me two very tired joints of some kind of grass and said, 'Here, try this.' It was your uproarious grass experience, laughing 'til you beat yourself. It was incredible dope. It flattened you out until you were like a piece of paper sitting in a chair. It was amazing dope."

While for many young people in the drug culture the pretensions of the psychedelic**gurus held true in their experience, in others they were caricatured. The vocabulary of liberation and human potential, in the mouths of the fatuous

---

*While it was possible to have a "bad trip" on LSD — horrifying hallucinations and grotesque sensations — the negativity was considered inherent, not in the drug, but in the subject. The hallucinogens were drugs of ecstasy, marvel and purification unlike, say, the amphetamines, which were drugs of dread and pollution. A "speed freak" described her condition this way: "My mind operated like a spider web connected to freeways and overpasses, upside down newspapers, dead cats, twisted elevators, people with three feet and hollow tomatoes." (*Georgia Straight,* February 1968)

**From a letter from a friend: "The term 'psychedelic' was coined in Saskatchewan where Dr. Abram Hoffer was pioneering research in the therapeutic uses of LSD. Ah ha! The U.S. counterculture was a CCF branch plant!"

and exploitative, became a justification for "doing my thing" to the exclusion of any consideration of the needs and rights of those affected by the action. Even Alan Watts, a scholar of Zen Buddhism and popularizer of the religious import of the psychedelic experience, cautioned that the existential posture of "anything goes" does not necessarily translate well to a social posture; in which case it is merely hooliganism and cynical self-interest.

In emphasizing the need of Westerners to "get in touch" with their deepest selves, to become aware and sensitive and communicative as "authentic" beings, the ideology of the stoned high evaded the question of the *social* genesis of alienation and *anomie* and became, in its later manifestations in therapies and encounter group philosophies, a containment of social conflict. For collective political action against the agents of oppression, it substituted elaborate ruminations of the self. The solipsism inherent in this insistence on the primacy of subjectivity emerges in the failure to see where the self ends and other orders of being begin, in confusing physical and metaphysical categories: "I once had a perception on acid, when I was really high, that when I died the universe ended."[6]

The busting of friends and associates would send waves of paranoia through the community, an omnipresent and nagging anxiety that knotted the stomach and corroded the brain as people imagined that they were being followed by plainclothesmen in their daily meanderings; that their telephone was tapped and their mail surreptitiously examined; that their new friends were undercover narcs and their old ones unreliable under pressure; that no matter how elaborately concealed was the stash of dope, the police would find it. This paranoia was a form of culture shock as the children of the middle class confronted the unthinkable: *they* would go to jail. By this singular act of smoking or swallowing a substance deemed offensive by authorities from whom in any case the "heads" had withdrawn assent, they, with stereos in their apartments and peace in their hearts, had become criminal.*

---

*By the provisions of the Narcotics Control Act of Canada, the penalty for simple possession of marijuana was $1,000 or six months or both;

Their homes were no longer inviolable as police came crashing in through the door, real tough, throwing their weight around, their big hands on your shoulders spinning you around to face against the wall, "You'd better tell us where your dope is, kid, we know you're holding," rifling through drawers and shelves, "Ah ha, what does this mean, this poem here, yeah *you,* this poster here, looks pretty obscene to me." They came crashing into a coffee-house and shut it down and busted everybody inside, unplugging all the band's equipment, "Put that fuckin' guitar down or I'll bust it over your head," parading an undercover narc with a paper bag on his head and holes cut out for eyes, "Okay, pick 'em out, the ones you scored from" — and just plucked these kids out one by one and into the paddy wagon. A guy is driving down Main Street, minding his own business, stops at a light, when *whack!* two sledgehammers come through the windshield and two hands around his throat — that was the routine, grab 'em by the throat before they can swallow whatever they're holding under their tongue — and they drag him out the windshield, slam him up against the car, shove his head back, and pry open his mouth with a flashlight. Nothing. "We'll get you next time," and take off, leaving him bleeding from his mouth beside the ruin of his car.

Consistent with the movement's critique of the repressiveness of government and industrial bureaucracies was its refusal to work in those milieux; consistent with its desire for a non-alienated community was its desire for meaningful work. Once they had chosen the work they would do, movement people worked devilishly hard: teaching in free schools, publishing from underground, operating a food co-op, making and selling handicrafts, manning a movement office, even peddling dope. Or take this one: working on the land.

"Drop out. Start your own country." Gluttony and greed, forecasts of the holocaust and horrid catastrophes, unendurable

---

for conviction upon indictment, prison for seven years; for trafficking, up to life imprisonment. LSD was not a restricted drug until 1968 at which point the penalty for possession and trafficking was imprisonment and ranged, depending on the seriousness of the case, between eighteen months and ten years.

cacophony, odours, insult in the city. Leave. Retreat into the country and "learn the berries, the nuts, the fruit, the small animals and plants. Learn water."[7] Slow down, take a deep breath, listen to the silence and begin the purge of the accumulated garbage of industrial/technological urban life clogging the nerveways of your being. Buy a little piece of land, it doesn't have to be grand, just a few acres of wood and water, join in self-supporting, self-sustaining community with others and in respectful equipoise with the spirits of the land, and get *real,* take responsibility for your own survival, for your food and water and heat and clothing. Pay back to earth what you owe.

To the West Kootenays they came. From Vancouver, Calgary, down east, California, especially California, they came to this paradise valley, green mountains, smell of cedar, sun shafts through the feathery foliage, sound of cold, clean water spilling down rock beds. They came in their twos, fours and sixes to settle where Doukhobors and Quakers and gold miners had already carved out little farms and villages. They came to Crescent Valley, New Denver and Salmo, Slocan, Riondel and Winlaw.* For $3,000 they could buy 150 to 200 acres, an abandoned farm with a clearing, a ramshackle cabin and chicken house, a creek.

They dug in. Scrounged boards and tools and fixed up the cabin, borrowed a broken-down tractor and dull old plough and ploughed up a whole field for a garden (ah, and then the laborious weeks of weeding), hauled water from the creek and bought a cow. In winter they hauled one-hundred-pound bags of rice, flour and lentils up the slope from the road on sleds, and one morning, when they woke up to twenty degrees below zero, they discovered they must have not just a stove but a heater too. And the truck broke down. In the spring, pockets empty, the men went to work, at the sawmill, with the Department of Highways, tree planting, driving the school bus; and it was up to women and children to turn this acreage of sod and cedar into a farm. The family farm.

---

*Between 1966 and 1971 the population of Slocan Valley increased by 420 to 2,861. It had been declining steadily since 1956.[8]

These new farmers were not pioneers. They were taking their place alongside settlers of an earlier immigration, alongside an established society. Their mutual relations were ambivalent. On the one hand some contacts were very friendly and supportive. At one commune, Doukhobor neighbours "took us to heart," brought over a plough and an old cook-stove and freely gave advice about gardening and animal husbandry. "Their own kids weren't interested in Doukhoborism but here we were, middle-class ex-professionals from California, putting the garden in in the nude, looking for alternatives to materialism and possessive relationships, and working very hard."

Initially skeptical, neighbours watched the greenhorns gradually transform abandoned and ruined farms into settlements again, prop up the buildings, clear out the junk, put in a lawn, fruit trees, berry bushes and flower beds, cut hay and milk goats and harvest honey. There were children again in the valley and talk again of schools and libraries and a community centre. "We'd been here a year when my neighbour up the road came down and said, 'I've got to take my hat off to you.' "

On the other hand there were other neighbours with whom there was little or no spiritual or political affinity. As far as the communards were concerned, they had moved into paradise and paradise it would remain. But for their neighbours, the Kootenays simply happened to be where they lived and made a living. From the perspective of the older inhabitants, who were these kids, so recently privileged in their cities, their jobs, their schools and now self-righteously chopping firewood and growing organic tomatoes, to tell them they should not want their money and their share of the goods of the twentieth century?

Who were these *Americans* to tell a Canadian what the good life was? If it weren't crazy Doukhobors and Japanese aliens, it was American hippie crazies taking over the valley, high on drugs and living together without regard for cleanliness or the diseases they could spread or for marriage and raising kids with discipline, without regard for the feelings of others — these hippies swimming nude for all the world to see, inviting their friends to set up camp on other people's property and growing marijuana plants, brazenly, like it was just like another crop.

Who were they to lecture us, they who knew how to get the government to give them grants and then, when the grants ran out, to give them unemployment insurance? Insurance *we* paid for by our weeks and months in the pulp mill, eleven months working, two weeks holiday, so *they* could, months on end, lie by the river talking with God. They got $24,000 for the Vallican community hall. We built ours with our own labour, our own pool of money and little bits of board — $24,000 and they never got further than the foundation.

> It was really arrogant of us, I guess, to come here to a logging economy and say, "You guys can't log because it's beautiful and I don't want to look at your clear-cuts. I don't want any clear-cutting behind my land where my water is." To tell them we didn't want to look at their clear-cuts when this is how they've been making their living for longer than we've been here, well, that's arrogance.

There were other miscalculations. They stripped the sod right off the ground, and in the hardpan of clay beneath, without a thought of applying manure, they tried to grow a garden. They got the cow in August and got rid of her in March. They couldn't take it: two people without close neighbours tied down to milking, twice a day, every day. The chickens didn't work out very well either. They hated killing them and then would kill the ones still laying. At one commune the garden was planted while consulting a book and the bugs got it all anyway. When they should have been weeding, they were meditating.

> The whole communal thing of course was a disaster. In a culture that represents 6 percent of the world's population and consumes two-thirds of the world's wealth, the young people are bound to be spoiled rotten. Growing up, they never had to wash a dish. They didn't know the first thing about work and they didn't know how to put it all together. They weren't project oriented, they had no linear skills. They couldn't add, subtract, multiply or divide and they couldn't drive a nail in straight.

Being close to the land, in harmony with it, being free of the garbage of the city. The woman in the house, literally barefoot and pregnant (they practised astrological birth control), kneading bread dough, canning the garden produce, preparing meals for however many mouths were around that day to feed ("Basically the work I did was eaten — nothing to show for it"), taking care of the babies, washing diapers on a scrub board, sewing and mending under a kerosene lamp ("Electricity was a no-no and of course it would have been 'unnatural' to go to town to the laundromat"). The man was outside with his friends, building a shed, a root cellar, cutting wood with a chainsaw ("Nobody said a chainsaw was unnatural"), learning about tools and lumber, foundations and insulation, roofing and finishing ("His job was always more important than mine"). There was almost no outside wage work for women. The man would work at the mill, take the truck and go. She was left in the house, stuck. Winters were the worst. Isolated! Snowbound with no electricity, no telephone. She would trudge uphill through the snow, a baby on her back, another following, wailing, in her tracks, to visit her nearest neighbour-woman.*

To the extent that the people of the back-to-the-land movement failed to overcome the sexual divison of labour (and the attendant disproportions of status, personal authority and social power), they failed to establish a genuinely "new community." What they tended to construct instead was a nostalgic throwback to the social organization of the frontier, where pre-industrialized society was speciously secured in the servitude of women.

Notwithstanding the groups down on the farm, the counterculture was an urban affair. It was in the cities that hippies congregated to live in communal houses, work at odd jobs, deal dope, hustle gigs and just hang out; they would hit the highway to get to another city and there join precisely the same hippie society they had left behind. From one end of the country to the other, these were their own public places: in Vancouver, Kitsilano

---

*The situation of women was rather better at the commune-farms where labouring jobs were rotated and women had a chance to learn carpentry and mechanics and were freed for days at a time from child care.

district and Gastown; in Calgary, Riley Park; in Edmonton, Middle Earth coffee-house; in Saskatoon, the Ritz and the Senator hotels; in Winnipeg, the Experiment head shop and 655 Broadway (a house where dope could be purchased — it had cachet: it was busted weekly); in Toronto, Yorkville district; and in Montreal, Mountain and Crescent streets and the notorious Swiss Hut tavern (the FLQ liked it too). These were all adaptations, to some degree, of San Francisco's Haight-Ashbury district, the quintessential hippie village of North America. In 1967 the "Summer of Love" was proclaimed from San Francisco, and from that date the continent was crawling with trekkers.

A house in Kitsilano, a few blocks from the beach. A job for a few weeks, waitressing, driving a delivery truck, and then welfare.* Get up late and go down to the beach. Meet somebody. Bring them home for dinner, barley stews, cold hamburgers and out again, up and down the avenue or over to English Bay, up and down the beach, rapping, offering tokes, listening in on someone with a guitar. A party back at the house. Dark, smoky rooms, music from the record-player, lying on your back, thinking, "Far out, far fucking out." Crashing right there and next day back to the beach.

Hanging out. At the Robson Street Library, at the courthouse, Stanley Park, the corner of Fourth and Yew. Just sitting there, on steps and sidewalks, slouching, watching to see if anybody you knew would go by. Fourth Avenue: meandering in and out of the Psychedelic Shop, Positively Love Street record store, Horizon bookstore, Rags and Riches used clothing, Phase 4 coffee shop, a snooker parlour. "All that people around Fourth want is to have a lot of warm loving going on. . . . We're pretty tight. Everybody is just trying to work out an okay life."[9]

---

*"The only thing that got us through that nauseating experience of going to the welfare office for our cheques was the reminder that we didn't have to be there. Like, we could go back to university any time we felt like it or write home for money. But for the mothers with their kids — the place was screaming with kids — it was awful. Waiting, waiting in line-ups only to be told, sorry, we don't have your cheque, come back tomorrow. Back on the bus for them, another precious dollar and maybe tomorrow still no cheque."

With a little bit of money, there was coffee and folk music at the Bistro, black walls and candles in Chianti bottles, light shows at the Retinal Circus and rock bands, folk music at the River Queen. Down in Gastown, near the waterfront, there were "freak" bars, the Gastown Inn, the Dominion, the Alcazar, comfortable places in which to drink and rub shoulders with old winos, to deal and to score. "Dealers walked among the tables like street vendors: Hash anyone? Acid, grass, MDA?"

The Easter be-ins at Stanley Park brought the tribes out in their Sunday best, streaming out of Kitsilano in flowers and beads, bearing balloons and sticks of incense, to congregate on the grass in little circles of friends, drumming and chanting and singing, handing out to each other the yellow daffodils that had been blooming gloriously in their beds. Of course there was much dope. It was here that many out-of-town dealers made their connections — and there were cops. But when the cops moved in on someone with a joint, the freaks surrounded the smoker and the pressure of their presence, utterly non-violent, made the cops back off.

Given that in that summer of 1967 many businesses refused to serve hippies and the media were predicting the disintegration of Kitsilano into a "psychedelic slum" and an alderman recommended that the "Communist" hippies be deported holus-bolus to a district more easily policed,[10] it fell upon the countercultural community to take care of its own. The IWW dispensed free clothing; the Radha Krishna Temple, free food; the *Georgia Straight* and *Yellow Journal,* survival information. And Cool-Aid provided a place to crash, but especially help to get through a "bad trip." Kids came in in various stages of freaking-out, laid their sleeping bags on the floor and through the long night moaned and thrashed, their hand held, a soft voice talking them through and down from the trip, while phones rang and the kid in the next sleeping bag had his knapsack ripped off and someone else, starving, fed herself with peanut butter and white bread from the kitchen. Talking, talking, what did you do today? What's your mother's middle name? What's your favourite band? No psychoanalysing, just anything to keep the kid from walking out the door and in front of a bus.

When kids ran into a bad drug trip they used to be taken to the Vancouver General Hospital and if they started to act up on bad acid they'd be arrested for creating a disturbance. They'd end up in Riverview Mental Hospital for the rest of their lives. There were kids with hepatitis going untreated. There were kids that were suffering from malnutrition and pneumonia and the existing agencies would treat them as criminals or as runaways and wouldn't give them a breathing space. That's what Cool-Aid was all about, to create a breathing space between the kids and their families and the authorities and help them get it sorted out and stay alive.

There were ninety-two raids on Cool-Aid in a year and a half. I'd get woken up at two in the morning as the lawyer and chairman of the board to go down because there were two paddy wagons, police dogs, cops with shotguns, looking for dope dealers and runaway kids. I'd see a policeman with his gun drawn and ready to kick in the door and I'd say, "Excuse me, officer, this is a door and it has a doorknob. It's a new invention and if you turn it like this, it'll open real nice."

1967: the Summer of Love in Yorkville, Toronto. On the face of it, why not? Yorkville Avenue and its cross streets were close to the heart of the city and yet were still the avenues of a neighbourhood. Funky old houses, big trees, the requisite head shops, sidewalk cafes, clubs, the Riverboat, the Penny Farthing, the best of the bands, the Paupers, Kensington Market, the milieu of artists, craftspeople, poets, film-makers, theatre people. And Toronto, although it was not a beautiful city, was a cosmopolitan city: it had a large, politically alert student population, an astonishing ethnic mix, large parks, islands a short boat ride away and nearby, every summer, the Mariposa Folk Festival, one of the largest, tastiest, happiest of its kind.* That May there was a love-in at Queen's Park, languorous crowds meeting under the sweet greenness of the

---

*The 1967 line-up of performers included Tom Rush, the Staple Singers, Leonard Cohen, Murray McLaughlin, Buffy Sainte-Marie, Ritchie Havens and Joni Mitchell.[11]

newly leaved trees, in long skirts and denims and hand-painted rubber boots, carrying enormous paper flowers and kaleidoscopes, there to play music for each other and join in large dancing circles around the flute players, to admire young men with earrings and a rose behind their ear and, in a soft suede jacket, Leonard Cohen, to whom one presented a sparkler, sighing. (L. Cohen, poet and songster, lyricist of melancholic marriages and sorrowful dissolutions and mocking self-disclosure, whom we shrove.) Yes, flower power in Toronto too.

The summer of 1967 Yorkville was overrun. With hippies and their admirers from across the continent and from the middle-class suburbs of Toronto. And with tourists driving along Yorkville, bumper to bumper, to have a gawking look. Yorkville was in crisis: it needed shelter for the runaways, the hitch-hikers, the vagabonds, the penniless street kids sleeping on park benches and in the laundry rooms of apartment buildings. It needed medical clinics, legal aid service and a counselling centre, and it very badly needed the avenue closed off to the noxious traffic.

As in Vancouver, it was the community itself that took care of its own, with help from friends. Digger House, for instance, at 117 Spadina, inspired by the Diggers of San Francisco who had come to the aid of the homeless and hungry in the Haight with a free clinic, free stores, free meals, free communes. ("Do not ask what free can do for you; ask what you can do for free.")

> The house had nothing — a few radios, a record-player, a few chairs, twenty bunk beds, some food and clothing — all donated. We had only two rules: no drugs, and you couldn't stay longer than three months. Kids kind of collapsed there. We had hundreds at first in a five-bedroom house. One hundred kids. Then we set a limit of only twenty in the house. They didn't have sleeping bags or anything. They just came in to get warm. They'd come to Yorkville in the summer and they hung around for the dope and the groovy times and then they'd get sick. Then the girls would get splashed by Satan's Choice or the Vagabonds. And we had a hepatitis scare, infectious hepatitis, passed on by dirty needles.

And the kids thinking that they were so emancipated, so free, and they had been spooked out of all the little towns by this dream of all this love that was going to happen. This youth world, a children's crusade all over again. I thought all we needed to do was to be kind and be fair to these kids, just for five minutes and it'll save their lives. But these kids, you'd have to hold them in your arms for the rest of their lives one way or another to do anything meaningful for them. So I had to learn to stop thinking that I was going to be able to help any of them and just do whatever it is they wanted me to do. Bail, a meal, twenty dollars for an an overdue hydro bill, simple things, and quit thinking that by extending this warm, middle-class friendship that I was going to be important to them.

Towards the end, the house was absolutely wrecked. I don't know how many thousands of kids had been through there. The plumbing didn't work, the basement was flooded, the furnace wasn't working, sparks came out of sockets, walls were coming down. And the city owned it. We stopped paying our rent because we said they had to make some repairs like the broken windows. In the end we moved out because they refused to make the repairs, we had no more money and the house was too dangerous for kids to live in. By that time they were all heroin addicts.

The Summer of Love had faded into the bitterness of police harassment, vagrancy charges, by-law charges, civic hostility to hippie merchants, developers sniffing the air for investment in "chic."* On the edge of Yorkville, on the other hand, was the experimental educational commune, Rochdale College, big, free, unstructured, nurturing Rochdale. Hungry, sick, stoned, on the lam, of course the hippies were taken in. All that space. The lounges, the corridors, the suites filled up with them. The

---

*An extensive campaign, led by Diggers, to have Yorkville Avenue closed to traffic had involved hundreds of hippies in a mass sit-in, protest marches, love-ins, arrests, head bashings and inconclusive meetings with Mayor Dennison. "It just blows the mayor's mind when we go in and sit on the edge of his desk," said David DePoe, Digger folk hero. The mayor recovered his mind, however, and steadfastly refused the hippies' demand.

kitchen fed them all, losing $12,000 a month to do so, not to mention the trays of eggs, say, they'd carry out with them to a window just to see how crazily they splattered on the walk below. Drugs. You could deal and smoke and shoot and swallow in Rochdale with impunity. And with the street kids came the speed merchants, bikers and thugs with killer dogs, who sold them the dope, stole it back and sold it to them again. Weekend hippies too, thousands of them, draining the life out of the place with their nonchalance and frivolity, refusing participation and responsibility, leeches, free-loaders on the commitment of the residents ("This is a free school, we can't throw them out"). Vandalism. Suites like garbage heaps; the plumbing broken down; walls punched with gaping holes; in the kitchen, dirty needles; in the bedroom, radios, televisions and record-players stolen from other residents. Illiterates, their education experience a devastation, hung around these others — the ones playing chess, reading science fiction and discussing God (Wow! I can be a poet too, an artist, a lover, we're all longhairs and freaks) — never knowing what hit them when they failed at this too.

Manoeuvring judiciously around these catastrophes, one could still have an exhilarating experience in Rochdale. Think of it: in the middle of millions of utterly lonely and hungry urban lives was a community — the door's open, come in — conversations in the hallway, by the elevator doors, with perfect strangers; on the edge of an intellectually cutthroat society of scholars, this collaborative cross-pollination of ideas, people seated cross-legged on the floor of the lounges, here a Hesse seminar, there a mathematics seminar. Into and out of this, coming potters, video artists, modern dancers, actors. You could live your whole life here with your friends: cooking for each other, putting dances and parties together, showing movies, turning each other on, sharing books and manuscripts and, while just outside the doors was disapprobation and ill will, holding each other in small circles of solicitude and admiration.

The visionary communities of the "new consciousness" (urban and rural communes, production co-ops, food co-ops, free schools, drop-in centres, alternate media and artists' collectives and so on) were deeply concerned with ethics of organization and behaviour. Against the ethical system of mainstream society they proposed precisely opposed equivalents.

The violence of society would be countered with a pacifist community in which all life was revered, relationships would be non-coercive, habits peaceable (dope was a drug of serenity and reconciliation; alcohol, a drug of turbulence and discordance) and tools creative. "There is no excuse," said Leary, "no explanation to God or the DNA code, which can justify the existence of one distance-killing machine on this earth."[12] In place of competitiveness and hierarchy, the commune or co-op attempted cooperation in work and in decision making and egalitarianism — no one person was more "important" or "useful" than another. And in this possibility of immersion in the collective and in the principle of mutual service — you give each other a hand, you make yourself available to the neighbourhood — the group struck a blow against isolation and atomization.

Where bourgeois society was organized around the insular nuclear family and private property, the commune was tribal — we are all each other's brothers and sisters — and owned property collectively, whether this was land or a printing press or pots and pans. By extension, commodity fetishism was severely criticized and the massive waste of middle-class lifestyles deplored: the alternate community purchased only what was needed for the dignity of the household and tolerated people who, having opted for a marginal economics of existence, panhandled, shoplifted and "crashed" for weeks on end in a sleeping bag on the living room floor.

The moral and emotional strictures of "straight" society perpetuated the repression of desire and delight and possessiveness towards one's friends and mates, and deferred gratification *ad infinitum* while one's life petered out in joyless labour and obligation. Rejecting such circumspection of fulfillment, the commune opened up a space where its members could exercise trust in each other — you are safe here — and learn in fellowship how to "let go" of neurotic needs, and indulge heretofore censored ones, and where it was "okay" to do now what the spirit moved you to do.

If the mass culture of bourgeois society was characterized by the uniformity of industrial and corporate processes, by mechanized and linear modes of expression, then communal culture would be idiosyncratic and experimental — here people dressed in bizarre combinations of garments in a theatrical projection of the complexity of identity; here men wore long hair and passed time in languid introspection, and women wore army jackets and rode motorcycles to the Gaspé; here everyone dabbled in music and fingerpainting and writing poetry. Despising the straitened and mechanical mind-set of logical, sequential, dispassionate "linear" culture — the culture of the printing press, of science and industrialization, of order and exclusivity and singularity — the commune valued instead electronic culture, the culture of TV and the stereo, valued sensory experience enveloping the subject in a "shower of perceptions."

In sum: communal culture is revolutionary because "the commune is the life-form of the future."[13]

In the best of them, the commune was a comfortable place, modestly furnished with old, overstuffed furniture from Goodwill Stores and decorated with prints and psychedelic and political posters — Che, the "Desiderata" and the pinwheel lettering of a dance poster — and the funky things that people collected. People sat down together at healthy meals they took turns preparing in a kitchen they took turns keeping clean. They had house meetings in which they aired their differences and in which they shared their eclectic interests, anarchism, Buddhism, yoga, Maoism, Taoism, massage therapy, native cultures, exegeses of the texts of Bob Dylan, and where men wept and women cursed. Members were monogamous or not, as they saw fit, and no one could be intimidated into doing or being something s/he didn't want to do or be.

In the worst of them, the place was a mess: the furniture was in permanent disrepair; the walls were streaked and grimy and covered with vulgar graffiti; and people's possessions were constantly disappearing out the door with a "crasher." People ate sporadically on junk food; the dishes piled up in foul disorder in the sink; and a carton of milk in the fridge carried the inscription, "This is Brian's. Fuck off." In corners, speed freaks gnawed on their fingers and upstairs in the bedrooms women were being raped. All organization was considered a form of militarism; on cleaning day the men went to the park, the women washed the floors. In spite of it all, it was, as a woman said of a place in Vancouver known as Rat Hotel, home.

II
HOPE I DIE BEFORE I GROW OLD

The last few years I've been advising everyone to become an ecstatic saint. If you become an ecstatic saint, you then become a social force. . . . The key to the psychedelic movement, the key to what's going on with the young people today, is individual freedom . . . .Liberals and left-wing people, Marxists, are opposed to this individual pursuit. . . . They're attempting to wash out these seedific energies. . . the hippies and the acid heads and the new flower tribes are performing a classic function. . . . The empire becomes affluent, urbanized, completely hung-up in material things, and then the new underground movements spring up. . . . They're all subversive. They all preach a message of turn on, tune in, drop out.

— Timothy Leary (from an interview with the California underground paper Oracle, *October 1967)*[1]

Subculture, the underground, flower tribes, counterculture, subversion: dissident youth cohered not simply around a shared life-style but around a shared consciousness of their collective integrity and of their incipient seditiousness. As "freaks," as celebrants together of music, drugs, sexuality and the commune, they were by self-definition simultaneously critics of the social order *and* prototypes of a new one. They refused cooperation with a post-industrial social, economic and political order that required their emotional and sexual repression, their joyless toil, loveless competitiveness, and suicidal submissiveness to fulfill grossly expansionist, colonialist and materialist imperatives. These they refused not only on their own behalf but in the name of planetary needs as well. In the arrangements of the *status quo* lay the prefigurations of mass death. In the freaks, in their fantasies of love and beauty, their eroticism, their mysticism, their playfulness, in their flexibility of life-style, adaptability to environmental changes and in the quickness of their reflexes as danger closed in, a new human personality was taking shape, along with new definitions of family, community, productivity and responsibility. "Open up your senses, shed your old skin, prepare yourself for an evolutionary leap out of sight."[2]

This sense of a special, collective and aggrieved identity was not gratuitous. As a group, youth endured high rates of unemployment;* minimal wages and salaries in low-skilled jobs; the forced migration from hometowns of poverty; enforced dependence as students; the repressiveness of the narcotics laws; and police harassment in their own communities. Unsurprisingly, they were smoulderingly resentful of the smug paternalism of adults that would "keep them in their place." Their demands for social services were similarly collective: youth hostels, drop-in centres, crisis centres, free medical clinics and labour education.[3] They were not merely insubordinate when they felt deeply offended by the procedures of bourgeois society and looked to themselves and each other for alternatives.

An American freak called the youth and its culture a "colony," a territory of discrete "post-industrial" institutions, technologies, and economic relations that was nevertheless threatened with abduction into the "mother-country culture" and that could save itself only with a movement of "national liberation" from the "colonialists."[4] In Canada, in an essay that provoked much interest among politicos at least, two academics in Toronto argued that inasmuch as youth "occupy the critical workplaces," the army and the universities ("the war machine and the idea factories"), and are exploited and impoverished in them, youth is a "class in itself." Inasmuch as youth are moving away from "individualist passivity" to "collectivist activism," they are also becoming a conscious

---

*In 1968, 42.6 percent of the unemployed in Canada were in the fourteen to twenty-four age group. Of this age group 20.4 percent were unemployed.

"class-for-itself."* In its confrontation with the "administrative imperialist system" a revolutionary youth is aborning.[5]

And indeed there were elements of the counterculture who saw themselves as potential revolutionaries. In their flight from the "living death of bourgeois culture," they were undermining the authority of that culture and its custodians. It was a German political philosopher, Herbert Marcuse, who saw this refusal to cooperate with the system as a whole as a "total" rebellion, sexual, moral, intellectual and political, an all-encompassing consciousness of "how much cruelty and stupidity contribute every day to the reproduction of the system."[7] But the counterculture was also politically *creative*. Envisioning an alternate society, one that tapped into the "great subculture" that runs subversively through all of human history — from "Paleo-Siberian Shamanism and Magdalenian cave-painting; through megaliths and mysteries, astronomers, ritualists, alchemists and Albigensians; gnostics and vagantes"[8] — the freaks submitted themselves to the rites of the underground, rites of deconditioning and purification, and emerged reborn, as prototypes of a new civil order. (You can't take acid, they said, and want to be a used-car salesman or to save money or to join the army or to hide inside the nuclear family household anymore.)

Self-conscious, the freaks were the new mutinous minority group — diggers are niggers, said Abbie Hoffman — and as such, the new recruits for the civil war that was raging in the heartland of capitalism. The culture of the commune, of ecstatic rituals, of economic marginality was nothing if not trenchantly critical of capitalism and its social relations. And in the counterculture one learned the life-style, the attitudes and values, however embryonic, of the post-capitalist, post-industrial, post-scarcity future. In the future, as in the counter-culture, truth would proceed from the experiential. All beings

---

*The argument was valid for American youth only, however. Given the economic underdevelopment of Canada, the voluntary character of military service and the relatively low enrollment of youth in higher education, "young Canadians do not share youth-specific work experiences and youth in Canada is not a class formation."[6]

would be interrelated in harmony and balance. All would have the right to their self-expression and self-definition, and all would have the right of access to the material surplus generated by the new technologies, that is, cybernation. ("Why should you have to work to get food?" the freaks asked.) The attempt to practise this incipient, liberated society was the "methodology of the revolutionary process."[9] It prefigured classlessness and communitarianism and intensified, to the point of intolerance, that "contradiction between the productive process which has provided the most highly advanced material base yet in the history of the planet and the anachronistic system of relationships used to operate that process."[10]

"Mankind has so far been restricted in developing its innovation and creative powers," remarked one hippie, "because it was overwhelmed by toil. Now we are free to be as human as we wish."[11] This is *the* revolutionary project, of course, this liberation of the human from the realm of material and historical necessity, and revolutionary authorities have ascribed to cultural renovation a revolutionary role: the critique of bourgeois ideologies, the mobilization of the energy of all the dissident forces of society, and the acquisition of "civil hegemony" preceding the actual revolutionary seizure of political power.

Those who articulated the ideals and claims of the counterculture may well have believed that these were precisely the tasks they had assigned themselves in their visionary community. But until they also articulated how broad masses of people were to get from the enslaving, bourgeois "here" to the liberating, post-revolutionary "there," until they articulated a strategy of change beyond the individualistic action of dropping out, the counterculture would represent nothing more than a pleasurable holding tank for social misfits in the bourgeoisie's backyard.*

---

*It was to this strategic gap between critique and revolutionary action that the American yippies addressed themselves. Melding the lifestyle freakiness of the counterculture with the political objectives of the new left, they came up with "pop terrorism." "Risk, drama, excitement and bullshit," as the notorious Abbie Hoffman put it. Revolution being whatever you can get away with, yippies behaved

In the fall of 1969, at a rock festival in Toronto, unruly members of the audience break through the line of security men surrounding the performing area and rush the stage. The frazzled MC tries to deal with them:

> Hey cats and chicks, like this is a groovy scene, right, and we don't want to blow it. You know you can smoke your grass and those narcs up there on the roof aren't going to bust you. We're going to take over because the revolution is coming so we don't want to blow our scene. You're gonna hafta get back from the stage, all right.[12]

The joining of the rhetoric of revolutionary struggle with an incident of transcendant triviality underscores the bathetic moment of the counterculture deprived of politics. Or, rather, of the counterculture's confusion of its spontaneous act and gestures of riot, mayhem and festivity with political strategy. Alas, "capitalism is still as powerful and resilient as ever. No winter palaces have fallen. No long march is being conducted across the northland of Canada."[13] By the end of the decade it was becoming clear that for every freak who had managed to carve out a space of tranquillity and self-sufficiency and for every yippie who, in the catharsis of theatrical skirmish, equated purgation with the strategic advance of the "revolution," there were hundreds and hundreds of youths stranded in the no-man's-land of a life-style that was gradually being reabsorbed into the mainstream of capitalist enterprise and exploitative, demoralizing and even violent relations. A highly conscious *counterculture* was degenerating into an unconscious subculture of reaction.

---

and gesticulated with theatrical excess and manipulated the media shamelessly, thereby circumventing the discipline, frustration and guilt on which they claimed new left organizations were based. Although yippie!ism took hold in Canada only on the West Coast, even there it was tempered by "Canadianisms": while the yippies of the Vancouver Liberation Front, for instance, performed an exorcism on the police station, and clashed with police on the beaches of English Bay, others, like the "structure freaks" of the new left, called for their own "city government" of hostels, coffee-houses and free schools and demanded that straight society fund it.

Style substituted for substance, gossip for communication, guilt-ridden accommodation of irresponsible behaviour for tolerance and compassion, and self-abuse for cultural disaffection — sleeplessness, bad teeth, malnutrition, constant colds, pneumonia and, from dirty needles, hepatitis. The adventures of the life of the self-assigned economic exile had become the bleak monotony of the economically dead-ended: no money, no education, no skills, no job opportunities. No home, no privacy, no sanctuary. Out there on the street, trying to find shelter in parks or lobbies, they were prey. Out there at the music festival, which cost them ten bucks to get in, it was a scene of rip-off prices at the food concessions, bad dope, litter and debris, clogged toilets and indifferent musicians who imitated the Rolling Stones because "that's where the money's at."

Cashing in. In Canada, the struggle for an indigenous pop music and business was one of the more desperate cultural campaigns. Legislation governing Canadian content of the airwaves did not exist prior to 1971. During the Sixties, Canadian musicians and their agents were battling uphill against the *status quo* of the commercial music scene. The Top Forty stations were locked into the American playlists drawn up on the basis of the songs that were being played in the U.S., deejays took their on-air styles from Los Angeles and London, and the vast majority of record companies were branch-plant operations involved mainly in distribution, not in the recruitment of local talent. The critic sensitive to the situation was lamentably rare, and a public de-Americanized enough to take its own artists seriously did not exist in large enough numbers to materially support those artists. Given this context, it is not to be wondered at that for every Canadian artist who made it to the charts of *Billboard* and *Cashbox** (the publications of the music industry), there were scores who never made it out of the local coffee-house/high school gym/tavern circuit. Or who,

---

*Among these successes were Moe Koffman's "Swingin' Shepherd Blues," the Guess Who's "Shakin' All Over," the Irish Rovers' "The Unicorn," and Gordon Lightfoot's album, *Sunday Concert.*[14]

having made it as far as the recording studio of a local company, lost their shirts on studio rental costs, engineer's overtime, instrument rentals and taxes. Since the group was not Crosby, Stills and Nash, the advances it received were token.[15]

To add insult to injury, the predominance of Toronto in the Canadian music business (such as it was in the mid-Sixties) was a powerfully inhibiting factor in the development of artists who were either not prepared to work in Toronto or unable to "crack" its tight society. (With the exception of the Guess Who who stayed in Winnipeg, every nationally successful Canadian act was based in Toronto in this period.) Toronto had four recording studios, several rock clubs, a nationally powerful Top Forty station (CHUM's playlist, which was itself compiled from American lists, was distributed to radio stations across the country and used as their programming guide) and a nucleus of rock entrepreneurs (managers, booking agents, promotors and producers), some of whom did very well indeed on the fees they extracted from their hopeful clients. (Jack Batten, a Toronto rock critic, described in 1968 one such entrepreneur, a twenty-five-year-old who was clearing $50,000 a year for himself.)[16] Sooner or later, any musician or group who wanted more than local or regional play and attention would think of going to Toronto. And over and over again their stories are the same: "We had no connections and the people inside the scene, who've known each other five or six years, had no time for 'outsiders' and treated us very condescendingly." "The competition was rough — every band from Halifax to Vancouver was converging on Toronto." "There was a lot of hype involved, double-faced, double-dealing ripoffs, and just to get them to *listen* to our tapes was a major battle, they had such preconceived ideas of what a Vancouver or Calgary band would sound like. I think we scored three gigs in nine months." And went home.

In November 1966, the CJCA Radio 93 Fab Forty list showed, right under the Troggs, Gordon Lightfoot's "Spin Spin" at number six. The situation for Canadian folk artists was rather different from that of rock and pop groups. Folk music, by definition, is rooted in particularity, in locales and events and personalities which are historically specific and are

named, and the singer-songwriter was valued precisely for the individuality and personality s/he brought to the corpus of the tradition. Thus it was not anomalous that an Ian and Sylvia, a Lightfoot, a Buffy Sainte-Marie, a Humphrey and the Dumptrucks, should sing of the foothills of Alberta, of the CPR, of the plains buffalo, of the Cargill Grain Company and still have a national, if not international, audience. But rock music was part of a continental culture produced by and distributed from the commercial and political centres of North America (that is, the United States) which, because of their metropolitan and corporate character, were deemed to be of universal significance and value. Thus it was that the Canadian consumers experienced no contradiction in interpreting musical references to Chicago, San Francisco or Baton Rouge as references to *their own* experience but were decidedly jarred by the Guess Who's "Running Back to Saskatoon." Saskatoon? Never been there.
Bad dope:

> I guess it would be the summer of '69 that we started doing junk. We'd been doing MDA very intensely and then it ran out and a friend said, junk's a nice way to come down, here let me show you what junk is. And as soon as there was junk in the community there was also heavy-duty cops. And paranoia. The police would pick you up and take you to a dark place for a little beating, then let the word out you'd talked. We started packing guns.
>
> Then all of a sudden people were actually going to jail for years at a time and people were starting to rip each other off. People were going crazy. Robbing drug stores, knifing other people. Putting together bags of milk sugar and selling it as heroin. It's very easy to avoid any kind of clear thinking when you've been hitting for weeks and weeks.

The streets did not belong to the hippies who wandered them: they belonged to the merchants, to the head shop proprietors who dealt in pricey trinkets; to the coffee-house owners who extracted profit from labour at a minimal wage; to the department store magnate who ran a boutique called Rip-Off ("Some jerk had picked up this piece of slang and thought it was hip"); to the record and music storekeepers who were agents of

Transamerica (owners of fourteen music-publishing companies), American Telephone and Telegraph (owners of Gibsons Guitars) and CBS (owners of Columbia Records). As early as May 1967, *Georgia Straight* reprinted a warning from the Diggers of San Francisco: "Tune In, Turn On, Drop Dead?" "Look — the psychedelic merchants are shit, low-grade deliquescent turds. . . . They are the System, playing the System's games in the System's way and they don't give a flaccid fuck about you or any of their sheep." To which the merchants replied: "Marxist bullshit."

By exploiting the contradiction between the subversive content of the counterculture and its dissemination through the mass media, capitalist commerce was able to pick up the "messages" of that culture and recycle them back into the community as merchandise. It was able to lure the most inventive, the most engagingly *outré* of the culture's exponents, with the irresistible rewards of money, status and power, and hand them to the community as entertainment packages. Sabotaged by their own anti-intellectualism and their own disdain of the political "hype"of the left, the hippies could not distinguish between their own legitimate aspirations for cultural alternatives and capitalism's "repressive tolerance" of those aspirations — its permissiveness, which sucked the vital juices from countercultural ideas and left only the dry husks of advertising copy. Initially innovators and creators of their own culture, the hippies became passive consumers of it as it became more and more organized outside their own collective relations.

(Theatre entrepreneurs produce the rock musical *Hair* for the middle class who want to go slumming tastefully and for hippie bubble-gummers who want to "discover themselves," to "become" what *Hair* "is."[17] Warner Brothers presents *Woodstock,* the film, and issues a special booklet for the occasion, a compendium of corporate psychedelic rhetoric, "surrounded by the wave/of the future/aquarian choral of mood," and in the trade papers announces that "WOODSTOCK IS BEAUTIFUL": ". . . first week, New York, $65,654, Los Angeles, $40,400. . . . ")

Outside such ubiquitous mercantilism there was seemingly

only the handicraft economy of the hippies in their storefront workshops, where they produced lovingly crafted goods that would somehow be distributed by some means of transportation to a market somewhere. The only clear idea was that the production would not depend on crass profit.

> There was a lot of talk about alternate structures but people never really thought through the ramifications of what they were saying. How could this alternative market work? Where was its raw material going to come from? People would go down and "buy" leather, but without any sense of where that leather came from. So all these raw materials would arrive — from where? From whoever was making them. How would the goods be marketed? People imagined we'll simply open a shop. But of course once you got to opening a shop you had to pay rent and utilities.
>
> Indeed they were quickly integrated into shopping centres. The old part of town was rediscovered from whatever past any given city had and this was a great place to incorporate boutiques. None of these people imagined how these renovations took place so that the old historical part of town was suddenly reusable. The boutiques became just retail shops and the indigenous production of items disappeared. We certainly had no conception of how production was organized in the society. And nobody, outside of a few obscure Marxists, thought that was an important thing to know.

As critical as the counterculture was of the obscenities of bourgeois society, it was not so much an assault on social structures as it was a retreat from them. The mythology of returning, even metaphorically, to the land was essentially nostalgic (and American),* recapitulating as it did that Western romance of the settlers' last stand against the barbarians of the government. In retreat, the counterculture evacuated socio-

---

*This point was made to me by George Melnyk, regionalist: Canada's "frontiers" were settled, not by adventurers, but by the CPR, the RNWMP and by families.

economic spaces that capitalism filled all too enterprisingly.

July 1970: Festival Express comes to Calgary. If Canada has a Woodstock,* this is it: a Woodstock travelling by train to Toronto, Winnipeg and Calgary, and on board are the magical ingredients: The Band, Janis Joplin, the Grateful Dead, Robert Charlebois, Ian and Sylvia, Tom Rush. The mayor of Calgary sets aside, for the incoming caravans of festival freaks, Prince's Island in the middle of the Bow River and here they camp out — tents, motorcycles, painted vans — build giant bonfires, feed themselves and pass the dope around. Meanwhile, outside the gates of the stadium, a bunch of new leftists and high school students, incensed at the price of the tickets (nine dollars), galled by the fact that one of the festival's promoters is from the T. Eaton family and another from the Maclean-Hunter empire, and demanding the reclamation of youth culture from the entertainment conglomerates, tangle with police as they attempt to crash their way through the gates. They are vigorously repulsed.

This was the swan song of the counterculture: young people shouting hoarsely at the police who stand between them and the artifacts of their own imagination. No admittance without a ticket. Behind the police lines, death at an early age. "You couldn't just hand somebody a joint and everything would be cool. They'd take the joint and shoot you anyway."**

"Choose your weapons," intoned the Diggers, "guns or flowers. Flowers shoot rotten bullets, guns make lousy flowerpots." To the freaks, politics was only about information, and about the processing of data, about material reality and the historical dimension of existence. Politicians, even revolutionaries, shortchanged the revolutionary future by ignoring the

---

*In September 1969 some 400,000 people gathered at Woodstock, New York, for a rock festival. Contained by the police and confined within fences, they tolerated rain, food shortages and garbage and cohabited peacefully for several days, stoned. The media congratulated them fulsomely and the Woodstock legend took off.

**Quoted in "The Sixties," CBC, producer Terry Hoffman. This is a reference to the Altamont, California, tragedy in later 1969: at a concert of the Rolling Stones, a young black man was killed by the Stones' bodyguards, the Hell's Angels bikers.

power of *awareness* and of the liberated consciousness, the complex of reality, inner as well as outer, and by insisting this didn't matter. It mattered very much said the freaks and the yippies. It mattered that people be able to break out of the cultural mould in which are the imprints of egoism, possessiveness, aggressiveness, neurosis. It mattered that they free themselves of the hypnotic pull of the historical forms of being in order to open a space within themselves in which the forms of the future personality could take shape. Without such "mental mutants"[18] the revolutionary generation would simply repeat, in the shabby garments of the *poseur*, variations on the culture of death. One could see these death-dealers in the movement, people hung up on control and personal power, on the refinements of arguments and the formalities of organization; philistines who supposed that only in politics was action humanized and not, say, in art or in friendship; incipient fascists, bullies, who advanced their politics through intimidation and the cult of personality; shrivelled people whose desiccated passions were useless in the joyous projects of the tribe.

For their part, the politicos criticized the acolytes of psychedelicism for being concerned only with the salvation of the self — as if the self were not a social as well as psychic construct — and for trivializing the desperately serious and *collective* struggle (it was collective or nothing at all) for liberation of oppressed peoples. A statement like "Every man has his 'thing' and Che was merely doing his thing — making revolutions"[19] filled them with contempt for such an ethic of laissez-faire, as though the socio-historical mission of colonized people against the institutions and machinery of imperialism could be reduced to this scenario of a voluntary, playful, *personal* decision to take up arms. The politics of the nervous system, the politicos charged, assume that one is unfree by choice. That unfreedom need not be confronted but only sidestepped by the retreat into a subculture where the values of freedom and fulfillment would be nurtured in *some other place* than right here: in the everyday society of pain and perplexity. That the person who is "aware" is "one for whom the revolution has already been won":[20] go tell these things, go explain yourselves, said the politicos, go to the Vietnamese and tell them that the war raining death on their heads is but a manifestation of bad consciousness and that they can win if only they'd "get in touch" with the syncretic mysteries of inner being.

Yes, the life-style of capitalism is frightful, the rat race, the gluttonous consumerism, the predatory nature of human relations, the tensions and frustrations and hostilities; and, yes, the search for ecstatic experience to escape from the pains of the world is the profoundly grave "sigh of an aching heart." But if this pain does not associate itself with history, with the possibility of human society freeing itself in the long run, then it can only express itself in pessimism, escapism and defeatism. In such quietism lies the real threat of fascism. As Warren Hinckle wrote of the hippies, when you drop out of the arduous task of attempting to steer a difficult, unrewarding society, "you leave the driving to the Hell's Angels."[21] If the consciousness, the awareness, of human potential is not manifested in the community of all souls, then it abandons that community to those who would appropriate it with deception and terror.

Yes, it is important to develop alternate structures of community, welfare and production. Indeed, these are a necessary condition for the construction of the new society: these materialized visions of camaraderie and reconciliation. But they are not sufficient in and of themselves to bring about the post-capitalist millenium. Unless there is direct *political* struggle with the state, its military and police agencies and its technological apparatus, the counterculture is doomed merely to coexist with these forces. Furthermore, with its anti-intellectualism, its anti-materialism, its mistrust of the uses of science and technology and its impracticable methodologies of change (mysticism, tribalism, subsistence farming, primitive hand production), the counterculture hasn't a hope in hell of terminating the rule of the bourgeoisie. Only the culture of the revolutionary process itself can do it — "the totality of ideas, politics, philosophy, morality, styles, art, methodology and codified experience"[22] — in the communalization of struggle.

These were the disputes between the hippies and the politicos. Except for the extremists of each type — the perfectly anti-social, hopelessly addle-brained acid head on the one hand, the utterly ruthless, unscrupulously demagogic new leftist on the other — the disputes were in fact fraternal.

For pothead or activist, the goals of all behaviour were that the dignity and worthiness of the person be confirmed; that all human relations be transacted with love, compassion and tenderness; that, in the morality and process of democracy and participation, powerlessness, meaninglessness and alienation be overcome; and that the split between the person and society, between personal and political values, be healed. Revolutionary change must embrace the *whole* of human potential, must speak to the reunification of all being in clarity of awareness and responsibility of action, if it is not to beach its warriors on the shoals of atrophy. Such an embrace is passionate, greedy and brawny with love. "If we are serious about our desire to build a movement, we must opt for the intellectual, emotional and spiritual freedom now. We must taste it and want it and become jealous for its survival."[23]

In the coherence of countercultural life-styles with the social criticism of the new left, in the proposals for a society where people live without illusions and beyond the clichés of egoism, where they live released into the liberation of meaningful work, free activity and modesty of consumption, in the balance of "being" and "acting," was the integration of the political and psychic projects: "Zen Marxism," as one new leftist called it.[24] The flower grows in the earth fertilized by the fire of the gun.

Indian activist Kahn-Tineta Horn speaking at the University of Alberta, 1969.
Photo: University of Alberta Archives

Rock Festival at Mosport.
Photos: John F. Phillips — Baldwin Gallery

Demonstration in support of Civil Rights movement, 1964.
Photo: Public Archives of Canada

"Get stoned, end marijuana prosecution."
Photo: John F. Phillips — Baldwin Gallery

The kids are alright: rock festival, Edmonton, 1969.
Photo: University of Alberta Archives

In support of Che and revolution.
Photo: John F. Phillips — Baldwin Gallery

Trudeau in the Sixties, the philosopher king, loved by all.
Photo: John F. Phillips — Baldwin Gallery

Amex: The American Expatriate in Canada, *a voice of resistence to the war in Vietnam, Toronto.*
Photo: Laura Jones — Baldwin Gallery

Demonstrating outside the gates of McGill University, Montreal, 1969.
Photo: Public Archives of Canada

Everdale Free School, Toronto, 1969.
Photo: Laura Jones — Baldwin Gallery

Rock Festival at Mosport.
Photo: John F. Phillips — Baldwin Gallery

Pro- and anti-war demonstrators at the U.S. Consulate, Toronto, 1965.
Photo: John F. Phillips — Baldwin Gallery

Yippie Abbie Hoffman addressing students, University of Alberta.
Photo: University of Alberta Archives

Street Festival in downtown Toronto.
Photo: John F. Phillips — Baldwin Gallery

Unrest on campuses across the country.
Photo: Laura Jones — Baldwin Gallery

Wedding celebration, Toronto, 1969.
Photo: John F. Phillips — Baldwin Gallery

Protesting the war in Vietnam, Liberal Convention, Ottawa, 1968.
Photo: John F. Phillips — Baldwin Gallery

John F. Phillips — Baldwin Gallery

PART IV
THE THIRD
WORLD WITHIN

I

WE HOLD THE ROCK

Leaning on the lectern, the better to defy her listeners, she launched a flood of complaints in the name of Indian people of Canada and a string of demands that left the room momentarily stunned and silent.

Canadian history books, especially the French ones, have always depicted the Indian as an evil savage, she said. The French have been raised with a hatred of Indians.

And now, along comes this French-Canadian gentleman, Pierre Elliott Trudeau, brought up on the hate literature of French-Canadian scholars, and he says he wants to tear up our treaties because he feels like it.

"Imagine his calling the new government Indian program a 'White Paper!' "

She stood in the glare of the SUB [Students' Union Building] theatre floodlights, in moccasins and buckskins, her black hair flowing over her shoulders, eyes shooting spears at her audience.

Confronting a packed house of white university students Thursday afternoon, Kahn-Tineta Horn, a former Indian princess of Canada and a full-time crusader for Indian rights, tried to shout the white man down and out of the country.

"Why don't you all go back to where you came from," she cried. "We were doing fine before you came. We own this land; we're your landlords. And the rent is due."

— *Elaine Verbicky ("Kahn-Tineta Horn Verbally Scalps Whites,"* Gateway, *19 September 1969)*

When the revolutionary Black Muslim leader Malcolm X was speaking in the Audubon Ballroom in New York, in February

1965 — his greeting (to the brothers and sisters), *"As-salaam' alaykum,"* ringing in the air — a bullet hit him in the chest and threw him backwards across the stage, where he died. In August, in Watts, Los Angeles, crowds of blacks, glaring insolently at the police, would not disperse from 103rd Street but set it aflame and looted it — the whole district going up like a brush fire — and stoned and stabbed white interlopers and careened jubilantly through the streets and parks that were *theirs*; when the National Guard moved in like the force of occupation it was, jeeps, machine guns and bayonets reasserting white supremacy, it seemed after these events that the pacifist Christian vision of Martin Luther King and of the hundreds of thousands of blacks and whites who had pressed their claims for justice had been eclipsed by the violence of murderers and the counter-violence of desperados.

In 1966 Stokely Carmichael, chairman of the Student National (formerly Non-Violent) Coordinating Committee, said he was working not for morality or love or non-violence but for power, *black* power, the power to get Whitey off his back and to build a black community of self-government.[1] And the Black Panther party,* bristling with guns, ammo belts and black leather, demanded "an end to the robbery by the *capitalist* of our Black Community," and, quoting the Bill of Rights of the United States, asserted the right of "black colonial subjects" to decide by plebiscite to throw off the despotic government of whites.[2] Clearly, as long as black people continued to suffer debilitating poverty in the ghetto and genocidal slaughter in the army in Vietnam, then voting-rights bills and anti-poverty programs had not delivered on their promise and the militancy of black communities would have to be stepped up. In 1964 Malcolm X had warned that if the white government didn't do its job, then the blacks would have no choice but to defend themselves: "It's the ballot or the bullet." By 1966 the Black Panthers were encouraging blacks to arm themselves in self-defence. And in 1968, in a speech in Oakland, with magnificent passion, the passion of the gospeller

---

*When it was formed in 1966 from the Lowndes County Freedom Organization, it had two members: Huey Newton and Bobby Seale.

and the *guerrillero,* Carmichael issued a declaration of war:

> We must first develop an undying love for our people, our
> people, our people. . . . If we do not do that, we will be
> wiped out. . . . We are a beautiful race of people, we can do
> anything we want to do, all we got to do is get up, get up, get
> up and do it. . . . We are building a concept of peoplehood.
> We do not care about honkies, but if in building that
> concept of peoplehood, the honkies get in our way, they
> got to go. There is no question about it, there is no question
> about it. We are not concerned with their way of life, we
> are concerned with our *people.* We want to give our people
> the dignity and the humanity that we *know* as our people,
> and if they get in our way, they gonna be offed. They gonna
> be offed.[3]

By this point, white activists had been drummed out of
SNCC, but from a jail cell in California, Eldridge Cleaver, who
was to become a Black Panther on his release, wrote in *Soul on
Ice* that there *were* elements of honky society with whom black
national liberationists could usefully make an alliance, youthful
elements who, like the blacks, were standing up to the
colonialist Man, were shucking the culture and values of the
"slave-catchers, slave owners, murderers, butchers, invaders,
oppressors," and identifying instead with the heroism of the
Third World, of Castro, Ho Chi Minh, Mao Tse Tung: "There
is in America today a generation of white youth that is truly
worthy of a black man's respect, and this is a rare event in the
foul annals of American history."[4]

In many of his speeches, Stokely Carmichael made reference
not only to the "brothers and sisters" of the black communities
of Nova Scotia but to the colonized peoples of the native
Indian nations as well and to the genocide visited upon them by
the white man. A Canadian Métis activist, Howard Adams,
studying at the University of California in Berkeley, heard
Malcolm X speak and himself participated in the civil rights
struggles. Black Panthers visited Montreal and Halifax in 1968
and met with local militants. In this manner were the ideas and
purposes of the continental "national liberation" movements
cross-fertilized. The American blacks were very inspiring in

their appeals to racial pride and bonding, in their furious militancy and in their vision of an emancipating nationalism of the racially oppressed. The native peoples of Canada looked to their own lives as a place to begin the subversion of Whitey and the reconstruction of their own community.*

To be "native" in Canada: in 1965, 75 percent of Indian and Métis families live on $2,000 a year or less in conditions of absolute deprivation (in parts of northern Saskatchewan the average income is $500 per family). More than half live in three rooms or less; less than 13 percent of households have running water. The infant mortality rate is twice that of the white population. Only 15.9 percent of employable natives are in the work force and then mostly in seasonal low-skilled, low-paying labour.[5]**Alcoholic, tubercular, malnourished, suicidal, they live on the social periphery, on reservations whose administration and revenue are controlled by the Department of Indian Affairs and Northern Development or in urban ghettos. (In Manitoba, for instance, half the province's eighty thousand Indians and thirty thousand Métis would be living in Winnipeg by 1970.)[6] In the ghettos they subsist likewise impoverished, dependent on welfare and bureaucratic caretakers, and are berated for "lack of initiative" and parasitism.

To be a native in Canada is to be despised and defamed: it is to be called a savage. At school it is to be sermonized in a foreign language about the depravity and barbarism of one's ancestors and the shame of one's people's history, never learning, of course, that it was starving and terrorized people who had signed the treaties. Never learning that it was the outraged and fearless ones who had fought back, had taken on the Canadian army and its guns and died a champion's death at

---

*Because of limitations of space, I have confined myself to an account of the native people's movement and do not deal with the civil rights movement among Canada's blacks. That movement included SUPA activities in Halifax, an identification with the ideas of black power among American blacks, and with the struggle of the Vietnamese, contacts with the Americans and, climactically, the occupation of the Computer Centre at Sir George Williams University in 1969, resulting in the arrest and trial of some ninety occupiers.

**Farm work, logging, fishing and domestic service.

the end of a rope. Nor did they learn about the pre-eminence of women in the pre-colonial native society, for the strength and power of women had been subdued by three hundred years of rape and concubinage and by a political edict that stripped women of the Indian nationality should they marry a man who was not a Treaty Indian.

The government's own Hawthorn-Tremblay study, published in 1966, found that fully 25 percent of the budget of the Department of Indian Affairs went to welfare payments to the reserves as against 10 percent for "economic development" on them; and that the total expenditures of the department averaged out at $530 per Treaty Indian per year as against the federal government's expenditure of $740 on the average non-Indian Canadian (not including provincial and municipal spending on schools, health services, roads, et cetera).[7] The vast range of responsibilities of the department — reserve management, education, revenue administration, relief, inheritance, treaty obligations, welfare projects, enfranchisement — made of it a "version of colonialism," according to the report, "... a quasi-colonial government dealing with almost the entire life of a culturally different people who were systematically deprived of opportunities to influence government, a people who were isolated on separate pockets of land and who were subject to different laws."[8]

Although Indians formed only 3 percent of the population, they represented a third of the population in the jails and training schools in the late Sixties.[9] Like ghettoized peoples everywhere (patronized by bureaucracy, manipulated by social agencies, infantilized by the church, harassed by the police, brutalized by poverty), when they strike back they strike each other and themselves. Hence the alcoholism, the suicides, the beatings, the abandonments, the petty theft and the random, raging destruction and demolition of their own households and neighbourhoods. It may be that there was something in the "ethos" of native culture that historically inhibited the assimilation of Indians into the values and behaviour of industrialism. It may be that, as a result, "native Indians were left far behind"[10] by urbanized, industrialized, capitalist society and condemned to death by slow degrees at the periphery of the

New World. But surely this is true only up to the point of consciousness: "Because I postponed my confrontation with [the] white oppressor, I postponed decolonializing myself."[11] At the point of decolonizaton, the native "ethos" suddenly is revealed as a repository of values not of a pre-industrial backwater but of contemporary resistance.

> Politics were always good for lots of discussion around the table with my family. We were half-breeds and people talked about Riel and Dumont like they were still alive or had just left the country a couple of years ago. We talked about the idea of a land settlement and "colonies" like the half-breeds have in Alberta, and the Saskatchewan government's removal of about fifteen hundred families to one such colony where they were supposed to farm except it was totally useless land and they were starving. They couldn't go back north because they'd sold everything and now they were so poor they couldn't even afford to move across the road. From what I know now, I can see that these people were relocated to make room for the uranium mining.
>
> A lot of the people were hard-core Communists, as were the Ukrainian farmers in the area. They were outraged and energetic people but they weren't bitter. They simply wanted to understand what was happening to them. When I moved to Alberta the only vehicle for analysing the situation was with the Treaty Indians. Because they had land, they had a political base, so I started to study the history of the Indian people and hang out with them. I'd go to the library and come home with everything there was on Indian history. And that's how I learned about the wars, the smallpox epidemics, the treaties. I wasn't so dumb that I couldn't put two and two together. I started to read about the history of Mexico and the Indians there, the revolutions, the slavery, and I compared this with North America.
>
> Without realizing it I was accepting the fact that I was an Indian. This was a shock. We half-breeds spoke the same language as they, but they had always been "the people across the road" who never fought back. With us half-breeds it's a matter of pride that you don't let people

walk all over you. Nobody can tell us what to do. We might envy the Indians for the free medical treatment they got, the free this and free that, but my dad and uncles would say, well, at least nobody can come along and tell us what to do with our lives. We might be poor but we own ourselves.

In February 1965, 111 Slavey Indian men from Hay Lake, accompanied by a police escort, marched in total silence from the Friendship Centre near the downtown railway tracks in Edmonton to the provincial legislature building. They carried placards — "Help," "We Want Work," "We're People First, Not Just Indians" — up the flight of stairs to the rotunda of the legislature; and there, still silent, frightened, shabby, they waited while their chief and band councillors talked with Premier E.C. Manning, telling him of the band's starvation, their leaking roofs, their children schooled hundreds of miles away. The premier said these were federal responsibilities.[12]

That same year, 1965, a group of young native people, fed up with the treatment they were getting in Edmonton hotels, stores, laundromats, restaurants ("The Riviera wouldn't serve you if you were Indian, and because the downtown hotels wouldn't let us in, we were forced to stay in skid-road places"), held meetings to discuss what to do about this. "We didn't have a clue about how to go about protesting, about contacting media or getting sympathy. But we were all excited and everybody was talking at once, with all kinds of ideas. And anger, especially the Treaty Indians. Out of this came a Human Rights Committee with no tie to whites."

Summer 1968:

I was feeling really mean about this time and I'd been doing a lot of reading about Indian history — and all set to go out and save the Indian nation. That's why I agreed to a $600-a-month job with the provincial government to go out to Saddle Lake Reserve and do a survey about social service needs. What I didn't realize at the time was that the government knew there was a lot of unrest among the poor and they were bringing in "community development" to take care of it. But the communities had to ask for community development first and that's where we researchers came in. Our job was to ask a lot of questions and then come up with a report that said the people need community development.

I lived in a trailer right on the reserve with one of the other researchers, an Indian woman who was really bright, a university student, but she was no bush Indian. The third researcher was a white male activist from the university. Since I was the only one who spoke Cree, I did all the interpreting, and I was embarrassed all the time. I mean *I* was one of the people the questionnaires were aimed at and I knew how I'd feel about somebody walking into my house asking me what I thought about being poor and did I have running water. It was spy work for the government. In the end we filled the questionnaires out ourselves.

In 1968, with a living allowance from the Company of Young Canadians and training from the National Film Board, a native film crew was put together as a project of the NFB's Challenge for Change program. The film-makers would put their expertise at the disposal of poor people, such as Indians on reservations. The crew went to Faust, Alberta, where there were people waiting for something just like this.

CYC workers had been up north in the Métis and Indian communities, living in shacks and sleeping on the floors and couches: "The little shack was a mess and I thought to myself, how the hell can these guys help, they're so skinny and small." They held public meetings, the white residents all sitting in a bunch and scowling, where they told the people just what their rights were, how much welfare they were entitled to, how to get a clothing order, how to organize a timber co-op. "The whites in the town wanted to kick the CYC out but I stood up and said, every time Indian people try to help themselves, you just look at us like we're dogs; we're not dogs, we're people and I say these guys should stay. I was letting it all out and talking so strong." The CYC had their eye out for potential militants, would talk to them in their homes: Why don't you work for us, we'll help you do whatever it is you think should be done, we'll help but you have to do it. "I liked that. I wanted to learn how to organize, all

I knew how to do was work and take care of my family, so, yes, I said, I'd hire on." The CYC workers brought government people and social workers up to listen and see, they brought the press, they fought for health care and housing and then, when they heard about the native film crew, they said, why don't you come to Faust?

The idea was to use the crew to film exposés of the conditions of native life in the north country, show the dying babies, the intrusion of the oil and gas companies into the bush, the pollution, the diminishing wildlife.

> We went out with the crew to Loon Lake, a Métis settlement, and the people came out to see us and the next thing I know is the guys on the crew are working slower and slower, they were getting drunk, they didn't show up where they were supposed to be shooting, they were in Slave Lake where the town put them in a hotel and gave them credit and took them on airplane rides — that was their way of buying them off. Next thing I know they've shipped back to Montreal and I was left all alone in the community with one crew member, Willie Dunn, who stayed behind.

CYC kept on organizing, set up a drop-in centre in High Prairie and were joined by Tony Antoine from the Native Alliance for Red Power (NARP) in Vancouver. "Tony used to say, 'I advocate violence in order to wake my people up and also to shake society up for the suffering we do,' and people were afraid of him." They would get run off the highway, they would be insulted and harassed, run into court for every little infraction of the law, they were threatened and even beaten, and then one day they were in the bar at Canyon Creek: "There was eight of us and fifteen whites and they started in on us, a big horrible fight, and when the police arrived they arrested two people, Willie and Tony, and grabbed me too, three of them grabbed me but I fought until they knocked me out and threw me in the car."

The three spent the night in jail in Slave Lake and next morning were marched straight to court; they were dirty and dishevelled from the fight ("They wouldn't even allow me a comb so of course I looked like a criminal"), were refused a phone call, refused a lawyer. "I was charged with assault, obstruction and resisting arrest. I got myself out on bail but they wouldn't allow me to post bail for Willie and Tony so they went immediately to prison and I went straight down to the university in Edmonton where I'd heard there was a group of radicals."

January 1969: Rose Auger of the CYC appealed to the students' council of the University of Alberta for help acquiring funds to bail out Willie Dunn and Tony Antoine — the council committed itself to a $100 donation and then held it back "under further consideration" — and then, together with Harold Cardinal, Indian Association president, and an anthropology professor, joined the appeal with the broad issue of "institutional racism" of the police and courts. Sponsored by the Student Christian Movement and the Students for a Democratic University, this appeal for a "native defence fund" ultimately raised enough money from the Native Alliance for Red Power, NFB employees and York University students to spring Dunn and Antoine.[13] "It was the students who said, we're going to get you the best lawyer we've got. That was Gordon Wright. He came up to Slave Lake, made everybody look stupid and got us off completely."

Summer 1969: in a continuation of the research project begun the summer before at the Saddle Lake Reserve, three researchers travelled to southern Alberta, to the beet fields in the Taber, Lethbridge and Picture Butte area where Indians may find summer employment.

> We drove out to the fields. It was appalling. Nobody wanted to talk to us because they were too busy getting their work done — they get paid for as many rows as they hoe. It was only Indians working there. We checked some things out; found that the farmer who'd hired these people also runs the commissary and sold used cars. When a car broke down, he'd charge to tow it into town. So whatever money he was paying out in wages he got back. The workers were usually broke by the end of the summer and had to borrow money to get home.

The work, done by children as well as adults, consisted of weeding by hand the long rows of sugar beets growing in irrigated fields, for which the wages were: three dollars *an acre* for light weeding and seventeen to thirty-five dollars for weeding and thinning. If the farmer believed the workers had done an inadequate job, he docked three dollars an acre from their pay, and docked more for accommodation if the family were using the "home" he provided (often a converted granary or chicken coop without plumbing or electricity, water or refrigeration). Such workers were ineligible for unemployment benefits.[14] "I started to understand some things. I remembered that my parents always owed money for groceries at the Hudson's Bay Company shop and it was to the HBC that my father sold his furs — he had no choice. I learned that this is what is called a monopoly."

July 1969: the Department of Indian Affairs released a "white paper," the main recommendation of which was the termination of "special status" for Indians, based on the argument that the treaties struck between the federal government and the Indian people are an "anomaly" in civil relations. Without the special status accorded the Indians by the treaties ("As long as the rivers run. . . "), the reserves become likewise anomalous, the federal services redundant and the guarantees of the treaties abrogated. "Should the main recommendations . . . be implemented," a writer objected, "the reserves will be lost, and the native people will be permanently pauperized, a skid-row culture."[15]

Native activists immediately responded to the affront of the white paper by publicizing its offensive and gloomy implications: extermination through assimilation ("The only good Indian is a non-Indian"), legal and moral irresponsibility of government, and official blindness to social reality. They gave notice too that Indians would resist any attempts to implement the nefarious policies suggested by the white paper.

> The supposed new policy is no different than the arbitrary dictations from Ottawa to the Indians that have been repeated down through our history. . . . In spite of all government attempts to convince Indians to accept the white paper, their efforts will fail, because Indians under-

stand that the path outlined by the Department of Indian Affairs. . . . leads directly to cultural genocide. We will not walk this path.[16]

November 1969: native Americans and Canadians occupied Alcatraz Island in San Francisco Bay. "We are a proud people! We are Indians! Our Earth Mother awaits our voices. We are Indians of All Tribes! *We hold the rock!*"[17]

The unrest of the internal "third world" was abroad in the land. As it developed in consciousness and experience, native protest moved from apologies and supplications to rigorous demands and counter-proposals to assimilation. The movement for "red power" rejected the paternalism of the bureaucracy and the social welfare agencies and insisted on the development of community self-reliance. Aroused by the vehemence of the advocates of black power in the United States, native militants in Canada defiantly reaffirmed their Indian identity: a cultural revival replaced hopelessness and self-disgust with self-confidence and self-esteem. Paradoxically, this insistence on their racial and cultural specificity provoked a spirit of "internationalism": against the Man of white imperialist North America all the oppressed races and nations of the world were united in resistance.

No different from the white movement activists who were demanding a fundamental revision of the distribution of wealth and authority, as capitalism expanded and generated ever more sophisticated forms of surplus, the native militants refused both relegation to the economic and political periphery and assimilation into a niggardly *status quo*. The more they understood of the relationship between racism and capitalism — in the underdevelopment of their communities, in their formation into an urban "lumpen" subclass, in the myths of white superiority — the more they accepted the imperative of a social and economic revolution that would transform the whole of North American society.

We need to liberate ourselves from the courts, ballot boxes, school system, church and all the other agencies that command us to stay in "our colonized place." This oppression of the native people is so deeply rooted in the capitalist system that it cannot be completely eliminated without eliminating capitalism itself . . . as the struggle widens, social class features will gradually become more prominent and the movement will turn into a class struggle.[18]

Granted that such analysis was arrived at by a very few, it represented nevertheless the tip of a broad refusal in the "third world" to accommodate itself any longer to white bourgeois society.

This refusal, apparent readily enough to the state, prompted strategies of containment and co-option — a process already underway with the establishment of the CYC. Particularly through the promotion of "community development," the state's manipulation of the burgeoning political restlessness of youth was extended into black and native protest groups. As it turned out, community development was a mechanism by which the potentially explosive frustration and impatience of an increasingly self-conscious dispossessed community were redirected into short-term goals, interfactional disputes and the launching of careers in the civil service.

Item: The community development people, who were almost always white, would present themselves to our organization as resource people; they were very egotistical, macho men who had a perfect way of working a crowd, like an evangelist does, and the reaction of the Indian leaders was we should be damn grateful that guys like that want to work with us because we sure couldn't afford to hire them.

Without anyone realizing it, they'd take over. They had all the analysis and the solutions and they did all the talking, but they were careful to praise the Indian leaders in front of us and, what do you know, our guys started parroting them, as though all these radical, militant ideas were their own. In the back of their minds, of course, they knew that without the advisors backing them up and giving them ideas they would lose their positions. What had happened is that the community developers had made themselves indispensable to the Indian leadership.

Item: The grants started coming in and suddenly all these really strong people, for whom we'd bent over backwards to get free babysitting and so on so they could get involved in the organization, got greedier than hell, started hiring themselves and giving themselves big salaries and expense accounts. S___would always wear a black suit because, he said, our people associate the black suit with the Indian agent and the priest: they associate it with power. This is one of the things you learn from community development training.

Item: The community meeting would be called to order, the speakers would be introduced and they'd get up and they'd talk. Everybody would clap and cheer. When the discusson would start, everybody would have something to say but there'd always be one or two people that would be really together and really strong and really talking. Those were the people that we'd discuss on the way home from the meeting. "You watch those people because they're going to cause trouble." One of the things we'd do then was go up to Faust, say, announce there's money for housing but the house would go to that guy or two who'd spoken the longest and hardest and strongest. Of course everybody else would then get mad at him, jealous, resentful, and that's the end of his local base of support. We didn't have to do anything else.

Further, in June 1969, a memorandum was submitted to the cabinet of the federal government by the minister of health and welfare and the secretary of state, advising of racial agitation in Nova Scotia since the fall of 1968, the growing threat of civil disorder, and the existence of "extremist elements" planning disruption of the Canada Summer Games. Its recommendation to cabinet was that the Black United Front of Nova Scotia, which represented the "constructive and moderate elements within the Black Community," be funded by a grant of up to $100,000 over five years. Without such support, there was a possibility that "black militants" might take over a discredited leadership. With support, the BUF could hold the militants off. ". . . given the climate of unrest in society, further consideration [should] be given by the Cabinet Committee on Social Policy and Cultural Affairs to methods of intervention by the federal government in matters of this nature."

The most trenchant refusal to cooperate, or collaborate, with the "hidden hand" of the federal bureaucracy and to play the part of the "professional Indian" was in the mobilization around red power. In casting off illusions about the capacity of the system to deliver redress of grievances and in going beyond the "ethnic nationalism" of the Indian cultural revival,* red power became a *political* formulation. However it began, whether in the simple fraternity of the reserve or ghetto or in the articulation of an ethic appropriate to the values of native culture or in the desire for separation from white society, red power was about *power*: the power of a nation/collective/ people to take back its rights to self-determination and the power to keep them once won. "We are learning from others," wrote Harold Cardinal, "about the forces that can be assembled in a democratic society to protect oppressed minorities."[19] Such an assembly would by necessity occur in the public arena of Canadian society and not behind the closed doors of negotiation between white bureaucrats and "professional Indians."

In contrast to the concentration of authority within an isolated leadership and its white consultants that was characteristic of the "official" native pressure groups (the federations, brotherhoods, councils and cultural centres), red power was in the neighbourhood. In contrast to the professional elites whose power rested not on a base of communal support but on their privileges (salaries, offices, staff, expense accounts, media attention, et cetera), awarded for good behaviour by the government, red power contested the authority and legitimacy of racist, bourgeois government. Red power rejected any kind

---

*In native customs, rituals, mythology, folklore and spirituality, many young natives rediscovered the idea that the native peoples of North America knew how to live in peace with the environment and that in this idea was the renewal of the race: ". . . the world we live in today, the electronic, tribal, total systems, cybernetic society, is the real manifestation of the Indian personality."[20]

of assimilation into the processes of white capitalist society and proposed that in "Indian nationalism" itself were the content and spirit of resistance to colonization and of the brave new world beyond.

In this revolutionary hopefulness, the young proponents of red power were very much like those of flower power: in Indianness, as in hippieness, the violent, greedy and egomaniacal stratagems of "straight" society would be confounded. *"Red power is the spirit to resist. Red power is love for our people. Red power is now."* In militant Indianness the inexorable dissolution of the Nation into the ideological and social hegemony of whiteness could be forestalled.

Between 1969 and 1970 red power had several moments in which it declared itself. Thousands of Indians from the United States as well as Canada converged on prairie reservations to dance to the drum, smoke ritual tobacco, consult the shamans and pray. "It gives me enough strength to go on for another year," said Willie Dunn, who was a songwriter as well as an activist. "What's the use of writing songs if you think you're going to die?"[21] Indians in Quebec began their agitation around land-claims settlements. Mohawks from the St. Regis reserve near Cornwall, Ontario, staged a sit-in on the U.S.–Canada border, demanding official accession to their treaty-right to unobstructed travel across the frontier. The Native Action Committee in Saskatchewan ran a red power candidate in Meadow Lake constituency in the 1968 federal election. And in its newsletter the Vancouver-based Native Alliance for Red Power published its demands: abolishment of the "Indian Act" and the "destruction of the colonial office (Indian Affairs Branch)"; an end to the collection of taxes from the Indian people by "racist government"; a cessation of the harassment of native people by the police and the courts; and compensation for the land lost by Indian bands who had not signed treaties. "We want the government to give *foreign aid* to the areas comprising the Indian Nation. . . . We want to develop our remaining resources in the interests of the redman, not in the interests of the white corporate elite"; *Red power is now!*[22]

The implications of red power were that, alongside the revolutionaries, rebels, protestors, dissidents and drop-outs of white society, the Indian youth were rejecting the apathy, resignation and fatalism with which the preceding generation had sought to defend itself from genocide. They were advancing — spiritual and ideological guns blazing — to that political site of the reconstruction of the race in democratic self-government and humanist "nationalism." In some white radicals, they had sincere comrades in this adventure.

It seemed that in the agitation and militancy of native youth was the emergence of a credible force of social change that would unsettle the affairs of white-dominated society in a ripple effect of transformation: start disturbances at the periphery of mainstream society and eventually the waves of seditious energy would swamp the core of (white-held) power. It was not possible that the demands of native radicals would be met without profound dislocations of the *status quo*. If this were true, it was not because of the Indians' numbers, because they were a handful, nor because of their geographic concentration, for they were scattered, but because the demands represented the aspirations of a group of people *strategically* situated at the points of expansion of corporate capitalism in Canada.*

I've never been romantic about the Indian struggle. The fact is their call for self-determination matches my own political feelings about decentralization and about people having control of their own lives. It also matches what I think is a world-wide struggle against the power of the transnational corporations. I always felt that a good part of the struggle in this country was to cut the tentacles of the corporations which operate from the United States. In this country that means taking on the resource industries. It's exactly these industries that the Indian people face in direct conflict. It's the mining and pulp and paper and oil and gas companies they're going to have to deal with in their struggle for community self-determination. I also know the exploitation that they put the Indian people through. So part of it was theoretical in the sense that this

---

*This analysis of the native peoples' strategic location in the continental economy is a far cry from the SUPA-type analysis of native power as the "power" of the dispossessed and alienated.

is a way to cut the tentacles, the other part was the absolute oppression that the Indian people were suffering at the hands of the resource corporations and so it is a simple struggle for justice.

Like the white radicals, many native activists had little faith in the probability of the organized working class taking up the revolutionary struggle. Not only were the workers completely absorbed by the economist imperatives of the bureaucratized unions, the white working class was as racist as the rest of white society and unlikely to serve a campaign snipping away at the supports of their privilege. But from the example of their ancestors' belief that this land was meant for the sharing and the benefit of all humankind upon it, and from the example of the strategic alliances of other national liberation movements with white radicals, the men and women of red power were prepared to accept from youth, women's liberationists and the nationalist workers of Quebec, comrades in a "new revolutionary class."[23] Wherever there were people "up against the Man," there too were the Indian dreams of people who own themselves.

Natives as well as blacks were reading the literature of black power and the writings of the Black Panthers ("Cleaver's and Malcolm X's books were like Bibles for us"), noting what they shared of the blacks' colonized situation and suspecting that somewhere in the vocabulary and visions of the black guerrillas was a key to their own release: "How did they get their people so strong?" So when Fred Hampton, twenty-one, chairman of the Illinois Chapter of the Black Panthers, visited groups of native militants in Saskatchewan and Alberta in November 1969, he was received with enormous respect, admiration and sympathy. Fred Hampton, the man in the black leather jacket, standing in the cold wind of a grey day. Fred Hampton who said the Black Panthers had come together as "peacemakers" to challenge the corrupt and atrocious power of the "sheriff" as Jesse James and his brothers had challenged him in the dusty streets of an earlier frontier. Fred Hampton, who had written that "you can jail a revolutionary but you can't jail the revolution; you can murder a liberator but you can't murder liberation," was murdered in his bed at four o'clock in the

morning, December 1969, by Illinois state attorney's police.*
With shotguns, pistols, automatic rifles and magnum shells,
they tore apart the apartment, the walls and the furniture, and
Hampton himself, with two shots in the head and one to the
heart. A photograph of the bedroom, taken after the removal of
the body, shows a hanger on a nail in the wall, a plain wooden
chair with an ashtray, wads of paper on the floor, and a blood-
soaked mattress: somebody lived here, somebody was sleeping
here.

Hampton died two weeks after his visit to Edmonton. For
many who had met him, shaken his hand, rapped with him, felt
his "warmth and legitimacy," his death cut off the last retreat
they had back into their illusions. Behind them was the
romance of reconciliation, ahead of them fear, and resolution.

---

*Hampton was the thirty-eighth member of the Black Panther party to
be killed by the police in 1969.

II
THE RISING OF THE WOMEN

Every woman should have the right to choose whether or not she wants to bear a child. Every child should have the right to know that he or she is wanted. As long as these rights are denied, thousands of women and children are condemned to death and thousands more to misery. Death comes to women through self-induced or "quack" abortions — in Canada there are at least 2,000 such deaths each year. Death comes to unwanted children as the constantly increasing number of "battered children" affirms. Evidence recently collected indicates that unplanned pregnancies can precipitate long-lasting mental breakdowns and since therapeutic abortions are so hard to obtain, the misery of many a woman will lead to this too. This leads to our demand that abortion be removed from the Criminal Code; any woman has the right to an abortion if she so desires.

— from the pamphlet "Abortion Is Our Right!" distributed by the Vancouver Women's Caucus, 1970

It was an ordinary morning in the cafeterias of the campuses, slats of sunshine coming through the windows onto our coffee cups, onto the hands of our companions gesticulating as they spoke of Freud and Plato and Voltaire, onto the pages of the book, a cheap paperback, dog-eared already, over which we bent our heads and read in the little cocoon of silence we hugged around ourselves. It was 1963 and we, the women, were reading Betty Friedan's *The Feminine Mystique.*

We read there about the "problem that has no name," about the women of North America who that very morning, as we sat with our coffee cups between lectures, were making beds and peanut-butter sandwiches and loading the laundry and meandering through the supermarkets, fulfilling perfectly the expectations of femininity. We read that these women felt tired all the time, felt weepy and despondent, felt sexless and barren of personality, and, in shame and guilt, got drunk in the afternoons from the bottle of vodka hidden behind the cans of furniture polish and spray cleaners, or sat in the armchair at the psychiatrist's office, resignedly accepting the prescription for tranquillizers as the appropriate remedy for their anxious queries: "Who am I?" and "Is this all there is?"

We read there of the grotesque discrepancy between the image of men in our society — men as revolutionaries and space travellers and physicists and mystics — and the image of women, of *us* — as childish, frivolous, empty-headed house-keepers whose cultural task was to beautify ourselves; social responsibility, to have babies; and economic function, to consume household goods. We were cheated, wrote Betty Friedan, of our self-esteem, disallowed our development as intellectual and moral beings and forfeited of our personhood. We had swallowed the lie of our inferiority and obliterated the genetic memory within us of women who had been mighty with the truth about women.

> Look at my arm! I have ploughed and planted and gathered into barns . . . and ain't I a woman? I could work as much and eat as much as a man — when I could get it — and bear the lash as well. . . . I have borne thirteen children and seen most of 'em sold into slavery, and when I cried with my mother's grief, none but Jesus helped me — and ain't I a woman?[1]

And weren't we women? But it was 1963 and there was none of us who did not believe we would be different from the brigades of defeated women in the suburbs. *We* were students. We would be clever and we would travel and have adventures. And then we would marry, and *we* would be in love. We would build an interesting home and raise bright children. We shut the book, shut out the plaintive women and shut out the forebodings that our lives might after all be reined in within the order of female prostration. Just a few years later, of course, the women came back to haunt us, and we saw that we were their sisters.

In spring 1967, at a SUPA conference in Kingston, movement

women met separately for the first time, marching off to have a women's caucus in a room of their own while the men giggled and made jokes.*

> We weren't quite sure what we were going to talk about when we decided to have our own meeting but it gradually came out. We talked about how it was men who did the writing and women the Gestetnering, about how our political influence in the group was directly related to how "heavy" the guy was that we were coupled with. We were feeling our way into talking about our experience as women but we weren't sure how to do it. For instance, there was a woman there who was pregnant and she said, "Yeah, all this discussion leads up to the fact that I'm sitting here seven months pregnant and I'm scared to death." I remember thinking, what does this have to do with anything? Why is she talking about this? Everyone wants to have babies so why is she saying this? We brushed over it. And I kept on arguing that it was wrong for us to meet separately because the only way we could prove we were just as good as the men was by sticking it out in the organization and arguing with them.

Which is what they did. By the fall of 1967, invigorated by the reports of women's caucuses meeting within SDS in the United States and by the appointment in Ottawa of a Royal Commission to "inquire into and report upon the status of women in Canada and to recommend what steps might be taken by the Federal Government to ensure for women equal opportunities with men in all aspects of Canadian society,"[2] Judy Bernstein, Peggy Morton, Linda Seese and Myrna Wood presented a paper at the SUPA conference in Goderich. It was called *Sisters, Brothers, Lovers . . . Listen . . .* and the women would never be so supplicatory again.

The tone of the paper is hopeful, defensive and conciliatory.[3] "We hope that it will not be taken as vindictive. . . . We trust that you will consider this paper with the seriousness with

---

*One such "joke" was that SUPA women, as their contribution to support of the Viet Cong, bake cookies to sell.

which it was written." Sensitive to the devaluation of women's intellectual capabilities, it defensively covers itself with a cloak of references to Karl Marx, Herbert Marcuse, the British Marxist feminist Juliet Mitchell and the French feminist philosopher Simone de Beauvoir. "[Woman] realizes in her subconscious what Marcuse says: 'Free election of masters does not abolish the masters or the slaves.' " It is heartbreaking in its need to argue the most self-evident of political truths about women's estate: "Unlike lower forms of life, human beings are capable of becoming . . . more than a living entity that is enslaved to the creation and maintenance of the species."

Nevertheless the paper raised themes that immediately reverberated throughout the new left and quickly laid the basis for the autonomous organization of women militants. Here were the beginnings of revisionist anthropology (in the references to the role of female labour and production in pre-capitalist and industrial societies) and the hints at the revolutionary potential of female demands. Here were the first expressions of the political content of sexual relations ("Woman is the object; man is the subject. Women are screwed; men do the screwing") and of the fundamental importance of women's right to the control of their bodies' use and function. And here, in the pointed references to the role of women in SUPA and, by extension, in the movement as a whole, was the proposition that would challenge the very *raison d'être* of new left politics: a movement in which women are as exploited and demeaned as they are in the society as a whole is a movement that will continue to reproduce the oppressive relations of that society. As such, the movement is a sham and a travesty of the struggle for liberation. "It is our contention that until the male chauvinists of the movement understand the concept of liberation in relation to women . . . they will be voicing political lies."

SUPA dissolved shortly after. And the women's liberation movement took off. Women across the country began caucusing separately within movement organizations (for instance, in the SDU groups at Simon Fraser University, the University of Alberta and the University of Regina) and from there quickly determined to make contact with women outside the campus locales. Although university women continued to be the support base of the women's liberation groups, it was not unusual when their meetings included young working women, high school students, middle-aged housewives, single mothers, women from old left groups. And it was here, at such meetings that two things happened. One was the formation of consciousness-raising groups* and the other the organizing of action projects around the related issues of sexuality.

Consciousness raising (otherwise known as c-r), getting together in a circle to talk, to hear, to open oneself in an environment of sisterly sympathy and recognition and to begin the extended and difficult process of expressing the hurt and anger and hate and fear in female experience that had been denied legitimacy elsewhere. To speak of housework and living alone and childbirth and body image and girlhood and bosses and lovers. "The insight I remember most vividly from consciousness raising was Christ! I've been crippled by the totality of my experience as a woman, I've been frightened and damaged and paralysed. As I began to acknowledge this I had feelings of unspeakable anger and from there I began to repair myself." Women read together *The Feminine Mystique, The Second Sex* by Simone de Beauvoir, *The Golden Notebook* by Doris Lessing and giggled and chitchatted over a bottle of wine, debating the pros and cons of using deodorant and shaving your legs and wearing make-up — the hilarity of it as the ribald and preposterous confessions came out: "I remember a lot of times feeling uncomfortable because we should be more *serious* but another part of my mind realized this was the first time I'd spent a whole evening with a bunch of women and just had *fun* with them." Women learned how to be articulate and get the ear of others for the first time, discovered

---

*"I remember countless SDU social evenings where the men talked and the women listened — we weren't talking to each other. And one evening I just got up and said, 'This is boring.' Everyone was very surprised. Shortly after that I joined a consciousness-raising group where we talked about make-up, our bodies, our relationships. At this point the men got paranoid and thought we were getting together to talk about the size of their cocks."

that, like a cork out of a bottle of champagne, women, pulled out from the confines of male-dominated groups, gushed with literacy and eloquence and intellect and prefigured, here in the sisterly circle, a politics all their own, a politics of absolute commitment, of unqualified support, of innovation. "We challenged everything that was male, their rationality, their logic, their intellectualism, I mean we saw that even the way buildings are built and streets are laid out is masculine; we felt that in the entire culture there was nothing that had anything to do with us because we had not made it, we had no history, no art, all we had was ourselves, our sisterhood." And finally, women dared to use the word "oppression" as the substantive of their condition; yes, *women* are oppressed, we whom you objectify and trivialize, abuse and humiliate, shackle and deform. As it had proved for the oppressed of the Deep South, the oppressed of the reservations and ghettos, the oppressed of the colonies, the word was the "open sesame" of the ranks of the women. With this concept they acknowledged that their pain was collective, objectively rooted in history and in society, and was redressable by action.

Arguing that female being has historically been defined and limited as sexual and that "woman's body is used as a commodity or medium of exchange,"[4] the women's liberation groups in 1968 determined that women's right to control the sexual functions of their bodies was the *sine qua non* of their liberation. And so began actions around the issues of birth control and abortion.

As early as 1962 branches of the Voice of Women had been campaigning for the legalization of birth control information-distribution.* Deliberately disregarding the law, the new groups set up birth control information and counselling booths and centres on and off campus where they made available printed literature on contraception, samples of available contraceptives, and lists of sympathetic doctors who would

---

*Since 1892 the Criminal Code of Canada had forbidden the sale and advertisement of contraceptives and the dissemination of information. The code was amended in 1969.

prescribe for single women. And when the *Birth Control Handbook*, a comprehensive digest of information and argument, became available in late 1968 from the McGill Students' Society, they distributed some fifty thousand copies of this, too, by the summer of 1969. At the University of Alberta, where since 1967 there had been agitation against Health Services' decision not to make the birth control pill available to students nor even to supply any information whatsoever about contraceptives, the Committee for the Status of Women accused Health Services of "abdicating its responsibility" to students and disseminated the information themselves.

> A number of us women were living together and we talked among ourselves about the sexual double standard, about our right to screw when we pleased, about all the women we knew who were dropping out of university because of accidental pregnancies. We were very frustrated because we couldn't get information and the University wouldn't budge: it was illegal, period. Finally, Lynn said, well, why don't we do something about it? At first I was appalled: to think one should *do* something about a grievance! And then we just up and did it.

For all the embarrassment and consternation aroused by the illegal actions around the birth control issue, the women's groups were in fact tolerated and allowed to operate in this regard. Their activities around the issue of abortion were, however, a different matter. Logically and politically, the two issues were inseparable, of course: as long as women were denied access to birth control, they would have no choice but to seek abortion in order to terminate a pregnancy they had not chosen. Up to 28 August 1969, abortion for any reason was illegal under the Criminal Code; therefore, in seeking an abortion a woman risked prosecution, not to mention disfigurement or death, as the result of putting herself in the hands of the only person who could help her: the abortionist. There was not a woman alive who did not fear the consequences of her sexual activity; nor one who did not realize, even instinctively, that this fear was a form of social control. Because she might become pregnant at any time, and be reduced to economic dependency within the family, she was denied employment of equal pay and value to that of men, placement in professional and graduate schools at the same rate as men, and mobility and independence in carrying out life-decisions as she saw fit. Clearly, women's liberationists were to argue, women's right to abortion on demand had to be secured before any of the other campaigns for the liberation of women could be undertaken. Only when freed of biological determinisms could women address themselves concretely as workers, intellectuals, artists or politicians. "Abortion counselling dominated our activity."

They set up offices and publicized their phone numbers. They answered calls from women who were hysterical and in tears; would talk them into composure and determine what their decision was; would give them the name of a handful of doctors who would abort them; would accompany them to the abortionist or would lend them money so they could travel to the nearest "safe" doctor; would talk to them after the abortion if they were depressed or fearful. It was agonizing work.

> I was sent a fifteen-year-old pregnant girl who had been a resident of Warrendale.* I couldn't get her into the doctor in Kingston and I had never tried this guy in Brockville before but I had been told that he was okay. His front was as a chiropractor and the address in Brockville was a lean-to on a house. I went in and he was sitting in this really sordid room, that's the only word for it. And he was drinking. I looked at the girl and she looked at me and I said, "Are you sure that this is what you want?" And the guy said, "Oh, don't worry about the drinking. I've done these things when I was so pissed I couldn't walk across the room." I looked at her again and I said, "Are you sure you want to do this?" And she said, "Yes." He went out to the garage and he brought in one of those boxes that carpenters keep their tools in and this is where he kept his medical tools. He wouldn't let me stay in the room with her. I went out and sat in the car for what seemed like hours. Then she came out and she said that the only thing

---

*At the time, a treatment centre for children near Toronto.

that he had said to her was that she had one of the cleanest twats he'd ever seen.

In Edmonton, abortion counsellors were harassed by obscene telephone calls, and in Regina the Women's Health Centre was under surveillance by the Department of the Attorney-General.

Closely related to the issue of involuntary pregnancy was that of child care: should a woman bear a child, she was held totally responsible for its care. As more and more women were employed, this responsibility assumed the proportions of a social crisis.* Given that the median weekly earnings of women in 1967 were fifty dollars, it was obvious that the typical child-care arrangement of a babysitter ate up the mother's earnings. Clearly, women required cheap and accessible day-care facilities if they were ever to function independently and remuneratively. The women's liberation groups took up this requirement and made it a demand.

In Toronto, in the fall of 1969, the University of Toronto Women's Group spearheaded the occupation of an empty house near the campus as a cooperative nursery. When the city demanded the occupants undertake $2,000 worth of renovations and the university vice-president refused to make funds available for them, the day-care people marched to the administration building and occupied the Senate Chamber. The number of sitters-in grew to two hundred, with the support of the students' council and the New Left Caucus. "People are singing, smoking pot, sleeping, and sharing sandwiches with the campus police. Everywhere there are discussions and arguments. The place is alive."[6] The next day the university capitulated and promised the $2,000. "Victory was ours! . . . we now had the base for the further actions of committing the university to the responsibility of providing day care. . . . Women's liberation had engineered the first occupation at the University of Toronto. . . . All power to the people — especially women!"[7]

---

*According to a child-care survey made by the Dominion Bureau of Statistics in 1967, 908,000 children required care arrangements.[5]

In 1969, after two years of review, a bill was passed by the House of Commons by which abortion was legalized under certain conditions. The conditions added fat to the fire of the abortion campaign and brought sharply into focus what had been previously obscured by the universality of the issue: the class discrimination of abortion legislation.

According to the reforms, abortion must be performed by a qualified doctor in an accredited or approved hospital. The doctor must first receive a certificate in writing from the hospital's therapeutic abortion committee stating that the continuation of the woman's pregnancy "would or would be likely to endanger her life or health";[8] and the committee must consist of at least three doctors. No hospital is *required* by this legislation to have a therapeutic abortion committee. It was immediately obvious to the militants of the women's movement that they had been cheated of the intent of their campaign, and once again the women's liberation movement geared up for another assault on the law. Women pointed out, in leaflets and demonstrations and briefs and speeches all across the country, that the hospitals' decision-making structures were entirely in the hands of male professionals and of a bureaucracy that could not be expected to act expeditiously and in the best interests of the woman herself.

They argued that, with grounds for abortion being for "health" reasons, "it will be the affluent middle-class women who know about and have access to a sympathetic psychologist. What help will such a law be for the women who are intimidated or refused by doctors and psychologists because they cannot pay?"[9] Women living in isolated areas, in Roman Catholic dioceses, in towns where no hospital establishes an abortion committee, are effectively prevented from exercising their right to a legal abortion. A legal abortion remains the privilege of women with money of their own who live in large centres close to liberal hospitals, liberal doctors and the support facilities of the women's liberation movement. The only humane and the only just solution to this cruel discrimination was the provision of abortion on the simple demand of the pregnant woman herself. Control of our own bodies! Repeal all abortion laws! Abortion is our right! Every child a wanted child!

In April 1970, a call came from the Vancouver Women's Caucus* for women across Canada to join a caravan that would travel from Vancouver to Ottawa, there to confront the prime minister: "We consider the government of Canada is in a state of war with the women of Canada. If steps are not taken to implement our demands by Monday, May 11, 1970, at 3:00 P.M., we will be forced to respond by declaring war on the Canadian government."

And so they set out from Vancouver, stopping in a dozen towns and cities en route to Ottawa, holding public meetings and swelling their ranks with supporters anxious to add their bodies to the demonstration planned for Parliament Hill. In Kamloops, Edmonton, Regina, Winnipeg, the Lakehead, Sudbury, Toronto, activists knew they were coming; they greeted them, billeted them, cooked up hot suppers.** Up and down the streets of downtowns, the caravan drove, blaring from a loudspeaker the Judy Collins version of "We Want Our Revolution," while women sang along and distributed literature and talked to people in the streets. They travelled with a coffin, symbolizing the women dead from illegal abortions and filled it, in one town after another, with petitions signed by thousands and thousands of women demanding the repeal of the abortion laws.

They drove into Ottawa with placards pasted on their cars and vans, drove in with women hanging out the windows, shouting and singing, and in the streets women waved V's and clenched fists back at them. Billeted en masse at a church, they hunkered down for strategy sessions, trying to arrive, by consensus and collective decision making, at a plan of action for the weekend, while the menfolk who had accompanied them cooked the meals and "did whatever we needed done to carry out our strategy." They decided that, "disguised" as respectable women and armed with forged passes to the House of

---

*The core of the downtown-based caucus had, the year before, been the women of the SFU SDU.

**Thirty-five years earlier, another generation of women militants had done precisely the same for another on-to-Ottawa trek of insurgents, travelling the same route.

Commons galleries (procured by sympathetic female support staff on Parliament Hill), they would disrupt Parliament by chaining themselves to their seats. Not everyone would go in: the action could provoke arrests and prosecution; no woman should feel compelled to participate. It was okay to be scared.

On Saturday, May 9, over five hundred women and their supporters marched to Parliament Hill and demanded unsuccessfully to meet with Trudeau, Health Minister Munro and Justice Minister Turner. (Trudeau was "unavailable" as he was preparing for a trip abroad; Munro was in Geneva; and Turner was playing tennis.) Instead they held a rally. Woman after woman stood up to denounce the abortion laws and the bureaucracy calcifying their implementation. They stood up to publicize statistics of death and sterility from abortion, to describe their experiences with hosptial boards and doctors, and to lead in songs and slogans: "Just Society Just for the Rich!"

And then, angered and fed up, they all marched to 24 Sussex Drive. Some, on the first march of their lives, came all the way from Vancouver and Calgary to shout and sing along with the women who had been in the movement for years; all of them sensed they were part of the same historical motion now; class and age and race and experience subsumed within this wave of women united in sisterhood against the regime of the women-haters and women-murderers and the women-crushers. "Woman-Power to the Women-People!" They marched their way past the dumbfounded RCMP guards at the prime minister's residence, sat in on the lawn for an hour, and marched out, leaving behind the coffin full of petitions — and coat hangers, Lysol and knives.

Monday morning. They got dressed that morning in their "disguises," wearing long-sleeved blouses over the chains wrapped around their arms, and strolled over to Parliament Hill, casually going into the galleries in their ones and twos, while a large contingent gathered for a demonstration at the steps of the Peace Tower. In the House of Commons, the honourable gentlemen were discussing the condition of the carpeting in the visitors' elevators.

At a quarter past three I stood up and started making my speech, demanding free abortion. It took the security guard a fair amount of time to reach me so that I was almost finished by the time he got to me. The woman beside me who had been really nervous stood up as he came towards her — one of those great decisions she had made — and said she wasn't going to let him touch me. She got totally into it. He grabbed me and he pulled me out and I think we reached the door before the next person started — I was shouting all the while. Outside he said, "Well, dear, you've had your little say, haven't you?" It must have taken us three or four minutes to walk down to the main office. By that time bells were ringing and people were screaming and running all over the place. Another guard came in and said, "There's thirty of them in there and they're all chained to their seats!" It dawned on him that I was not a nut; or that if I was a nut, then there were a lot of nuts in there with me.

As soon as she had been dragged out, the next woman, chained to her seat by the ankle, stood up and shouted out a statement about the right to the control of her body, and then another woman and another, in this gallery and that gallery, while the guards rushed frantically from one to the other, unable to drag them out until they got hacksaws and cut them free from the chains. As they chanted over and over, "Free Abortion on Demand" and "Every Child a Wanted Child," the Speaker adjourned the session. It was the first time in the history of the Canadian House of Commons that it was closed because of a disturbance.

Still high and buzzing with the fervour of the united actions of the Abortion Caravan, women's liberationists from across the country convened in Saskatoon in November 1970 to answer the question: What next for us? In the debates that followed, the unity of the springtime dissolved.

There was a contingent in Saskatoon, largely Trotskyist, that argued for a continuation and intensification of the free-abortion-on-demand campaign. It made sense, they argued, to concentrate energy on a single issue, given the appeal and importance to *every* woman of the abortion issue. Besides, though the battle may have been fought, the war was scarcely won.

But there were militants who chafed at the limited aims of the abortion campaign, and fearing the ultimate co-option of the movement by liberal legislation, they wanted to press for radical change across the broad spectrum of women's condition. The movement itself, well before the Abortion Caravan, had already begun to take up the issues of women's work, women's education, child care, socialization and sexism. The women's caucus at the University of Regina had been divided up among those who did work on campus, those who set up a women's centre downtown, and those who organized a working women's group. The Vancouver Women's Caucus had already acknowledged the need to organize "beyond" abortion (their first public action had been to involve themselves in a SFU day-care centre) when they, two months earlier, had organized semi-autonomous workshops: Women in Education, Women in Teaching and Working Women.

And there were the New Feminists of Toronto who had broken completely with the (male-dominated) left and with (male-ideated) socialism, arguing that "we must eradicate the sexual division on which our society is based if women are to be liberated."[10] They had worn red scarves on the Abortion Caravan as a badge of distinction.*

It should have been no great surprise to anyone when no single, broad, all-encompassing union of women's liberationists emerged from Saskatoon, but, instead, a large number of militants variously organized around this program or that, this theoretical position or that. It may have seemed, depressingly enough, mere squabbling at the time. The disputes were, however, a sign that the women's liberation movement had engaged the *realpolitik* of radicalism.

If it was female sexuality that first impressed the women's liberationists with the distinctiveness of their oppression, it was

---

*"I remember asking somebody, 'Who are these people?' 'Oh, they're the New Feminists, they're the people who think men are the enemy.' I thought they were wrong because obviously it was capitalism that is the enemy. I mean, it's one or the other."

female labour that convinced them of its universality. As women had always borne children, so too had they always laboured, and it would be a superficial movement indeed that did not seek them out where they worked, and were exploited.

The Royal Commission on the Status of Women, reporting in 1970, learned that: pay is generally lower for traditionally female professions than for other professions; equal pay laws are inadequate; paid maternity leave is rare; few women reach senior levels; women have less opportunity to enter and to advance in many occupations and professions.[11] Only 17 percent of waged women workers were organized in unions in 1967 — not that this did them much good. In 1969 only between 3 and 5 percent of all collective agreements in force at that time included clauses providing for equal pay for male and female members employed at similar jobs.[12] Housework, of course, is unpaid labour,* and the housewife experiences debilitating dependency. ". . . it should not surprise anyone to learn that the women of this country are particularly vulnerable to the hazards of being poor. . . . The Commission received a great many briefs dealing less with abstract rights than with economic justice."[13]**

Here then was the constituency for the women's liberation movement: working women, poor and isolated and distraught. If, while still active within the male-dominated new left, the women militants had shared their male comrades' low estimation of the potential for radicalism of the working class, they no longer shared it as they began their efforts among working women. "I think," says a male activist now, "if you want to locate the first *analysis* of the workplace done by the move-

---

*In 1967, pre-dating the wages-for-housework campaign of the women's movement itself, delegates from the Prince Albert, Saskatchewan, constituency to the provincial NDP convention moved that housewives be paid a salary.

**Of the 2,558,000 women in the labour force in the third quarter of 1969, fully 2,003,000 were employed in the service industries where they earned an average weekly wage of $97.60 compared to an average of $137 in the manufacturing industries.[14] Although women represented in 1967 roughly one-third of the labour force, they received only 20 percent of all reported income.[15]

ment you'd find it was done by women, on women in the work force."

In these efforts the Vancouver Women's Caucus was exemplary. In January 1970 the Working Women's Workshop was formed within the caucus to "acquire the tools for organizing" and almost immediately after were in contact with women members of the Hospital Employees Union and of the Pulp, Paper and Woodworkers of Canada. In March they joined the picket line of the striking employees of Tilden Car Rental, and in June set up a series of noon-hour meetings with downtown office workers. In August they became involved in what was to be an eighteen-month-long strike and boycott of Cunningham Drugstores (workers at their warehouse were on strike and trying to become certified). In fact the Working Women's Workshop organized a boycott of the drugstores and distributed "tens of thousands" of leaflets five months before the B.C. Federation of Labour saw fit to do the same.[16]

> The campaign is meeting with mixed reaction. At some stores the Caucus claims to be turning away from a third to a half of the customers. At the Cunninghams outlet in North Vancouver, however, the lone picketing woman was assaulted by an M.D. who spluttered that "You're the women who led the Abortion Caravan." The woman had to knock the doc to the ground twice before he would fuck off. And remember folks, "It takes a clever pig to be a Cunning ham."[17]

Also that summer, caucus and workshop members first raised the question of organizing a union of working women independent of the existing labour unions. As the caucus newspaper, the *Pedestal,* argued, even organized women were relatively inactive in their unions. They were unrepresented in the leadership and were thus unable to have their needs (for equal pay, for day-care facilities, for job de-ghettoization) taken seriously. "The organization of working women must be a major long-term task of the women's liberation movement."*

---

*At the Canadian Labour Congress convention in Edmonton earlier that summer, of fifteen hundred delegates, seventy were women. Of 461 resolutions submitted by union locals, only the last 5 concerned

Both the American and the Canadian women's liberation movements initially began as women's or feminist caucuses within the new left organizations, but the Canadian movement, unlike the American, for all its splinterings and contradictory tendencies, continued to operate within the orbit of left-wing politics. (The exceptions to this were the New Feminists in Toronto and, later, various lesbian feminist groups; but the exception proves the rule — the New Feminists had a core membership of Americans recently emigrated to Canada.)

American feminist ideas did, of course, circulate among Canadian women, socialists and otherwise, and were taken very seriously. It was from the American sisters that we appropriated the concepts of "sisterhood" and our oppression as a "class," of "male supremacy" as an ideology, of the "matriarchy" as the prehistory of women, of lesbianism as "politically correct" sexuality, of the women's liberation movement as a form of struggle against "imperialism" in the Third World.

But, in the same way that the Canadian new left as a whole was never as alienated as the American from its socialist antecedents, neither was the Canadian women's liberation movement. For that matter, the Communist party and the CCF-NDP had raised, a generation or two earlier, the issues of women in the labour force, of equal pay, of the right to abortion, birth control and day care. In the Women's Labour Leagues and the Congress of Canadian Women "we saw the struggle against capitalism as a struggle that would enable women to take their place as full human beings and citizens." From this generation of women radicals, the women's liberationists of the Sixties inherited the expectation that the left would advance the cause of justice for women. This meant, on the one hand, that the Canadian movement avoided certain exaggerations of rhetoric ("Housewives are political prisoners!")[18] and solipsisms ("We question every generalization and accept none that are

discriminatory practices against female workers. The Reform Caucus, a progressive grouping within the CLC, proposed a women's committee but "the convention defeated the resolution with the rationale that the problems of all workers were inseparable." (*Pedestal*, Vancouver, June 1970) not confirmed by our experience")[19] that were inevitable among the American feminists once the total burden of revolutionary analysis and strategy fell entirely upon the single contradiction of *sexism*. It meant, on the other hand, that the men of the new left were held accountable to the women for their failure to fight for the liberation of women.

This failure damaged women radicals, hurt them, humiliated them, and for years diminished their effectiveness as political cohorts. As unmarried sex partners, low-income earners (very often a movement woman would work at menial labour to free her man for political work), office staffers, charwomen, confidantes, women were an anonymous and individually invisible army of labour on whose efforts the "careers," the charisma, the status of the male heavies were erected, but for which the women themselves received little or no recognition or reward. In fact, there was no prestige in the work that women did, in the movement as well as outside it; there was prestige only in intellectual work, in being able to argue and debate and theorize and analyse, in writing position papers and drafting manifestos and making rousing speeches. Socialized into passivity and self-deprecation, intimidated by machismo, ill-confident with the rhetoric of the new left, unfamiliar with the jargon of political organization, the women of the new left were neither seen nor heard by their male comrades.

If, as Ernest Mandel argues, one of the main aims of the socialist movement is to abolish the distinctions between manual and intellectual labour, within socialist organizations as well as in the larger society (for they "cannot but breed bureaucracy, new inequalities and new forms of human oppression which are incompatible with a socialist common-wealth"),[20] then the organizations of the new left were pro-foundly compromised in this aim.

During the occupation at Columbia University, demonstrators engaged in "theoretical discussions of radical ideology, the faults of the university and the nature of American life,"[21] while, nearby, "girls" managed food and housekeeping details, made peanut-butter sandwiches, vacuumed the floors and cleaned ashtrays. ("Girls," I suppose, are to be distinguished from "demonstrators.") During the May–June events in Paris, a pamphlet, circulated from the Occupation Committee of the Sorbonne, was illustrated with a photograph of a nude woman on her back and printed with this text: "Some comrades from the *council for maintaining the occupations* are going to come and fuck me violently. Judging from their practice, their theories must be truly radical."[22]

Eldridge Cleaver of the Black Panther party, speaking before an SDS convention, called on radical women to mobilize around "pussy power," and David Harris, a draft-resister who went to jail, when asked what women could do to effectively protest the draft, advised they could refuse to sleep with anyone who still carried a draft card.

Revolutionary women of Quebec pointed out in a manifesto that not a single woman's name, apart from those associated with the October Crisis, was known in movement milieux; that in none of the FLQ manifestos, in none of the propaganda, was a single line written on the situation of the women in Quebec; that, while movement men had always had the time to go drinking on weekends, they never had the time to help organize a day-care centre; that in the minds of the leadership, women's liberation was "not important" and could be postponed. "We have typed their papers, painted their placards, listened to their speeches, marched in their demonstrations, marked the measure of their slogans 'Power to the Workers!' "[23]

In the analyses of the collapse of SUPA, not a line was written about the particular experience of women in the organization, nor any insight provided into the function of sexism in that collapse. Only in retrospect would the criticisms of "elitism" and "liberalism" and "manipulation" in SUPA seem to hint at the discouragement of women and to anticipate their withdrawal.

According to the analysis that emerged from the theoreticians of women's liberation, it was the sexual vulnerability of women, the reduction of their personality to mere sexuality, and the appropriation of that sexuality as "property" that allowed men to patronize them, to exploit their labour, to disregard their intellectuality and relegate them to anonymity and indifferentiation. And indeed it was from the odium and the anguish of their sexual experiences that movement women made some of their first cries of rage and formulated some of their first demands for justice. In the clamour and tremor of sexual rage was the cutting loose from victimization and terrorization at the hands of the sexual thugs of the new left.

Women, brought into new left organizations as the lovers of male members, were the "camp followers" of the new left. "There were a couple of good-looking, well-dressed sorority women in SDU who were passed around the male leadership like a tray of hors d'oeuvres." If a woman had any status, it was the reflected one of being the property of an important man, and in this role she was expected to be "loyal" and support his views. The "sexual revolution," as has often been pointed out since, simply served to increase the access men had to women, without the attendant responsibilities of traditional male-female relations. The woman was on her own with her fear of pregnancy, her pregnancy in fact, her "frigidity" if she would not consent to sex, and her desolation when she did. "In the name of free love we indulged in orgies. Or more correctly, gang bangs." It was the women's liberation movement that exposed the fallacy of the sexual liberation movement: that real sexual liberation could take place without upsetting the social superiority of men.

The women of the new left deserted the "male" organizations in droves to continue and expand their work as radicals in the autonomous women's liberation movement. The account of the flourishing of this movement properly belongs to the history of the Seventies. Contained still within the late Sixties is the motivation for the final break with the sexist new left. As the women developed their feminist politics, it became obvious they were being forced to choose between these politics and the new left organization. They chose their politics, which is to say they chose growth, development and power. The constraints of the new left milieux had become intolerable.

It was a commonplace of the first broadsides from women's liberationists to draw an analogy between racism and sexism, between the deprivations of blacks' lives and the spoliation of female lives, between the righteousness of the civil rights and black power movements and that of the women's liberation movement. In retrospect there is something appalling in this analogical impulse, for it speaks of the necessity of the women to attract men's attention to the gravity of their grievances by turning them into a metaphor: the metaphor had more power to move men than did the undiluted concreteness of women's oppression. Furthermore, the analogy evoked identification with a movement that itself was profoundly anti-woman.*

Yet women's liberationists continued to identify their movement with the liberation movements of other people and to appropriate the militaristic slogans and symbols of guerrillas. At one level this was an expression of healthy self-interest and of genuine support for anti-imperialist struggles: "We are engaged in the same struggle as the Vietnamese, the Laotians, the Palestinians, the Koreans, Black and Brown people, Gay people and Native Americans. It is a wealthy, white male authoritarianism. We have begun to feel that when bombs strike Vietnamese bodies they strike our own bodies and when they win, we win."[25] Imperialism is, after all, a system that exempts no one from its effects. But at another level this identification was a posture of self-contempt and defensiveness. For some time the "women's caucuses" themselves had accepted that their projects were subsumed within the "larger" and "more important" one of student radicalism; and in their anxiety to be taken seriously by their male comrades, these caucuses rigorously studied the Marxist texts for material that would justify their feminism and locate their female oppression not in the "patriarchy" or "male supremacy" — Heaven forbid! — but in capitalism and imperialism. Given the right kind of analysis and leadership (it was written), given guns and ammunition, given the acceptance of the absolute priority of anti-imperialist struggles, women can be as heavy as men. To fight "only" as women, to struggle for something as "limited" as women's rights was unacceptable; for had not the male comrades accused women's liberationists of being divisive, a mere minority group, neurotic and, most importantly, "incorrect"? To the demand that the men of the new left examine

---

*In Huey Newton's thesis that racism is rooted in the white "administrator's attempt to bind the penis of the slave,"[24] for instance, where is the voice that mourns the devastated womanhood of the female slave?

women's issues came the reply: "Tell Lady Astor's chauffeur that Lady Astor is oppressed." To the challenge that revolutionary politics include the demands of women came the reply: "Imagine Chairman Mao at the siege of Peking and he gets a call from his wife: Stop the taking of Peking! Women need birth control first!" When women sloganeered that "participatory democracy begins at home" and called on men to participate equally in housekeeping and child care, to support wages for housework and abortion on demand, they were dismissed as "bourgeois" appellants. In any case such tasks were beneath male dignity. When Juliet Mitchell came to Edmonton, forty women were packed into a tiny living room, discussing production, reproduction and sexuality while in the kitchen, resolutely uninvolved, the men discussed the workers' occupations of factories in Turin, Italy.

"That whole period of time during 1968 and 1969 we debated continually, men and women, whether or not it was okay to fight in your own interests." If the men could not see the exigency and momentousness of the women's revolution, so much the worse for them. The debate was resolved the day the women marched out into the streets, leaving behind the typewriters and the soup pots, to take their liberation struggle into their own hands.

PART V
TWO NATIONS, ONE ENEMY

I
CREATE TWO, THREE, MANY VIETNAMS

And best of all is finding a place to be
in the early years of a better civilization.
For we are a conquered nation: sea to sea we bartered
everything that counts, till we have
nothing to lose but our forbears' will to lose.
Beautiful riddance!
And some will make their choice and eat imperial meat.
But many will come to themselves, for there is
no third way at last and these will
spend their lives at war, though not with
guns, not yet — with motherwit and guts, sustained
by bloody-minded reverence among the things
    which are,
and the long will to be in Canada.

— Dennis Lee
(from Civil Elegies and Other Poems)[1]

When SUPA dissolved at the end of 1967 and the post-mortems were undertaken, there was an acknowledgement that the new left in Canada had failed to analyse its national context. By this failure it had fallen victim to the idealist notion that people could be mobilized around such niceties as "participatory democracy" without reference to the realities of national economic organization, national political structure and national social stratification through which this "democracy" was to be processed. However admirable the internationalist urges of the peace movement (the canny mistrust of the nation-state as the political embodiment of violence and massive regulation; the will to transcend its unhappy borders and to make contact with the peace-loving populations of the world), these had turned SUPA away from investigating what it needed to know about the specifics of its context — the

191

nation-state of Canada. Just what sort of a state is it? who runs it? whose interests does it serve? how is it like other Western capitalist states and how is it different? how does it control us? In the last analysis, "the fact that we are Canadians, colonials, has worked to turn our attention away from our own nation."[2]

The very fact that by 1967 the word "colonial" had entered the radical's vocabulary of self-attribution not as a metaphor but as a succinct and pointed description of the economic and social reality of Canadian existence indicates that already the movement had begun to come to grips with "the national question."

It did so, with some preparation. The government of John Diefenbaker (1957–63) had popularized the proposition that the Canadian government spoke for interests that were definably and exclusively Canadian: "We must decide," said Diefenbaker, "that our role is to determine the right stand to take on problems, keeping in mind the Canadian background and, above all, using Canadian common sense. In effect, the time has come to take an independent approach."[3] The Progressive Conservatives and the NDP had combined to oppose in 1956 the Liberal plan to loan $80 million to the American-controlled Trans-Canada Pipeline. In 1957 the Report of the Royal Commission on Canada's Economic Prospects (the Walter Gordon Report) had warned that to "do nothing" about the increasing measure of control of the economy that was passing into foreign hands was to "run the risk that at some time in the future a disregard for Canadian aspirations will create demands for action of an extreme nature."[4] By 1965, however, Walter Gordon was out on his ear, having failed to win the support of his Liberal party colleagues in cabinet for some very moderate restrictions on the operations of foreign-owned business and industry in Canada.

Also in 1965 the sociologist John Porter published his monumental *The Vertical Mosaic* in which he demonstrated that not only do a relatively small group of firms control a disproportionate amount of economic activity[5] (constituting in effect an economic elite) but that these firms are no longer contained within a national economic system and so neither is the elite.

Still in 1965, the slim volume *Lament for a Nation: The Defeat of Canadian Nationalism* by George Grant had posed the question that pierced the hearts of all those who felt, seemingly irrationally, an attachment to their Canadian being: if we believe that the "universal and homogeneous state" into which we are all being inexorably absorbed by the industrial civilization of the United States is a tyrannous state, then we must resist with all the resources available to us that doleful absorption.[6] Your enemies will be legion, Grant warned, even within the nation itself, and they are called "liberals." They confuse the people with claims that what is good for the ruling class of Canada is good for the nation as a whole. They enact policies that reflect their belief that Canada is merely an "undeveloped frontier" within the totality of North America.

> The power of the American government to control Canada does not lie primarily in its ability to exert direct pressure; the power lies in the fact that the dominant classes in Canada see themselves at one with the continent on all essential matters. Dominant classes get the kind of government they want.[7]

In dissolving the "taboos" around corporate expansionism, liberalism has become the "perfect ideology" of neo-capitalism and continentalism. But nationalism stands in its way, arguing as it does against the disappearance of Canada into the continent.

It was from the lessons of its own experience that the Canadian new left finally made its commitment not only to describe the contours of Canada but to struggle for their integrity. From the general turn toward Marxism in the search for "ideology" came the revelation that political ideas are rooted in a society's economic relations. If "continentalism" and "liberalism" were plausibly rooted in Canada's peculiar economic interrelationship with and dependency on American capitalism, as Porter and Grant had indicated, then "nationalism" was conceivably the political idea of socialism.

George Grant himself, for all his Red Toryism, had argued that it was only through a combination of socialist economic planning and mobilization of the "electorate" with its grievances against the (anti-national) elites, in support of such centralized planning, that continental absorption could be resisted.[8] The socialist Gad Horowitz, writing in *Canadian Dimension,* unmincingly equated the socialist and nationalist projects: the one was served by the other because through nationalism the Canadian people could free themselves from the Medusa-head of American ideology and finally awaken the life of the nation to the rest of the world. It was not America as American that must be challenged but America as capitalist:

> If the United States were socialist, at this moment, we would be continentalists at this moment. If the possibilities of building a socialist society were brighter in the United States than in Canada, or as bright, we would not be terrified by the prospect of absorption. We are nationalists because, as socialists, we do not want our country to be utterly absorbed by the *citadel of world capitalism.*[9]

A year earlier, in a seminal essay, "Conservatism, Liberalism and Socialism in Canada: An Interpretation," Horowitz had argued that the very presence of an influential and legitimate socialist movement in English Canada is an "un-American" characteristic of Canadian society. So are, accordingly, the notions that the national community is made up of classes, not individuals, that the real social achievement is "equality of condition" not mere "equality of opportunity," and that the community "does more than provide a context within which individuals can pursue happiness in a purely self-regarding way." Such a community is incipiently socialist.[10]

1963: the bombs of the FLQ. *1964:* students and police in the Saturday-of-the-long-sticks battle it out on the occasion of Queen Elizabeth's visit to Quebec. *1966:* Pierre Vallières and Charles Gagnon go to the gates of the United Nations in New York to publicize the liberation struggles of Quebec. *1967:* René Lévesque quits the Liberal party to found the sovereignty-association movement. *1968:* the Rassemblement pour l'Indépendance Nationale organizes demonstrators against Trudeau at the St. Jean-Baptiste Day parade. The demonstrators are violently repulsed by the police. *1969:* the McGill Français movement brings twelve thousand marchers out into the streets and the protests against Bill 63 rally fifty thousand. The movement was as irrepressible as it was massive,* and smouldering at its core was the indomitable urge of a *nation* to realize itself, to be liberated as much from the federalists of Liberalism and of resident corporations as from the agents *in situ* of foreign capital. ". . . let us answer Quebec," said the English-Canadian new left, "by developing our own equally strong struggle aimed at freeing Canada from U.S. domination by taking . . . our resources and industries out of U.S. hands. Let us advise the profiteers that the plunder called development is at an end."[11] Let us advise them that as Quebec is being torn from their grasp so shall Canada be. Two nations, one enemy.

For the Canadian new left, there was also the question of what kind of society was being shaped by the peculiar mix that was the Canadian economy, at once an industrial economy seemingly at the very profitable centre of "advanced capitalism" and yet also a "semi-peripheral" entity, controlled by interests outside its borders and only semi-industrialized. At the same time, this was the era of America's relative weakening internationally when it was prosecuting the war in Vietnam. As a new leftist was to argue a decade later, the Canadian nationalism of the Sixties gained strength precisely as "American imperialism was economically weakened and politically and militarily under attack,"[12] as the dollar was devalued, and as the domestic consensus regarding foreign policy was broken by the anti-war movement at home and abroad. Into these chinks in the imperial suit of armour the Canadian new left inserted and twisted the blades of its nationalist logic. And it was the war in Vietnam that had handed them the knife.

> We saw that there was a world imperial system, the U.S. was at its centre, and the Vietnamese were resisting, not only for themselves but for all people who were in the process of becoming aware of that imperialism. Canadians were at the beginning point of this process, just starting to distance ourselves from the idea of Canada as an *American* nation.

Granted, the people of Vietnam were in a bloody fight for their

*See Part V, Chapter II.

lives, but if their stupendous national effort to throw the imperialist beast out of their villages and their fields was one instance of the thrust of national independence against American capital, then the Canadian movement against the American domination of national life was surely another, for it was all connected. The material of the University of Toronto teach-in in 1965 had first pointed to this, and then had come the evidence of Canadian government and business complicity in the war, the conscious identification of Québécois militants with the Vietnamese patriots, and the student power movement's revelations of the involvement of American corporations with the government of the university. Who was to say that the anti-imperialist struggle should be engaged over there and not here; that the helicopter gunships and the napalm and 2,4-D dropping out of the skies of Vietnam would not one day threaten the security of Canadians; that it was not the duty of Canadian radicals, as it was that of Vietnamese guerrillas, to expel Uncle Sam beyond the borders so the real life of the nation could begin?

The left was preparing its case. From George Grant they took the forebodings regarding the ideological intent of technology — technological advance entails the disappearance of indigenous differences that give substance to nationalism[13] — but gave them an optimistic twist. If labour's target is the Canadian state, and if working-class politics are anti-capitalist and pro-Canadian,[14] then clearly workers' control of technology would support nationalism. In any case, it was still debatable just how technologized the Canadian economy was.

From the Marxist economist André Gunder Frank came the intriguing argument that the very structure of world-wide capitalism rests on the systematic underdevelopment of satellite countries in relation to the "metropolitan" countries. Not only that, but within the satellite country itself, metropolitan-satellite relations are replicated in the underdevelopment of the "hinterland." (One thought of Cape Breton, Manitoba and the North in relation to southern Ontario.)

Not accidentally was there a revival of interest in the writings of the University of Toronto political economist Harold Innis, who showed how economic, social and political superstructures of Canada have been shaped by the symbiotic relationship of "metropolitan-satellite" or "centre-margin."

In 1968 the Report of the Task Force on the Structure of Canadian Industry, commissioned by the then finance minister, Walter Gordon, and chaired by the political economist Mel Watkins, was tabled. The report recommended among other things that the government establish a special agency to coordinate policies with respect to the behaviour of multinationals. It was a mild enough proposal, considering the dimensions of the problem. Nevertheless, the report was received with great hostility both in government and out. As a result, Watkins moved over to the left wing of the NDP, a move that earned him the attention of the new left nationalists, for this seemed to demonstrate again that only socialism could contain the idea of national liberation.

Between 1945 and 1967 the percentage of foreign long-term investment in Canada that was *direct* investment increased from 40 percent to 60 percent; 85 percent of this direct investment was American. Through this investment, two-fifths of the Canadian economy, outside the sector of finance, was owned by non-Canadians.

By 1963 non-Canadians controlled 60 percent of Canadian manufacturing, 74 percent of the petroleum and natural gas industry, and 59 percent of mining and smelting. Since these are the most profitable, the most highly technological and the most capital-intensive sectors of the economy, the degree of their non-Canadian ownership was thoroughly alarming. As the economist Kari Levitt wrote in the book *Silent Surrender,* which represented in 1970 the culmination of all the disparate studies and expressions of alarm and anxiety concerning the meaning of the multinational corporation,

> The brutal fact is that the acquisition of control by U.S. companies over the commodity-producing sectors of the Canadian economy has largely been financed from corporate savings deriving from the sale of Canadian resources, extracted and processed by Canadian labour, or from the sale of branch-plant manufacturing businesses to Canadian consumers at tariff-protected prices.[15]

What did it all mean? It meant, for instance, that when the prime minister, faced in 1965 with a vast balance of payments deficit with the U.S. in auto trade, had to choose between continentalism and a protected market for Canadian-produced cars, he chose the continentalist Auto Pact. It meant, in that same year, when a bill was passed in the House of Commons to cancel the tax-deductibility of expenditures on Canadian advertising placed in Canadian editions of foreign magazines, *Time* and *Reader's Digest* were exempted. It meant that because the branch plants imported technology, in Canada research and development languished and the country's technologists, scientists and engineers were underemployed or forced to seek work outside Canada. And it meant that "to the degree that Canadian business had opted to exchange its entrepreneurial role for managerial and rentier status, Canada has regressed to a rich hinterland with an emasculated, if comfortable, business elite."[16]

Sharing with a political elite the opinion that an autonomous and self-determining nation-state thwarts the progressive absorption of the Canadian national community into the more "efficient" transcontinental market of corporate production and consumption, this business elite presides over the dismantling of Canadian national sovereignty. Effective economic decision making is transferred to the parent companies where they are beyond accountability to the Canadian electorate. Canadian government is then helpless to do much about inflation, regional disparities, unemployment and industrial stagnation. One may expect Canada to become "de-industrialized" as there is ever more economic reliance on the extraction and export of primary products (including energy), dependence on the "metropolitan" country for machinery and manufactured goods, and lack of resistance to even greater penetration by the multinationals as local business and industry weaken and collapse. One may say that this kind of country is an underdeveloped country and not the much-touted advanced, capitalist, industrialized nation of the continentalists' vision. By the late Sixties, Canada, to the new left nationalists, for all its privileges relative to the Third World and its "mini-imperialism"[17] practised by Canadian-owned corporations and banks in the Caribbean and elsewhere, was an economic community uncertainly erected upon the shifting sands of dependency and colonization.

The well-documented process of "Americanization" of cultural and intellectual values of Canadians with the apparent acquiescence of the population underscored the ideological, as well as economic, penetration of the American multinational corporation into everyday life. To the Canadian new left, this was no more apparent than in their own milieu, the university. Alarming statistics were coming in fast and furiously from this sector of the "multinational" too, largely due to the thankless efforts of Robin Mathews and James Steele, academics at Carleton University. According to their research, between 1961 and 1968 the proportion of Canadians teaching at the universities had diminished by 25 percent with some universities in particular showing a very high concentration of non-Canadian faculty. A survey at the University of Alberta in 1968–69 showed that from a high of 60.8 percent in 1961–62, the proportion of full-time Canadian faculty had dropped to 47.2 percent.[18] Nationally, the situation was exacerbated by the efficacy of the "old boys' network" in which non-Canadian heads of departments favoured the appointment of other non-Canadians of their acquaintance. In 1969 the political economy or political science departments in Glendon College, York, McMaster and University of Toronto all had American chairmen, and three out of five members of the University of Toronto's promotion and tenure committee were American.[19]

The non-Canadian (principally American) academics were attracted to the rapidly expanding social sciences and humanities faculties. For instance, almost 40 percent of the academic staff at the Ontario Institute for Studies in Education, making recommendations to the provincial Department of Education on curriculum and teaching methods, were American.[20]

Not surprisingly, of the seventy-nine undergraduate and graduate courses offered by the University of Alberta's sociology department in 1968–69, only one pertained to Canadian society; in the political science department, only seven of sixty-six.[21] "Across Canada not more than half a dozen courses appear to be offered in such important areas as the dynamics of federal-provincial relations, provincial politics, the political sociology of Canada and the politics of French Canada."[22]

Alarmed at what these statistics gauged for the employment opportunities for Canadian university graduates and for their ideological development, Mathews and Steele proposed, modestly enough, that Carleton University make it a practice to employ enough Canadians to ensure that Canadians become a clear two-thirds majority of full-time faculty in each department and that no non-Canadians be hired before all reasonable efforts to solicit applications from Canadians have been made.[23] The proposals were received as "immoral, illiberal, racist, neo-Nazi, proto-fascist, chauvinist, anti-American. . . intellectually obscene."[24] No less than their American colleagues did many Canadian academics react as though their very *raison d'être* had been impugned, as indeed it had. Wrote one such Canadian to the *Globe and Mail,* "Canadians should be grateful rather than distressed that academics from other parts of the globe have chosen to grace us with their presence in Canada. How else are the students of Canada's universities to acquire the research skills and knowledge which make them a part of the international community of science and humanities scholarship?"[25]

Such justifications, as the student movement was quick to point out, ignore the economic basis of intellectual "internationalism": that, where imperialist economic systems establish themselves, imperialist culture (or, euphemistically, "world" or "international" or "universal" or "cosmopolitan" culture) is sure to follow. As Peter Warrian, president of CUS argued: the role of the intelligentsia within the "American imperium" is to deny and mystify the cogencies of social class in the client-state, to rationalize its colonial status and to train the intellectual labour force that the "continental capitalist economy" requires for its stabilization.[26] It then becomes the task of the student movement, said an Ontario new leftist in 1969, to attack "American imperialization" of the economy at its Achilles heel: the cultural imperialists at the university. In this way are "class politics" unloosed at the university, for the cultural imperialists are members of the resident bourgeoisie, and here may the socialist and national liberationist projects again be conjoined.

Against the imperialism of the university — its authoritarian structures, its concentration of decision making within an administrative elite, its continentalizing curricula — the student movement posed democracy, decentralization and Canadian studies. It confronted in the classroom such "American" ideas as behaviourism and micro-analysis and end-of-ideology ideology and disrupted liberalism's symbolic occasions with pamphleteering, guerrilla theatre and occupations of "strategic targets."

As for the American faculty and graduate students who were radical, here was a contradiction indeed. On the one hand they played a very important part in the education of the radical — in the classroom, where they introduced Marxist texts and perspectives, and outside, in the student power movement where they offered their bodies and voices to the campus struggles.* But they were also Americans and it was as *American* radicals they profoundly impressed the Canadian undergraduates.

> In the Political Science Department at Calgary (there was one Canadian prof) we'd all get together in the coffee room and talk about American issues. The war, the presidential election, the American unions. I idealized the American outlook. On one level, of course, I was glad I wasn't going to get my head split open by a cop's truncheon; on the other hand, I felt a little envious, a little sad that *the* struggle wasn't here in Canada.

Who was there to tell him it was?

In November 1969, the students' council of the University of Alberta sponsored a teach-in: "The American Domination of Canada." About sixteen hundred people attended, mostly

---

*A personal note: I grew up in Social Credit Alberta and the influx of draft-resisters and young Marxist professors from the States to the University of Alberta in the mid-Sixties blew my young, wondering, rebellious mind wide open.

students, who, according to a student observer, were "groping for a new definition of Canadian values and purposes, as opposed to continental attitudes, and seeking politicians who will be their spokesmen."[27] Offered, among others, for their consideration was Mel Watkins. He spoke for forty-nine minutes, and there was hardly a rustle in the audience.

Mel Watkins at the teach-in:

> There's the big question whether capitalists, who run the show under capitalism, have the will or the means to struggle for independence. . . . Even if it could be done, to build an independent capitalist Canada hardly seems worth the effort. The U.S. has given that option a bad name. . . . With nationalism on the agenda of Canadian politics . . . it is my function, as I see it . . . to work to put socialist content into it. . . .[28]

September 1970. The students' council of the University of Alberta had decided to have a freshman orientation week aimed at telling the students "what the university was really all about" and to this end organized teach-ins and an acid rock festival in the quad, and as headline speaker, invited the American yippie Abbie Hoffman. (The council had agreed to pay Hoffman $1,750 plus air fare from the students' funds.)

Several thousand people were packed into the Kinsmen Fieldhouse the day of Hoffman's visit. Rock bands were on stage, and the atmosphere was dense with marijuana. Hoffman arrived, in a suede jacket and blue jeans, jumping up and down and hugging his entourage. "It was supposed to be a total happening. We hadn't told Hoffman what we wanted him to talk about; we expected he would just do his thing."

When Hoffman took the stage, two figures appeared alongside him: one was a local hippie radical, widely known to have been recently busted on a possession charge, dressed as himself, and behind him, prodding him along with the butt of a rifle, was an activist from a street theatre group, dressed as "Sergeant Sawchuk of the RCMP." When they reached the microphone, "Sergeant Sawchuk," in a thick Ukrainian accent, introduced himself and his hippie "captive" and, with further prods of his rifle, "forced" the hippie to hand over to Hoffman the large roll of paper he held in his hand. This event, announced the sergeant, was the second annual presentation of the Imperialist of the Year Award. When the bewildered Hoffman unfurled it, he and the audience saw this: a picture of a beaver with a bandolier of bullets across his chest and "a funny look in his eyes," and behind him, shoved up against his tail, an eagle with its head up in the air and drool coming out the side of its beak. The caption: YANK OUT! "Hoffman held it very politely, as though it were an Academy Award, and asked, 'Can I keep it?' I'll never forget saying to him, 'Yeah, but it'll cost you $1,750.' "

As it was Hoffman's style to begin his addresses in the United States with a rip-roaring 'Fuck Amerika!" he took the microphone in Edmonton and, mindful of where he was, yelled, "Fuck Canada!" Stunned, shocked, resentful, the crowd shifted gears and began booing and hissing. One man from the audience shouted, "You're putting me on, Hoffman, you're in a different nation now. You're in a colony of America named Canada Nation." "Canada," said Hoffman, "is the only nation that rolled over and died without firing a shot." And launched into a stream-of-consciousness narrative about his travails at the Chicago 7 trial.

> He understood nothing. Neither that we were far from wanting Canada to get "fucked" any more than it already was nor that we shared his perspective on the trial. To him it was a question of his personal, American, constitutional freedoms; to us, it was the inevitable result of capitalism. Because his concern was not with the external manifestations of imperial power vis-à-vis a nation like Canada but rather with his own liberty vis-à-vis the American government, you couldn't trust him, or any of the American radicals, to have your Canadian interests at heart. We came away with the impression that we were much more serious radicals and that he was a bit of an asshole.

There was no doubt that the nationalist new left had a constituency among students and that it ideologically distinguished its nationalism from simple "bourgeois nationalism" (patriotism and anti-Americanism) as the radicalism of anticolonialists and anti-imperialists. In a 1966 essay in *Our Generation* two former SUPA activists, Art Pape and James Laxer, dismissed the Liberal party, the NDP, the federal Parliament, the civil service, the universities and technology itself as all being incapable of undertaking the project of national liberation. It was only around student activists that a national liberationist program was emerging because it was the students who were struggling for "radical democracy": grievously alienated from a society reproducing itself as an American province, students were imaginatively creating an "un-American" one in which the rule of the elites would be abolished.[29] To be a student was to be a democrat was to be an anti-imperialist was to be a liberator.

By 1968, when the student had been identified as an intellectual "worker," the university, like the industrial plant, was seen as a branch-plant workplace and the student within it a "colonial." The way out was to repudiate liberalism, embrace radicalism: "To attack Canadian liberalism becomes therefore an attack on the colonialism of the Canadian market society. . . ."[30]

And by 1969 the New Left Caucus was arguing that "the question of the specificity of Canada" was actually of *strategic* importance if Canadian radicals are not to become, along with every other intellectual worker in Canada, "branch plants" of American radicalism. If higher education in Canada has been "underdeveloped," if autonomous Canadian intellectual traditions are difficult to discern, if throughout the educational system are the texts and ideas of American "liberal and reactionary scholars," it is because education takes place within a "colonial economy," and one cannot expect or hope that American radicals will see that or understand its implications within a "bourgeois" state such as Canada.[31] CUS, in its position papers of the period, also made the connections between the structural and ideological sameness of American and Canadian universities, the so-called "interdependence" of the national economies, and the "emasculation" and "servitude" of the Canadian people.[32]

It was through CUS, in fact, that very many students who lived beyond the range of the new left or student power organizations of Montreal, Toronto, Regina and Vancouver, made contact with the nationalist debate. At the Guelph conference in 1968, for instance, Mel Watkins gave early-morning seminars on American ownership of the economy.

In the summer of 1969 Mel Watkins, Giles Endicott, Gerry Caplan and Jim Laxer, all in the NDP and committed to transforming it into a genuinely socialist party, wrote and issued what came to be known as the Waffle Manifesto, a position paper on independence and socialism aimed at the federal NDP convention to be held that October in Winnipeg. The socialist nationalists were about to intervene in politics.

Posing the "very survival of Canada" as the most urgent issue for Canadians, the manifesto called on the NDP to begin a "process" and formulate a "program" that would replace capitalism and dependence with socialism and independence. The elements of the process and program, according to the manifesto, are, *inter alia,* the extension of working people's influence into every area of industrial decision making, "community democracy," extensive "national planning" of and public control over investment and "nationalization of the commanding heights of the economy," the encouragement of "full expression and implementation" of Quebec's history and aspirations, the unity of the two national groups as the only "successful strategy against the reality of American imperialism" and, finally, electoral success, of course.[33]

Only a few months later, at the University of Alberta teach-in on American domination of Canada, Watkins was to pose "democracy at every level of decision making" as the demand that separated the old left from the new left. With those proposals in the Waffle Manifesto that called for workers' and community control over the institutions that govern peoples' lives, the new left surely had no quarrel. They had been the very stuff of their own movements in the community and on the campus. But with the *substance* of the manifesto (its involvement in the policies and practices of a social democratic parliamentary party), and with the manifesto's appeal, in the name of anti-imperialism, to "national unity," the new left was decidedly unhappy.

Here in sheep's clothing was the old left. The new left, committed to the notions of radical democracy, was profoundly suspicious of notions of "planning" and "control" and "nationalization" as quasi-socialist clones of bureaucracy. Which social class would be the planners? To whom would they be accountable? How could government administration of industry substitute for "workers' control" of the industrial workplace? The new left, by contrast, visualized a socialism won only through the "self-emancipation of activized masses in motion, reaching out for freedom with their own hands . . . as actors on the stage of history."[34] And the new left, as national liberationist, had allied itself in sympathy and solidarity with national liberation struggles everywhere, including in Quebec. It rejected as spurious any strategies of "unity" between English-Canadian and Québécois radicals as long as the Quebec national liberation project had not been fulfilled in the independence of Quebec.

Supporters of the Waffle Manifesto would refer to the "Canadianism" of social democracy, that "Canadian" progression of Methodism to social gospel to CCF,[35] and to the necessity of situating anti-imperialist strategies in the "organic" political traditions of Canada. The new left would take a closer look at those traditions and conclude that in Fabianism (that variety of socialism introduced "organically" into Canada by British working-class and union militants) class struggle and uprising and revolution were inanities, and "managerial, technocratic, elitist, authoritarian, 'plannist' " solutions were *de rigueur*.[36] The new left had been there before, in the early Sixties, when it had first made the distinction between itself as a popular movement for social change and the NDP as a reformist party so compromised as to be a collection of "tinkerers" within the system. The NDP was not then, and was not now, in 1969, even on its nationalist left, capable of revolutionary politics.

> The new left, on the other hand, was an international movement of the student left which supported the national liberation struggle of Canada because that's what was anti-imperialist. We respected the possibility that people who are engaged in local struggles just might be trying to

express an internationalist aspiration of solidarity with each other.

The whole point of resisting the American domination of Canadian life was to throw the unbearable weight of peremptory structures off the backs of people so that, upright, they would be free to fashion — not be compelled to hand over to a state bureaucracy — *who they were.*

Unfortunately, this debate and others* were cut short. In 1970 Quebec was on the agenda. Dramatically, the question of who owned Canada was overtaken by the questions of who owned Quebec and who there was, in Canada, who would gainsay the owners. Here, at last, was *the* national question.

---

*Also under discussion were the danger of focussing on imperialism and not the "local class enemy," the need to investigate the anti-capitalist traditions of the Canadian working class, the confusion between economic colonialism and cultural and psychological malaise, and the need to distinguish the dominated capitalism of Canada from the Third World of classically imperialist capture.

II

LE QUÉBEC AUX QUÉBÉCOIS!

Dans la langue douce de Shakespeare
avec l'accent de Longfellow
parlez un français pur et atrocement blanc
comme au Viet-Nam, au Congo
parlez un allemand impeccable
une étoile jaune entre les dents
parlez russe parlez rappel à l'ordre parlez répression
speak white
c'est une langue universelle
nous sommes nés pour la comprendre
avec ses mots lacrymogènes
avec ses mots matraques

Speak white
tell us again about Freedom and Democracy
Nous savons que liberté est un mot noir
comme la misère est nègre
et comme le sang le mêle à la poussière des rues
     d'Alger ou de Little Rock*
          — Michele Lalonde (from "Speak White")

The Quiet Revolution, as Québécois nationalists reminded English Canadians, accomplished in ten vigorous years what the Western world experienced in a hundred years of experimental evolution. Within the decade of the late Fifties to the late Sixties, the farming classes of Quebec resettled in the cities as increasingly literate, skilled and disciplined workers. When only 23 percent of students in the Fifties were finishing

---

*In the sweet tongue of Shakespeare
with the accent of Longfellow
speak a pure and gruesome white French
as in Vietnam, in the Congo

secondary school, by the mid-Sixties more than 60 percent were doing so. The nationalization of electricity, the beginnings of a medicare program, and the extensive educational reforms all provoked a "revolution of rising expectations" in the population of Quebec: there was the possibility that the people could realize themselves materially and culturally as Québécois.

However, the Québécois in 1965 were a people who, within the borders of their own province, were the third lowest income-earning group,* whose incomes, in the city of Montreal, were $330 below the average, while Scottish-Canadian incomes were $1,319 above the average. The Québécois were a people who, when bilingual, still earned considerably less than unilingual anglophones; and unilingual francophones, of course, were at the bottom of the heap. Francophone representation in the key positions of industry had not increased since 1931.[1] More than 53 percent of the labour force of Quebec worked for Anglo-Canadian or foreign owners of industry. The "language of command" in these enterprises was English.

In 1965 tuition and living expenses for one year of university training were valued at approximately half the yearly earnings of at least one-third of the family heads of Montreal.[2] Almost half the families and single people of metropolitan Montreal were living on incomes of less than $5,000 a year, and their

---

speak an impeccable German
gnashing a Star of David in your teeth
speak Russian speak order speak repression
speak white
it's a universal language
we were born to understand it
with its tear-gas words
with its black-jack words

Speak white
tell us again about Freedom and Democracy
We know that liberty is a black word
just as misery is Negroid
and as blood mingles with dust in the streets of Algiers or Little Rock

*Only Italians and native Indians earned less.

youth were not at university but in the work force, or unemployed.*

Doctors working in the "inner city" districts of Montreal in the late Sixties came across alarming rates of malnutrition, physical retardation, bad eyesight and language difficulties in the children.[3] There were no subsidized day-care centres in the city core nor, until the end of the decade, any health clinics. It was by no means uncommon, in the housing in the east end and in the St. Henri districts, to have neither bath nor shower, to have no hot water nor, in many cases, any running water at all.

It was a mean life, this life of the Québécois majority. It was a life doled out on the cheap, cramped by fear and resentment. It was a cheapness and a contraction that generations of priests and paternalistic politicians and *vendu* intelligentsia had counselled the demoralized masses to accept as their destiny as Québécois. So they accepted it, more or less, until now. Now, with the promises of vast social wealth and collective pride of Québécois being, this destiny was no longer acceptable.

In the Rassemblement pour l'Indépendance Nationale (RIN) in the early to mid-Sixties and in the Parti Québécois (PQ) of the late Sixties, certain elements of Quebec society found the expression of their frustration, impatience and resentment. They spoke uncompromisingly of the need to throw off the "Anglo" institutions and structures, and of the need to assert the province of Quebec as the *state* of the French-Canadian nation if the Québécois were to progress towards mastery of their own household. They drew into their ranks the thousands of middle-class Québécois — mid-level managers, engineers, technocrats, university teachers, lawyers, accountants — who had been engendered by the "bureaucratic revolution" of the mid-Sixties. As urban institutions had expanded and become specialized, as new channels in the public sector had opened to upwardly mobile professionals, and as new intellectual skills had been required to operate enterprises, this new social class took its place as the managers of modern Quebec society

---

*Compared to Ontario's rate, 4.4 percent unemployment, 8.9 percent of Quebec's labour force was unemployed, half of whom were under twenty-five years of age.

— and there they were stuck.[4] Perceiving their mobility to be constrained by the dead weight of Anglo ownership and bossmanship, they called upon a nationalist political party to shake loose the Quebec state from these constraints and to expand its base of independent operations so as to secure the role these workers hoped to play.

It was a call viewed by the union and student radicals with odium. Where in the rhetoric of "self-mastery" was the connection between colonialism and exploitation? The association with working-class and socialist elements? The denunciation of U.S. capital and its domination of the Quebec economy? The proposition to transform not just the nationality of state management but the whole of political and economic structures? All, all, of these conditions of Québécois life must be challenged, said the radicals; otherwise the PQ and its ilk would simply deflect the consciousness and rage of the people into party games of "moderate" programs to win the nationalist allegiance of the "moderate" middle class. There was another way of championing Quebec, said the radicals, and that was to be a revolutionary.

The young radicals of Quebec had, along with the rest of the continent's youth, witnessed against Selma in 1965; had, three thousand strong, packed MacGregor Street in Montreal from Guy to Simpson and sung "We Shall Overcome" in French; had crowded around a truck on which James Foreman of SNCC had stood, in his dungarees, fresh from the South, and had spoken to them, in French, of the heroic labours of his people; had made the connection between these labours and their own as a people struggling for nationality. Of the tactical possibilities of direct action and civil disobedience, they also took note. They had marched, too, in the United States. Starting off from Quebec City, students, peaceniks, labour activists, *indépendantistes,* they had set off for Guantanamo Bay in Cuba to touch base symbolically with the Cuban revolution, but had got no further than the southern states, this rag-tag collection of pacifists meandering to Miami.

They came to a town in Alabama and were told by the cops they could not have an integrated march down the main street; they would be allowed to march only in the black neighbourhood. The marchers said, "We're sorry but we have to go down Main Street." So of course they were attacked and brutalized and taken off to jail. They were eventually paraded out, totally unresisting, of course, and tortured with red hot cattle prods up their vaginas or on their testicles by cops who were weeping as they did it. That was the sum total of the non-violent philosophy: they suffered and their torturers cried. Thank you very much, Albert Camus.

It was Algeria that saved the young radicals from the pit of self-abnegation: the war cries of Ferhat Abbas and Ben Bella and the Front de Libération Nationale; the battle of Algiers, Arab women with bombs in their shopping baskets moving among the French colonialists in the sidewalk cafes, intent on murder; Arab youths dying on the rack, the will of emancipation passed on to the next guerrilla in line, and the next, and the one after that. It was Frantz Fanon, black Algerian psychologist of colonialism, whose book *Les Damnés de la Terre* had been published in 1961, who saved them: a colonized people is never alone, the victory of the Vietnamese people at Dien Bien Phu is no longer, strictly speaking, a Vietnamese victory but belongs now to the annals of *all* the oppressed in their violent efforts to throw off the colonial master.

Goodbye to non-violence and to the negotiations around the "green baize table" meant to forestall the inevitable: the masses, listening to their own voices, take up arms. Decolonization, like colonization, is always a violent process, Fanon argued, but in the process, violence pushes the oppressed to the point beyond which they can no longer fall back into alienation and helplessness. The terrorist sheds his/her inferiority complex and is rehabilitated. The terrorist act is the first act of the people's autonomous history, as Hubert Acquin, separatist writer, put into the mouth of a Québécois revolutionary separatist: "Our history will begin at the unknown moment when the revolutionary war begins. . . . That day, with open veins, we will enter the world. . . . Actions will prevail."[5]

By violence the guerrilla is not introducing a new element into politics. (Quebec was conceived in the violence of colonial settlement and mercantile trade, was surrendered to the English in violence, and lives violently in the modern conditions of poverty, depression and dejection.) The guerrilla simply "democratizes" the violence monopolized by the modern state and its instruments.[6]

In taking up violence, Fanon warned, the revolutionaries will abandon all (false) hope of a decolonization undertaken by their own bourgeoisie, for the nationalist bourgeois "loudly proclaims he has nothing to do with these Mau-Mau, these terrorists, these throat-slitters."[7] Here was what the Black Panther Huey Newton would call the "house nigger," the slave a cut above the rest, granted privileges not accorded the "field nigger" and terrified of losing them.[8] And here was Léandre Bergeron's description of the Quebec premier, Jean Lesage — a *"roi-nègre"* whose policies of nationalization of electricity and road construction and a state mining authority and Labour Code modernization were all designed to deliver an "efficient" society to the foreign capitalists.[9]

The culture of a colonized people, wrote Fanon, was a culture condemned to secrecy and surreptitiousness, but nevertheless, in the underground, there was still the refusal to submit, to disappear. Given the power the colonialist exercises through control of culture and personality, the role of the artists in providing a counterculture and counter-personality cannot be overestimated.

Accordingly, the combative artists of Quebec in the early Sixties rejected Americanism and picked up the European novels of Malraux, Camus, Sartre, the novels about colonialism, fascism, communism, terror; refused any longer to "speak white"; and revived in their literature the benighted language of their people — *joual* — the language from the pavements, alleyways and balconies. They put on record for the first time in their history how they felt — angry and insolent and crazy and immovable. Said Gerald Godin: "We appeared on the scene and said, 'The language is in a mess and we're going to sit here and write in it, make you listen to it, until the reasons for this mess have been recognized.'"[10] No longer would people be encouraged to dream dreams; now they would be made to rub their noses in the stuff of their lives. In their journals, *parti pris,*

Socialisme 64, Révolution Québécoise, the writers and the politicos reiterated the recrudescent themes of national liberation struggle.

In 1968 all this came together in the "Songs and Poems of the Resistance," a raucous and boisterous evening of music and poetry: Quebec's best artists — Pauline Julien, Robert Charlebois, Louise Forrestier, Georges Dor, Gaston Miron, Jazz Libre du Québec — yelling and stomping and howling their rage and their joy in a benefit concert for Pierre Vallières, a revolutionary separatist recently convicted of involuntary homicide. Two years later they would do it all again, in the same place, the Jesuit-owned Gésu Hall, for "The Night of Poetry," poetry up on posters, poetry on computer print-outs, the poetry of *joual,* the poetry of resistance. Thirteen hundred people witnessing a veritable assault of solidarity in a generation finally rid of solitude and disjunction.

Before the Sixties, there was no revolutionary Québécois left. As Malcolm Reid, in *The Shouting Signpainters,* points out, the radical youth of Quebec had no revolutionary tradition to draw on from twentieth-century Quebec. While our English-Canadian parents were caught and involved in the swirl of events around the formation of the CCF and the Communist party, the marches and strikes of the Depression, and the antifascist war in Spain, the Québécois were saying prayers for delivery from such demons. The asbestos workers' strike in Murdochville in 1957 and then finally the expulsion by the electorate of Duplessis three years later broke the ground for the revolutionary separatists of the Sixties.

1963. The first of four incarnations of the Front de Libération du Québec (FLQ) is organized by a Belgian who had been active in the anti-Nazi resistance. In March they throw Molotov cocktails at Canadian army installations, paint the dripping white FLQ on walls and hoardings, and send to the news media their manifesto: "The Quebec Liberation Front is a revolutionary movement of volunteers ready to die for the political and economic independence of Quebec." In April a bomb, apparently abandoned in a garbage can by two Felquistes scared off by patrolling policemen, explodes and kills a nightwatchman.

September 1963. The Armée de Libération du Québec holds up a bank on Sherbrooke Street. In April the members of the ALQ are arrested.

August 1964. The Armée Révolutionaire du Québec, headed up by a former paratrooper in the Foreign Legion and composed of young working-class men "trained" at a camp in the Laurentians, raid a firearms store on Bleury Street. The store manager is shot dead and the police themselves accidentally gun down an employee. The five ARQistes are arrested. Of such spectacular actions, it has been said: "These members of the revolutionary groups believed that the people of Quebec would, at the sound of bombs, rise up spontaneously as one single man and forthwith make their independence."[11] No such thing happens. The people remain stolid and the FLQ lies low. In the meantime, the journalist Pierre Vallières and a group around *parti pris* form the Mouvement de Libération Populaire (MLP). They argue that it is necessary, in order to have a political base for militant action, to politicize the workers. The MLP distributes political tracts at the gates of the factories in the St. Henri and Point St. Charles districts of Montreal.

May 1965. On the occasion of Victoria Day, large crowds of youths in Lafontaine Park and in the surrounding slum districts skirmish with the police.

A year later, members of the revived FLQ are successful in stealing dynamite from a construction site, rifles and ammunition from a cadet corps, and money from a theatre.

5 May 1966. A bomb explodes in the strike-bound La Grenade Shoe Company, wounding three strikers and killing a union secretary. Shortly after, Vallières and Charles Gagnon, who are in New York publicizing the Québécois struggle for national liberation at the United Nations, are arrested by New York police and held in the Manhatten House of Detention before being deported to Canada and the RCMP.

Summer 1967. During Expo madness in Montreal, General Charles de Gaulle, president of France, makes an automobile trip from Quebec City to Montreal and is everywhere greeted with enthusiasm. In Montreal he stands on a balcony and exclaims: *"Vive le Québec libre!"* The government in Ottawa is horrified but the crowds exult.

1968. Revolutionary separatists who have split from the moderate RIN form the Front de Libération Populaire. Defining its struggle as part of a global movement of anti-imperialism, the FLP calls for an independent, unilingual and socialist Quebec, for workers' control and for direct democracy in the factory and neighbourhoods. Taxicab drivers, to protest the monopoly on airport traffic and prime downtown pick-up space held by the Anglo firm, Murray Hill, organize as the Mouvement de Libération du Taxi and together with twenty-five hundred students clash with police at the airport. The Ligue pour l'Intégration Scolaire, to protest the provisions for state support of English-language schools in the government's Bill 63, contest the school board elections in the district of St. Leonard, a mixed French and Italian east-end district. They win, and two years of pamphleteering, meetings, demonstrations and riots ensue.

February 1968. After two and a half years of incarceration, Pierre Vallières is brought to trial on charges of sedition and murder in the La Grenade Shoe case. In March, Operation McGill brings together student radicals and the Confederation of National Trade Unions in a campaign to turn McGill into a "working-class university integrated into Quebec society and serving the majority of people in Quebec and not the ruling corporations that exploit the Quebec people."[12]

April 1968. Pierre Vallières writes to his friends and comrades from prison: "Even if violence is a phenomenon detestable in itself, it is nonetheless true that for exploited and colonized people like ourselves, freedom grows out of the barrel of a gun."[13]

24 June 1968. Against the "renegade" federalist Pierre Trudeau, the RIN organize a demonstration on the occasion of the St. Jean-Baptiste Day parade at which Trudeau is in attendance. All night long, street battles rage between the demonstrators and the police on horses and motorcycles, and demonstrators fall beneath the policemen's nightsticks.*

---

*Twelve years later, according to some conversations I have had, it seems generally assumed in separatist circles and among those close to such circles, that the St. Jean-Baptiste Day demonstrators were

October 1968. Dynamite and detonators stolen from a quarry are deployed in renewed FLQ attacks on industrial enterprises, government buildings and the clubs of the Liberal and Union Nationale parties. And students occupy their CEGEPs.

13 February 1969. Twenty-seven people are injured by a bomb explosion in the Montreal Stock Exchange.

28 March 1969. Government army troops are brought out to contain the tens of thousands of demonstrators amassed by the McGill Français movement at the gates of McGill. *In June,* construction workers, civil servants and teachers besiege the Union Nationale's leadership convention in Quebec City to protest the government's labour policies. The demonstrators are driven back by police and by tear gas thrown at them from helicopters. At the annual St. Jean-Baptiste Day parade there is another riot. Ten to fifteen thousand working-class youths form up behind the official parade in a clamorous parade of their own. Charging down St. Catherine Street, they break windows and loot.

7 October 1969. Montreal police go on strike for wage parity with Toronto police. The Quebec Provincial Police and six hundred men from the Fifth Combat Group of Mobile Command at Camp Valcartier are brought into the city.

8 October 1969. The Mouvement de Libération du Taxi brings out 150 cabs to the depot of Murray Hill Limousine Company. Somebody throws Molotov cocktails, and a Murray Hill security guard fires a twelve-gauge shotgun erratically into the crowd. A QPP officer, an *agent provocateur* among the demonstrators, is killed.

10 October 1969. The FLP organizes a demonstration calling for the resignation of Montreal mayor Drapeau. The demonstration is declared illegal; the Riot Act is read and six hundred troops with machine guns and tear gas surround the city hall. The offices of dozens of left-wing and nationalist

---

incited by police *agents provocateurs* into the display of violence that led to the demonstrators' arrest and to the widely publicized gesture of "bravery" by Pierre Trudeau (then on a federal election campaign), who resolutely refused to leave the viewing stand in the face of flying Coca-Cola bottles.

organizations are raided, including the Company of Young Canadians, and declared subversive.

7 November 1969. Two thousand marchers demand the release of Vallières and Gagnon, who have been in jail for three years. The crowd storms into St. James Street and smashes the windows of the banking and financial establishments. A few days later, Drapeau's city council passes an ordinance (of disputed legality) banning all demonstrations. Political meetings and leafleting are banned in all the schools, students and teachers are expelled, citizens' and tenants' committees are raided, and their books, papers and copying machines seized.

Early 1970. Several Montreal-based citizens' and union committees for political action form an alliance, the Front d'Action Politique (FRAP), to fight Drapeau in the upcoming civic election in October. The slogan is *"Les salaires au pouvoir!"* (Power to the Workers) and the program is for a "true urban democracy" based on worker participation in decisions made at all levels concerning housing, health care, transportation and recreation.

February 1970. Postmaster-General Eric Kierans announces that in the interests of "efficiency" the Montreal postal area is to be divided up among four trucking companies, thus, in effect, breaching the contract which had been held exclusively by G. Lapalme Transport, whose workers, after bitter struggle, had the year before won certification as a CNTU union and a decent contract. The Kierans announcement threatens the workers' contract, their job security and their union. *"Les gars de Lapalme"* go on strike. Six months later the toll is: 662 postal trucks attacked, 104 postal workers' stations hit, 75 people injured, 102 arrested, 7 dynamite bombings and 1,200 postal boxes damaged.[14] And there are still two years to go!

29 April 1970. Another provincial election. The Liberals have engaged in a "scare" campaign, warning the population that, in the event of a separatist victory at the polls, industries and businesses will pack up and leave Quebec. Two days before the election, Royal Trust of Montreal had made a show, before TV cameras and reporters, of loading all their securities into Brinks trucks and driving them in the direction of Toronto. Election results: with 24 percent of the popular vote (34 percent of the francophone vote) the Parti Québécois wins 6 percent of the seats in the National Assembly. With 45 percent of the popular vote (30 percent of the francophone and 90 percent of the anglophone vote), the Liberals win 70 percent of the seats.

Summer 1970. The citizens of Cabano, a lumber town in the Gaspé, form a Committee of Survival. At issue is the fact that, although the lumber company of K.C. Irving had promised, back in 1966, to build a lumber mill in Cabano in return for cutting concessions from the government, it has now announced that it "cannot afford" to build the mill. The unemployment rate in Cabano is a disaster, and in retaliation the citizens barricade the town, blow up the bridges leading to Irving's lumber site, blow up the company trucks, burn the lumber and threaten to burn the forest unless the mill is built.

21 June 1970. Montreal police raid a house in Prévost, in the foothills of the Laurentians, and seize arms, ammunition, disguises and revolutionary literature. They also come across copies of a prepared statement to be distributed among the news media in the event of the kidnapping of the American consul in Montreal.*

> There is first the humiliation . . . it's the problem of all minorities and I do not accept the givens of the problem. . . .
> There is also the fatigue, which goes hand in hand with the

---

*Although it wasn't until 1970, after the October Crisis, that a special unit within the Security Service of the RCMP, called G Ops (for Operations), was activated with the specific responsibility of surveillance of, maintainance of files on, infiltration into and recruitment of informers from among terrorist, separatist and unionist groups in Quebec,[15] such operations had been ongoing in Quebec throughout the Sixties as part of the police's nation-wide repressive campaign against "subversion." The military, too, according to Pierre Vallières in his *The Assassination of Pierre Laporte,* as far back as 1966 had "systematically" infiltrated separatist groups, the labour movement and student circles in Quebec. Vallières goes as far as to suggest that such police and military operations and particularly the use of *agents provocateurs* in the demonstrations, strikes, et cetera, of the period manipulated the developing "revolutionary consciousness" of the Québécois and distorted it into a "revolutionary threat."[16]

humiliation. Fatigue, humiliation, powerlessness. . . . It's bizarre but I believe there is also joy.[17]

So speaks a character in Pierre Gravel's novel of the first "generation" of Sixties separatists, *A Perte de Temps*. By 1970 they had come a long way from such existentialism, had advanced from the haze of their despondency, irresolution and spasmodic adventures to the point where they had linked up the national liberation struggle with that of the workers' movement: the two were indivisible. It was beyond the individual's choice now, this motion in the streets, and "history" was no longer executed by this or that combative intellectual or emboldened terrorist. History was the process of hundreds of thousands of anonymous compatriots envisioning together, en masse, the desired, if improbable, future. It was not a simple vision. It was, as Vallières enunciated it, a program of expropriation of foreign capital, nationalization of banks, resources and industries, the disappearance of the parasitic classes, the socialization of culture, the communalization of relations. It was not a simple vision but at its heart was the most intelligible of ambitions: "It is because I cannot bear to be a nigger. . . . "[18]

There was, over the long haul of the liberation struggle in Quebec, much that English-Canadian radicals, CUS among others, could recognize of their own movement in the features of Québécois anti-colonialism. Recognizable were the rejection of the path of electoralism and parliamentary democracy and of the principle of non-violence. Recognizable too were the emphasis on community action, the passionate attachment to the accomplishments of the Vietnamese, the Cubans, the Black Panthers, and the nausea provoked by the ways and means of corporate capitalism. And, by the end of the Sixties, the English-Canadian radicals had "Canadianized" themselves, sharing with their Québécois counterparts acceptance of a national, historical and cultural particularity.

In fact, by 1968, CUS recognized Quebec as a "sovereign geo-political society," its right to national self-determination, its "victimization" within federalism, and its oppression at the hands of the anglophone society of the country.[19] There were also those, on the English-Canadian left, who hoped that from

LONG WAY FROM HOME

such mutuality of perspective could be forged an "anti-imperialistic alliance."

> Here were people who were obviously light years ahead of everyone else in terms of political development, and for them to turn their backs on the rest of us and the rest of the country, I thought was a terrible waste. They had a program of action which conceived of a socialist nation. No one else that I ever talked to saw anything more than maybe medicare or possibly singing songs about the Spanish civil war. If we could just plug into it!

Pierre Gravel: "But since October or November, since one had begun, one felt the words come: one must speak the city, for it was for the idea of a city that one had struggled. The idea of one's own capital city. The idea of a place."[20] On this adventure the English-Canadian national liberationists had also embarked: the pursuit of the architecture of a place called Canada and the naming of the streets in which its people lived, and the meditation on how one was to fight and to make love and to dream dreams in the new country. Adventuring, the English-Canadians said to the Québécois that, yes, it was at this point a question of two different countries — two historical experiences and two national possibilities — but that, when "translated," it could be seen that in their efforts, the two communities of contestants confronted the same political and class adversaries for whom the escape of the French *and* the English into nationality was insupportable. We share your enemy, they said, if not your city. In October 1970, they had their chance to test the mettle of this proposition.

III

FREE QUEBEC, FREE CANADA

Trudeau: So long as there is a power in here which is challenging the elected representatives of the people, I think that power must be stopped. It's only weak-kneed bleeding hearts who aren't prepared to take these methods. . . . Well, there are a lot of bleeding hearts around that just don't like to see people with helmets and guns. All I can say is: "Go on and bleed." But it's more important to keep law and order in society than to be worried about weak-kneed people who don't like the looks of an army.
CBC Reporter: At any cost? How far will you go with that?
Trudeau: Just watch me.   *Ottawa*
13 October 1970

On 30 April 1970 President Richard Nixon announced on television that he was ordering U.S. troops into Cambodia. The war in Vietnam had become *ipso facto* the war in Southeast Asia. In a fury of loathing and reprobation, anti-war activists throughout America escalated their resistance: they marched, occupied their schools and burned down ROTC buildings. On May 4, Ohio State National Guardsmen, who had been sent two days before to occupy the unhappy campus of Kent State University, shot and killed four students.

On May 9, a thousand people — hippies, yippies, draft-resisters, new leftists, Maoists, women's liberationists and the Vancouver Liberation Front — gathered at Peace Arch Park on the U.S.–Canada border south of Vancouver, stormed through the Customs crossing at Blaine and "invaded" the United States of America. A thousand people flowed off the highway and over and down the hill and into town, yelling, screaming, "Gook! Gook!," throwing their fists at the local "rednecks," smashing windows, hurling rocks at automobiles

223

("We weren't just protesting, we were *showing* these people something of what it's like to have your country invaded") and raced back, the same wanton, insubordinate wave of crazies, to Canada.* There they stood, in a line along the forty-ninth parallel, nose-to-nose with the National Guardsmen who had been in pursuit, there they were standing when up from the United States along a coast-side railroad came a train loaded with automobiles for Canada — "There it was, the whole Canadian-American issue, chugging across the border." They picked up rocks and smashed the cars, *take that, General Motors!* In their own piece of theatre, they imitated the splatter of Viet Cong rifle fire against the helicopters of the U.S. Army.

On May 11, in Toronto, the May 4 Movement** spearheaded a demonstration of fifteen thousand at the American consulate on the broad boulevard of University Avenue: "I remember having been in tears about Cambodia and the Kent State events, and then phoning people, saying, 'We've got to do something.' I mean, when were they going to turn their rifles on *us?*" It started peacefully enough. Church people, Quakers, community organizers, kids in strollers, as well as the May 4 Movement people in black armbands, the Communists, the Trotskyists, the Maoists. Banners, slogans, "Give Peace a Chance" and "Escalate People's War," ill-aimed stones thrown desultorily at the windows, a buzz through the crowd that the police had boasted there might be somebody killed this day, another buzz of May 4 Movement propaganda that the consulate would be attacked.

I had said, in response to an inane question at a press conference, that we would be attacking with Sherman

---

*Mourned a Blaine newspaper: "Saturday, May 9, 1970, may live in the minds and hearts of this nation as a day of indignity. For what was perpetrated on the United States-Canadian border is one of the saddest and most degrading incidents suffered by the people of this country since the Alamo."[1]

**An *ad hoc* coalition of new leftists, radicals and student activists named for the Kent State killings *and* the day in 1919 when students and intellectuals in China mounted a mass protest movement against the warlords, out of which came the Chinese Communist party.

tanks and bazookas. In fact, plans were vague. We weren't keen on real violence but the mood was that if the police were going to attack then people would not be restrained from fighting back in self-defence.

By five o'clock the demonstrators were ready to disperse. Suddenly there were hundreds of police, scores of them on horseback, charging into the crowd. Packed shoulder to shoulder for blocks, sealed off from the side-streets by more police, the people could not move. Sitting ducks. *Wham! Thunk!* Mass confusion. Frightened horses, rearing, their studded hooves kicking out in all directions. Batons, hysteria and mayhem. Police pulled off their horses, police attacked with stones, pieces of sod and even apples. Demonstrators beaten and pummelled and flung about. They scattered and ran to save themselves as best they could, chased by cops all the way up Yonge Street or up to the campus. Some ran over to city hall square where a hundred motorcycle cops charged them again. Swooped down on them with batons. "I was standing beside a kid whose head was split open, he was gushing blood, I was yelling, 'Somebody help! This boy's dying!' and a cop came after me, flailing away. It was positively American."* But that was before October.

Monday, 5 October 1970. The five members of the self-designated Liberation cell of the FLQ, Louise Cossette-Trudel, Jacques Cossette-Trudel, Jacques Lanctot, Marc Carbonneau and Yves Langlois, kidnapped the senior British trade commissioner, James Cross, from his home in Westmount. They demanded in return for his release: the immediate release of twenty-three "political prisoners" (Felquistes who had been arrested and convicted of various illegalities over the

---

*On May 14, five hundred National Guardsmen and numbers of state and civil police converged on the girls' dormitory of Jackson State University (the largest black college in Mississippi) where a couple of hundred (unarmed) students were "hanging out." A seven-second barrage of a thousand rounds of ammunition — from automatic weapons, shotguns, rifles, pistols and hand-guns — left two students dead, shot in the back.

years) and their own transport to Cuba or Algeria; $500,000 in gold; publication and broadcast through the media of their manifesto; the cessation of the police manhunt; release of the name of an informer; the rehiring by the government of 450 Lapalme mail truckdrivers who had lost their jobs as the result of a reorganization in the post office.

October 6. The federal and provincial governments announced they would not comply with the ransom demands, but that some other deal might be possible.

October 7. Liberation cell refused any negotiations other than those to do with their original demands but extended the deadline on Cross's life to Thursday.

October 8. Premier Bourassa travelled to New York to negotiate a sale of Quebec hydroelectric power. The French-language network, Radio-Canada, broadcast the FLQ manifesto. The first army troops were moved down from Valcartier to the vicinity of Montreal.

October 9. The Montreal police made several raids throughout the city. *La Presse* newspaper printed the manifesto.

October 10. The four members of the days-old Chenier cell,* Paul Rose, Jacques Rose, François Simard and Bernard Lortie, kidnapped the provincial labour and immigration minister, Pierre Laporte, and reissued the original demands of Liberation cell.

October 11. Federal troops were moved into Ottawa and some small units into Montreal. In the midst of the civic election campaign, FRAP announced it was in agreement with the objectives of the FLQ.

October 13. Michel Chartrand of the Montreal Central Council of the CNTU announced his "unequivocal support" of the FLQ manifesto.

October 14. At the University of Montreal, three thousand students staged a boycott of classes in a show of support of the manifesto. At the University of Quebec and at several CEGEPs, students participated in mass assemblies to indicate their approval of the manifesto and to call on the governments

---

*Dr. Jean Olivier Chenier was a rebel killed in battle with the British at St. Eustache in the uprising of 1837.

to negotiate with the FLQ. René Lévesque of the Parti Québécois, Claude Ryan, editor of *Le Devoir,* seven union executives and several academics issued a declaration:

> ... the primary responsibility for finding a solution and applying it must rest with Quebec.... We feel this urgency all the more strongly because we fear, from certain quarters outside Quebec especially, the terrible temptation of embracing a political stance favouring the worst, i.e., the illusion that a chaotic and thoroughly savaged Quebec would at last be easy to control, by any means whatsoever.[2]

October 15. In response to Bourassa's request for federal troops to "assure the security of the population," Hercules C-130 troop and vehicle transport aircraft, helicopters, jeeps, truck convoys, supply vehicles, ambulances and combat troops moved into Montreal. That evening, at Paul Sauvé arena, Pierre Vallières addressed a massive crowd of students. "We cannot afford to encourage the police to take reprisals against us. We must be solid." The students chanted: "FLQ! FLQ! FLQ!"

October 16. At five o'clock in the morning the government of Canada proclaimed the War Measures Act.* The provisions of the act suspended all civil liberties, eliminated the need for search warrants, suspended the right of *habeas corpus* for up to six months, provided for stop and search, and declared that the "FLQ and its sympathizers and *any* succeeding organization and *any* other group or individual who advocates the forceful overthrow of the government is *outlawed* and membership in such organizations is punishable by up to five years in prison." (Italics mine.) Likewise punishable were *past* membership in the FLQ or similar organizations, and any action that might in any way aid such organizations, if only by speaking well of them. Sections 3 (1) (a) and 4 of the War Measures Act imposed censorship. By the time dawn had broken, 242 people were in jail: artists, lawyers, journalists, doctors, members of

---

*The War Measures Act was adopted by a vote of 190 to 16. The 16 opponents were all NDP MPs. The act expired in April 1971.

FRAP, independentist groups and citizens' committees, publishers and teachers.

That evening the prime minister explained himself on television. The kidnappers, he said, were people who "are attempting to destroy the unity and the freedom of Canada." They were "a handful of self-selected dictators" and "those who gain power through terror, rule through terror." By application of emergency measures, the government could "root out the cancer of an armed, revolutionary movement."[3] The three major trade unions of Quebec, CNTU, QFL and CEQ, expressed in a statement their concern that the suppression of civil liberties threatened democracy more than did terrorism or "anarchy."

October 17. The body of Laporte was found by radio reporters in a car in a parking lot of St. Hubert air base.

October 30. Trudeau announced that the government had "solid information" that an effort to form a "provisional government" had been made by certain Quebec nationalists at the height of the crisis. The inference was that the conspirators were the signatories of the declaration of October 14.

October–November. Except for three batallions posted abroad, the armed forces had moved virtually every infantryman and paratrooper under its command into Quebec (five thousand men from New Brunswick and the West alone). Also used were aircraft from Air Transport Command, three regular and four reserve squadrons of 10 Tactical Air Group and even a fighter-reconnaissance squadron from Bagotville with its CF-5 jets. Police conducted 5,000 raids and made 465 arrests* from Hull to Gaspé. In spite of the latitude provided them by the War Measures Act, the police failed to find any evidence to support a criminal charge in 403 of these cases. Ultimately some 30 persons were brought to trial but charges of "seditious conspiracy" failed to hold up in court.

Outside Quebec, an American deserter was arrested in Toronto because while in Montreal he had stayed at the home

---

*Among them: Pierre Vallières, Charles Gagnon, Michel Chartrand, Robert Lemieux, Gaston Miron, Pauline Julien, Gerald Godin and Stanley Gray.

of FLQ sympathizers. The mayors of both Toronto and Vancouver publicly stated that the War Measures Act might be just the tool they needed to rid their cities of draft-dodgers and hippies. A teacher in Vancouver was fired for reading the FLQ manifesto to his class. In Winnipeg two people from a bookstore were jailed for having posted a "Free Quebec" sign in their window. Two University of Toronto students were detained several hours by police for wearing the letters FLQ, clipped from the headlines of the university paper, on their jackets. In Guelph, police confiscated all copies of a special edition of the student paper carrying excerpts from the FLQ manifesto.

December 3. Surrounded by police, army transport helicopters, troops, ambulances and a fire truck, the members of Liberation cell negotiated the release of Cross in exchange for safe passage to Cuba. Three weeks later, the members of Chenier cell were flushed out of their hide-out at St. Luc, thirty miles out of Montreal. Both cells had been tracked down by conventional police methods. No other active insurgents were identified.*

---

*Ten years later, certain additional facts and information about the October Crisis must significantly alter our perceptions of that event. For one thing, the kidnapping of Cross came as no surprise to government and police: they had been waiting for something very much like this. According to a *Globe and Mail* report of December 1971, the federal cabinet had decided, back in May 1970, to set up an interdepartmental committee to consider "steps to be taken in the event the War Measures Act comes into force by reason of insurrection." According to CBC research, a Strategic Operations Centre grew out of this committee. Comprised of officials from the Prime Minister's Office and representatives from the RCMP, it reported directly to Trudeau. For months the Centre amassed files on the FLQ. The FLQ centres and operatives were all known to the police. For another, the circumstances surrounding the kidnappings of Cross and Laporte are more than ever perplexing. It was faulty RCMP intelligence reports that linked the two cells in a conspiracy. In fact they were not in communication with each other. For many years speculation centred on a sixth member of Liberation cell. In July 1980 Nigel Barry Hamer, a married teacher living in Quebec, was charged with kidnapping the trade commissioner. He pleaded not

Popular resistance to the actions of the governments and to the intimidating rhetoric surrounding and justifying those actions was sporadic and fainthearted, especially outside Quebec. But even inside Quebec, where the Mouvement pour la Défense des Prisonniers Politiques Québécois organized demonstrations in front of the prisons holding people arrested under the War Measures Act and the Quebec Committee for the Defence of Civil Liberties called a few public protest meetings, the rage and humiliation (and even the principled support of the FLQ's objectives) did not erupt into mass resistance.

I didn't see any factory workers or office workers go off on strike. I didn't see a single trade union call for a general strike against the War Measures Act. I didn't see a single school close down in protest. If people continue to go to work, continue to go to school, if the public transportation

---

guilty. As for the Laporte kidnapping and murder, Chenier cell was the beneficiary of some remarkable coincidences. Police protection of Laporte, his family and his house was pulled just days before he was kidnapped. He was hauled into a car in full view of his wife and his neighbours and offered no resistance. The car carrying him happened to be the very last one to pass out of the district before the police put up roadblocks. The Rose brothers and François Simard had been under surveillance since 1968, and their house on Armstrong Street was known to police. It too was put under surveillance the day of the kidnapping and in fact was raided several times while Laporte was supposedly being held there. Yet Laporte was never discovered there. Chenier cell has never been materially linked with the death of Laporte. The communiqué announcing his "execution" was signed by an unheard-of Dieppe Royal 22nd cell: the FLQ never did claim credit either for the murder or the communiqué. The day of Laporte's death, Paul Rose was in downtown Montreal, Bernard Lortie was visiting friends and Jacques Rose and François Simard were in police custody! The car containing his body had been driven completely unnoticed in broad daylight onto the federal territory of the St. Hubert air base in the middle of the general mobilization under the War Measures Act. The "confessions" of Chenier cell to the murder were never signed. In summary, writes Pierre Vallières in his *The Assassination of Pierre Laporte,* "the facts on record fail to prove beyond a reasonable double that Laporte was in fact kidnapped, sequestered and murdered by the four men who have been imprisoned in connection with this case, or that they acted alone."[4]

continues to function, that means that the occupier is either being tolerated or supported.

In Toronto the *Varsity*, the University of Toronto student paper, published a special issue, "Crisis in Quebec," which delineated the history of colonialist conquest and exploitation of Quebec, the manipulations and corruption that have passed for the electoral process in Quebec, and the events of a decade of protest leading up to the FLQ action. It told readers that, under the War Measures Act, "all strikes can be banned. Demonstrations, canvassing, meetings for peace can be banned. All public meetings can be banned. Any newspaper declared to be in violation of the act can be closed down" and so on. In other words, all of the activities of the peace and anti-Vietnam and draft-resistance and women's liberation and student power movements into which people had entered as democrats and citizens were suddenly, categorically and unilaterally declared illegal. The paper editorialized: "When it becomes illegal to organize and work for fundamental social change — as may be the case in Canada at this very minute — a revolution will begin to take shape." It printed the photographs of soldiers in full battle regalia standing in the ordinary streets of the Canadian city, an image that so many people were regarding with disbelief. *It did happen here.*

Several meetings were held on the University of Toronto campus: "The question wasn't why are there half a dozen people willing to do a dumb thing like a kidnapping but, rather, why, when they write a manifesto which poses that kidnapping in terms of the national and class questions in Quebec, there's a massive, popular echo?" A city-wide Committee for a Free Quebec organized, not a demonstration, but a panel discussion with a variety of points of view represented, including the federalist. At York University, a "very cautious" civil libertarian rally, called to protest the suspension of civil liberties, was drowned out by two thousand students singing "O Canada," and it was reported that some students were carrying guns. "They were out hunting for 'frogs.' "

Up in Ottawa, Canadian University Press (CUP) news service was "pumping out" material on the crisis and its background, which university papers across the country picked up and reprinted.

> There were tanks at the airport and soldiers everywhere downtown where the CUP offices were. I was very afraid because the act had said that it was illegal to publish the FLQ manifesto and here I was pumping it over the wire anyway. I was all alone and waiting for the cops to come breaking down the doors to haul me away.

In Winnipeg, NDPers held meetings to discuss the Communist Manifesto and the FLQ manifesto and "we were afraid the whole time of the meeting we were going to be arrested. Actually, we needn't have worried. Western Canadians didn't see that the War Measures Act had anything to do with them." To people in Calgary the act meant that "friends in Quebec might get thrown in jail but Calgarians were probably safe. And we were. We did our little bit, took the afternoon off and marched downtown with placards. Someone took pictures of us and that was that." In Edmonton the remarks of the police chief that he might use the act to run the draft-dodgers out of town created not a little paranoia: people huddled in their houses, too frightened even to talk politics on the phone. Radicals on the students' council of the University of Alberta organized a protest rally but "there was a tremendous resistance to the idea of doing anything. We had a hell of a time getting anyone from the faculty to speak out against the act — even the dean of the Law Faculty wouldn't touch it." In the end, about two thousand people showed up to hear "a couple of left-wingers" and the dean of Collège St. Jean. RCMP officers in brushcuts circulated visibly in the crowd and the mood was in fact hostile to the statements of the protesting speakers. "Students by and large felt Trudeau was right."

A Friends of Quebec Committee in Vancouver had a meeting on the steps of the courthouse and read out the FLQ manifesto. Nothing happened. The *Peak,* the student paper at SFU, ran the CUP material, the FLQ communiqués, an excerpt from Vallières's *White Niggers of America,* a feature from *Last Post* magazine ("The Santo Domingo of Pierre Elliott Trudeau") and an editorial:

The Felquistes are taking on a very violent opponent, this we must recognize. Self-defence is necessary, sure. But there's got to be more to a revolution than that.

South American revolutionaries know this. In Argentina last week four revolutionaries intercepted a truck carrying 2,400 quarts of milk and distributed them in a slum district. The Tupamaros in Uruguay have done the same thing with trucks carrying meat. And these groups are gaining tremendous support.

All power to the imagination!!!

And the yippie paper, the *Yellow Journal,* came out at the end of October as *le journal jaune* with material prepared in cooperation with the Free Quebec–Free Canada Committee. It reprinted the FLQ manifesto "as an exercise of our democratic rights, unwilling to be intimidated by totalitarian legislation and in support of the people of Quebec who are fighting for their national liberation."

Brave words, brave gestures, and the least that self-respecting radicals could do. But the resistance was riven with timorousness as though the questions were not "How dare they do this?" but "What if they do it to me?" Here was a revelation: the movement which had so recently and so belligerently boycotted, disrupted and intervened in the processes of the authoritarians who governed their lives as students ground to a halt when that same authority turned on the Québécois. When forced to choose between the well-being of the colonized people of Quebec and the well-being of the Canadian state, for all their anti-colonialist rhetoric, the English-Canadian radicals could not choose Quebec. It was as though in the English-Canadian heart of each and every one of the radicals was this: that the federalist state, in all its baneful ways, was still their history, their condition and their aspiration.

The Front de Libération du Québec is not the Messiah, not a modern-day Robin Hood. It is a group of working people of Quebec who are committed to do everything they can for the people of Quebec to take their destiny in their hands.

The Front de Libération du Québec wants the total independence of the Québécois, brought together in a free society, purged forever of its band of voracious sharks, the patronage-dispensing "big bosses" and their servants who have made Quebec into their private preserve of "cheap labour" and of exploitation without scruple.

The Front de Libération du Québec is a movement not of aggression, but of response to aggression — the aggression organized by high finance through the marionettes of the federal and provincial governments (the Brinks "show," Bill 63, the electoral map, the so-called "social progress" [sic] tax, Power Corporation, Doctor's insurance, the men of Lapalme. . .). . . .

We live in a society of terrorized slaves, terrorized by the big bosses: Steinberg, Clark, Bronfman, Smith, Neapole, Timmins, Geoffrion, J.L. Lévesque, Hershorn, Thompson, Desmarais, Kierans. (Beside these Remi Popol* the gasket, Drapeau the "dog," Bourassa the Simard sidekick,** Trudeau the faggot are "peanuts."). . .

Working people in the factories, in the mines, and in the forests; working people in the service industries, teachers, students, unemployed: take what belongs to you, your labour, your determination and your freedom. And you, workers of General Electric, it is you who make your factories run; you alone are capable of producing; without you, General Electric is nothing!

Working people of Quebec, begin today to take back what belongs to you; take yourselves what is yours. You alone know your factories, your machines, your hotels, your universities, your unions; do not wait for a miracle organization.

Make your revolution yourselves, in your neighbourhoods, in your workplaces. And if you do not make it yourselves,

---

*Remi Paul, former Union Nationale minister of justice, used to appear on campaign platforms with the Quebec Nazi party.
**A French-Canadian family with extensive corporate holdings and into which Robert Bourassa, then Quebec premier, married, it is a financial supporter of the Liberal party.

more usurpers, technocrats or others, will replace the handful of cigar puffers we now know, and everything will have to be done over again. You alone can build a free society. . . .

Our struggle can only be victorious. Not for long can one hold in misery and scorn, a people once awakened.

These are excerpts from the FLQ manifesto, which was broadcast and widely disseminated, briefly, during the October Crisis. This is the language of the "bandits," the "criminals," the insurrectionaries from whom the government of Canada sought to defend the people of Quebec. Here they were in all their iniquity: revolutionaries who acknowledged that no mere spectacle of terrorism was sufficient to bring on a revolution, that such change could only be wrought by the exploited and humiliated masses themselves, in their places of collective desolation; who named the agents of exploitation and aggression; who drew the picture of what could be, down independence road. Against this vocabulary the government posed its own, an "official version" of events that, reduced to the simple formula of law-and-order, precluded, it was to be hoped, the "ideologization"[5] of those events, that is, the transformation of FLQ propaganda into a vision. Or, as a media wag put it, "This is the first time in this country we've had a counter-revolution before having had a revolution."[6]

Thus, one heard from John Turner, minister of justice, that the government had been placed "in a position of immobility whereby all the action in terms of public opinion was left to a bunch of renegades."[7] The secretary of state Gérard Pelletier stated that the FLQ "advocated" selective assassinations (it had advocated no such thing) that "might well have" resembled the Nazi's Night of the Long Knives in 1938.[8] One heard from "sources high in the provincial government" that there were at least thirty-five hundred Felquistes armed to the teeth with automatic weapons and ten thousand sticks of dynamite,[9] and from Montreal mayor Jean Drapeau that there was within Quebec a group attempting "to set up the provisional government that was to preside over the transfer of constitutional authority to a revolutionary regime."[10] Jean Marchand, minister of regional economic expansion, complained that the Criminal Code was not instrument enough "to get those people [the FLQ and its sympathizers] and question them."[11] And Prime Minister Trudeau asserted that "society must take every means at its disposal to defend itself against the emergence of a parallel power which defies the elected power in this country, and I think that goes to any distance."[12] In this manner, nine kidnappers, with only a handful of supporters providing direct assistance, with very limited funds (the second day after their kidnapping of Laporte, Chenier cell had exactly one loaf of bread in their house) and with six firearms and twenty pounds of dynamite among them — this was all they had, absolutely all — became a cunning, ruthless and conspiratorial battalion of desperados poised for a *coup d'état* who could only be stopped — they were, insidiously, *everywhere* — by the suspension of the rule of law.

Such scenarios were, as FRAP pointed out at the time, the hallucinations of men fearful, for good reason, of the vengeance of those they had violated and terrorized for so long,[13] the people of Cabano and St. Henri and Lapalme and the textile mills. They were, too, the rationale for moving against the whole dissident motion of the Québécois, for if it was not simple *criminals* with which the government had to contend (they had the Criminal Code for that), it was perforce all those thousands in the labour unions and the Parti Québécois and the CEGEPs and the citizens' committees who represented a *drift of opinion*[14] away from the justification of a federalist and capitalist state. The ideological monopoly of the state had been contested and its monopoly of the means of violence counter-vailed: "For Mr. Trudeau, that kind of challenge to established authority was illegitimate, and justified a very severe official response."[15] In the nakedness of the War Measures Act, the government of Canada was on record that it need not derive its authority from the consent of the body politic; simple preroga-tive would do.

To a degree, the government was correct. A Gallup Poll taken in late 1970 showed that 89 percent of English-speaking and 86 percent of French-speaking Canadians approved the deployment of the War Measures Act. This did not surprise

those pro-Quebec radicals who had been deeply disappointed
in their efforts to rally public opinion against the government's
rationalizations: they had come up against widespread antipathy
towards "the French," distaste for the "Communist"-sounding
rhetoric of the FLQ, horror at the kidnappings and murder, and
the conviction that however severe were the measures taken by
the state they were preferable to the disruptions and confusion
provoked by the separatists and were, in the end, "for our own
good."

In a sense the government had triumphed over the radicals
too. It had caught them by surprise ("Nobody saw it coming.
Nobody apprehended just how formidable a bourgeois leader
Trudeau was and that he really was absolutely willing to go to
the wall on the question of Quebec") and was able to capitalize
on the English-Canadian movement's isolation from Quebec.
Beyond Ontario it was, of course, a case of the isolation of
distance (in Edmonton, for instance, the radicals had difficulty
in getting hold of a copy of the FLQ manifesto), but it was also
the isolation of their unilingualism, of the general lack of
contact with the Quebec left and its movements, and of the
diffuse nature of their nationalism. "Explicitly we all supported
the right of Quebec to self-determination, but implicitly we
were pan-Canadian nationalists who feared that the separation
of Quebec would lead to the break-up and balkanization of
Canada. We failed to examine critically this idea." They had
also failed to examine the repressive capacity of the state so
that when the crunch came, they were frightened rather than
enraged. Intimidated by the provisions of the War Measures
Act ("Machine guns pointing at you in the streets *are*
intimidating"), by the arbitrary withdrawal of the freedom of
speech and assembly, by their alienation from their public,
Québécois and Canadian, who were convinced at the discovery
of Laporte's body that the nationalist movement did breed
murderers and thugs, and by their own ambivalence about the
"adventurism" of the FLQ, they abandoned the streets to the
police who rounded up their comrades in Quebec with
impunity.

Perhaps in October, 1970, the Trudeau government and
the military accomplished more than just the neutralization

238 LONG WAY FROM HOME

of thirty people and the rescue of a captive, abandoning the other to his fate. They profited from the isolated instance of terrorism to intimidate all Québécois nationalists and the progressive left. Trudeau was not playing at just catching some fish, he was after emptying the whole pond. . . .[16]

It was like a nightmare, as if it wasn't real. Repression had always been something that happened somewhere else and didn't immediately affect us. Now, as it sank in, it crystallized my feelings about Canadian politics. Horror at the lack of accountability. Then I began to feel very isolated, from my own family even. A very lonely feeling. In incredible loneliness and isolation, I began to question my whole politics.

Into the vacuum created by the dispersal of the Québécois student left into the Parti Québécois, the citizens' committees and *ad hoc* mobilizations, and by the scattering of the English-Canadian student movement into splinter groups, into the Waffle, into women's caucuses, the state had successfully inserted itself. The activists of the summer had been the last gasp of the united new left; the campuses had been quiet that fall of 1970.

Having said this, however, the story is not told. Within two years, Quebec was convulsed by a general strike, the most massive general strike in the history of North America, with the ports of Montreal and Quebec City shut down, major institutions paralysed, radio stations occupied, plants, mills, factories and mines abandoned, and whole towns taken over by the strikers. "It had been building up over the whole Sixties. When you have more than three hundred thousand people on strike, you obviously have the culmination of a process which has preceded them."

As for the English-Canadian radicals, there was to be no such drama. Rather it was a process of disillusionment with the state as they took the measure of its doleful mandate. Between the First World War and 1970, the War Measures Act had been in force no less than 40 percent of the time,[17] beginning with "arrest, detention, exclusion and deportation" of anti-conscriptionists, carrying through the eviction, dispersal and defrauding of Japanese-Canadians on the West Coast, and ending with the political imprisonments of 1970. There was an undercurrent of understanding too that the English-Canadian student movement had had its moment of truth about just what it was prepared to put on the line. The sobering realization that it had not picked up the tear gas cannister that was the act and lobbed it back behind the lines of the state's menacing advance persuaded a good many radicals that they had some hard thinking to do so that, the next time out on the streets, they would be very, very clear about what was happening and what they must do.

"If we fight back," wrote *le journal jaune* in October 1970, "and if we begin to be successful we too will be seen as an 'apprehended insurrection,' whether we use physical means or moral suasion. At the point we become effective in challenging *their* system, *their* values, all the power of the state will come down on us. They do violence to us every day, in a million little ways. . . . *They have declared war.* What should our response be?"[18] It was a question that went resonating down the corridors of the new decade.

PART VI
THIS IS NOT A REVOLUTION, SIR, THIS IS A MUTATION

I

MOVEMENT NATION

.... who is it that is getting fed up? Who is it that is getting disgusted with what Marx called "all the old crap?" Who is it that is thinking and acting in radical ways? All over the world — in the bloc, outside the bloc and in between — the answer's the same: it is the young intelligentsia.

— C. Wright Mills[1]

1962. Out they came, from out of the four cozy walls of home, out into the streets, kids, eighteen-year-olds, twenty-year-olds, kids, out into the public property of the city, the *polis,* the political boulevards of citizenship, to sit down in them, march through them, squeeze their bodies through the iron grilles of the gates shut tight against their passage. They were out there because they hated the Bomb and feared its poison, feared it not just for themselves but for all people everywhere (and for people still to be born) upon whose utterly human flesh its radiation might throw a lethal heat, hated the governments who grew fat with the transactions of the Bomb, hated the policies carried out in their name against populations with whom they ached to be in bonds of fraternity. They were out because at the root of their hate was an idea that one could live otherwise than in fear and confusion and solitude, that against the institutions of war and propaganda and profligacy one could erect imagination. Imagine: "alternatives to helplessness." Imagine that the owners of these institutions could be displaced. Where was it written that the fat men in the boardroom were safe from the shifting winds of history?

The kids were out because they had been handed unfinished business, and who were they to say, no thanks, it's not possible? It was Paul Goodman who had drawn up the list: a humane technocracy, community planning, workers' management,

economic egalitarianism, democracy, justice and honesty.
That's all. Nothing less was worth their enterprise and nothing
less would save them.

By 1965 this was an international event, this heaving up of
the young from their haunches of resignation to grasp hands in a
collective moral commitment to peace and generous order, to
perform, finally, actions of self-emancipation. Studies would
show that these activists were "liberal, tolerant, humane,
intellectually democratic, truly autonomous, warm, rather
impulsive and thoroughly decent,"[2] and so they were, young
utopians who gave themselves over heart and mind to fantasy,
to that moral realm where "nothing is forbidden" (or where that
which is forbidden is the malign and the cruel) and where, out of
respect for another's integrity and for their own dream of
mutual charity, they would be non-violent. In their activity they
would be loving and in their politics very, very ethical, for
politics is that ethic written by action into history and one
would not pass this way again. In the name of this love, of the
possibility of kindness, tenderness and succour, each to each,
young people everywhere refused the givens of their situation,
refused the "false authority" of the attitudes, customs, values,
relations, institutions and culture that were the work of
warmongers, slave-traders and commodity-fetishists. In their
place — for the territory they had deserted was vast — they
proposed the "movement," the collecting point of freedom-
seekers in motion, freedom from war, from bigotry, from
privation, freedom from politicians and managers, freedom
from indoctrination, "public opinion" and television, freedom
from bad sex and Big Daddy. No doctrinal program here, just
everything that had to do with the struggle to live well and with
joy. "The unrealistic sound of these propositions is indicative,
not of their utopian character, but of the strength of the forces
which prevent their realization."[3]

1968. Their movement had carried them away from the
places where their forbears had struggled — the industrial
plant, the mines and the mills — and dispersed them wherever
life had been cheapened and threatened and despised in the far-
flung empire of the "system" and its minions, had carried them
beyond the pale of traditional politics to the "helpless," among

whom they sought that "revolution from below" that would sweep them all, all of them in their hundreds of thousands and millions, up to the front gates of the citadels of Capital (within which were those who were accountable). It was not exactly clear what would happen next, and in any case the millions did not attend, but in the clenched fists of challenge (of trying even) the socialist project was recovered. In this they had the inestimable assistance of the people of Vietnam, for it was obvious from Vietnam, if from nowhere else quite so, that being "upset" was not good enough. Only winning was good enough. And one won through political action — up against the wall! — based on a thorough and implacable understanding of *what was going on*. "Once the policy critique of the war had been supplanted by the structural critique of the empire, all political therapies short of socialist revolution appeared to become senseless."[4] One could do worse than imitate the example of the ineffably courageous socialist revolutionaries of Vietnam. One could do worse by ignoring where the Vietnamese war touched the connecting wires that pulled at the executors of one's own existence, pulled at the bureaucrats in the university, at the decadents in mass culture, at the racists in the social sciences, at the woman-haters in the family: it was all connected, for it was all one body of unconscionable authority.

> God knows how many times there is a certain feeling that a kind of liberation of the soul cannot occur without a really cathartic event. How many times I wanted a revolution to happen just so I could go into a Safeway store with a sledgehammer and smash the shit out of it, smash all its decadence and stupidity. With impunity.

Massive black rebellion, constant strikes, gigantic anti-war demonstrations, draft resistance, Cuba, Vietnam, Algeria, a cultural revolution of seven hundred million Chinese, the FLQ, occupations, red power, the rising of women, disobedience and sabotage, communes and marijuana.

1970.

"It is not properly youth's role to bear so great a responsibility for inventing or initiating for their society as a whole."[5]

The movement generated ideas, ideas on how to live, how to examine things, how to make an organization, how to be a revolutionary, and just as the movement was an international phenomenon, scattered across borders and grounded in community after community, so too were its ideas flung about and passed around, refined and honed and involuted by an experience here and a debate there, until no one could say they were not everybody's. This was not surprising. Sharing the conditions of existence, the broad body of radical Western youth shared too the ideas of what their situation was. Everywhere they were in university, in the deadening circumstances of the classroom, being prepared for work they despised (or for the army, if they were not lucky) and for that mess of pottage called their comfort and their security. Everywhere intruded the news that the order that propped them up was not immutable, was indeed at this very moment under attack by some band or other of subversives and guerrillas. Their ideas took account of all this.

Praxis. The practice of the organization, the group, the collective. The radicals must be prepared to answer the question "What is the alternative?" with their own actions. The alternative is embodied in their praxis: note, they said, that we assume that people are capable of understanding their situation; note that no solution that has not derived from their/our participation in its determination is worthy of us. Without consensus, openness and *interdependence* of the members (you are my sister, you are my brother, we are in this together), there is no democracy, and where there is no democracy, the group breaks down into hierarchy, coercion and bureaucracy. Into violence. "The praxis is politics (theory, practice) *and* other acts. All tied together. The praxis rescues politics from terrorism by always recalling the obvious, the daily needs that make it necessary, and rescues daily things from nonsense and dispersal."[6]

Ideology. The separation of moral from political problems is phony. Within the human being, within the human life, the two are inextricable, for what power is and how it is to be negotiated are questions deeply rooted in what is the good and what is the ill. To separate out "politics" and to set it above all other inquiries is to separate out "politicians" (or ideologists) from the community, to endow them with "science" and to transform the brothers and sisters into "masses" in whom political life is not quickened until the ideologists invoke it. No, ideology *evolves* in the course of the movement meditating on its collective experience; it is situated in the *context* of the movement. "There has ultimately been no more worth or cogency in any ideology than a man infuses it with by his own action."[7]

The extra-parliamentary opposition. It is not possible to mount radical opposition within the political system because the system, far from being transformed by conflict, manages it. The movement places itself elsewhere. The movement is not a political party; it is a coalition, a united front of oppositional elements who seek to recover their power *from below,* from within the cells of civil society — culture, social relations, values — where social change occurs or not at all. The extra-parliamentary opposition therefore not only criticizes existing institutions of society and politics but also, by its activity, proposes alternatives, a "counter-milieu" in which new kinds of human relations are formed outside the existing apparatus of control and management."It's very important to withdraw from the established political institutions in our society and to undermine their legitimacy in order to create a new climate where people have the self-confidence to build new institutions. Of course that is a revolutionary process."

Cultural revolution. "Talk about the colonization of everyday life; they pull out of India to entrench themselves a little more deeply in your skull."[8] The human being is not just an economic and political construct; the human being is also a psychic and cultural event, and the revolution that will liberate us is the one that will expel the oppressor not only from the workplace but from the personality as well. The fact is we are mutilated people, condemned to the intellectual, emotional and spiritual life of the marketplace, and only the revolution can heal us, the revolution that implicates all our comings and goings, all our busy little doings, all the private fastnesses in which we cower and make believe we are happy. "The more I make love, the more I want to make the revolution. The more I make the revolution, the more I want to make love." The cultural life of the revolution, then, is the imagining, in embryo, of the personality and the life-style of the liberated future. In the visionary surrealism and psychedelicism of the movement, in its ecstatic epiphanies, its cooperative households, its renovation of the ego, its playful arts, and in its acknowledgement that every human has something to do with pleasure and beauty as well as labour and struggle is the synthesis of poetry and revolution. "But when their rhythms/mesh/then though the pain of living/never lets up/the singing beings."[9]

Student power. The radicals ask: What is a university for? Their movement rises in the cleft between the demand of industry that education be streamed along the needs of industry and the social need to allow a certain amount of intellectual freedom. The movement arises in the cleft between the fact that students as the "new working class" represent the producers of technocracy and the fact they are being restrained from fulfilling the liberating potential of that technocracy by the repressive regulations of neo-capitalism. What is the university for? If the final goal of education is to organize and direct consent for repression and regulation, then the radical students would withdraw their consent. Happily the university cannot be permanently policed (and still carry on its function); here, where social control is just a little less thorough, a "Red base" of anti-capitalist commotion can be organized and run on the energy of a hundred thousand fellow students' antagonism to what they must put up with in their daily lives and to what is being prepared for them in the cubbyholes of intellectual toil.

Capitalism. Although they leaned heavily on the work of left-wing or "oppositional" economists like J.K. Galbraith, Harold Innis, Paul Baran, André Gunder Frank, Ernest Mandel and André Gorz (not to mention the originals: Marx and Engels), it cannot be said the movement produced anything very remarkable in the way of political economy. It was, after all, made up of students. But from their readings and their lessons and their lives, the radicals did become bottomlessly hostile to capitalism and its pretensions. The "problem of production," they said, had only apparently been solved. The tremendous productivity of the industrial and service plants masked the social costs with which it was purchased: inequitable distribution, exploitation of labour, manipulated consumption, unemployment, waste, systematic impoverishment of women, the old, the non-Anglo, monopolization of resources, price rigging, growth for growth's sake, government by corporation. "But every step forward entails some human sacrifice and instead of being liberated man is being enslaved — ground up by the wheels of progress."[10] We categorically refuse all this, said the movement; we have in mind instead another conception of property and labour, we have in mind a world where work is self-managed play and where people see, not their production, but *themselves* as a social end.

The new left. In the 1960s, the world needed to be understood again. The knowledge that had been passed along from one generation of leftists to the next ever since the 1840s, as precious and fundamental and ingenious as it was, no longer explained enough. The world of the twentieth century had undergone such radical transformations of the economy, of the work force, of popular culture, of family relations, of education, that the left had to take up again the responsibility of figuring out what it was socialist revolutionaries had to deal with. By the same token, the left could no longer assume that its inherited structures of opposition and insurrection were equal to the task.

Think again. The Bolshevik model does not apply. Oh, yes, its glorious moment of the overthrowing a semi-feudal order for peace! land! bread! was an inspiration, still, but what then had happened? Of course the revolution is not a tea party, but must the post-revolution be a workhouse? Engels: "A revolution is certainly the most authoritarian thing there is." But after the revolution, what of that? Tomes of rules and regulations. A vanguard party progressively so isolated from the people that for the purposefulness and the self-generated activity of the working class it substituted itself, its dismal, mechanistic manipulative, terroristic self. This was a revolution? Eugene Debs: "I would not lead you out if I could; for if you could be led out, you could be led back again."

What then of the social democrats, the gentlemen and ladies of Parliament who observed the niceties of Roberts Rules of Order so that the party might progress from one election to the next to — what? The nationalization of industry and government by party hacks in the name of — who?

A plague on both these houses. "The bureaucratic forms of organization shared by communism and capitalism were embodiments of insult to the ideals of individualism, spontaneity, mutual trust and generosity that are the dominant themes of the new sensibility."[11] For such ideals the new left was accused by the old of naiveté, infantilism and sentimentalism. So be it. "Those who take their desires for reality are those who believe in the reality of their desires" — scrawled on the walls of the Sorbonne, 1968.

It was not possible, said the new left, that democracy in the locale could be realized in undemocratic organization, in the supercentralized, rigidly hierarchical, secretive and rigorously disciplined vanguard party at the head of the working class. Nor was it possible in the fetishism of technology and "technique," that "brave new world" of the earlier socialists and social democrats in which the agents of the workers, placed at the gearbox of industry, would liberate society through rational planning and scientific order. Remember, said the new left, we were born in the shadow of the Bomb; and reason, efficiency and progress are not everything. Democracy, if the word still had any credibility, was by definition a function of decentralized activity under local control, a function of overt, diffused and flexible structures dispersed throughout society. Modern industrial society had become much too complex and differentiated, polycentric and polymorphous, for one to dream again of seizing control of it by one fell swoop for power at the top. Rather, society must be penetrated at all its levels by "insurrectional cells" and "nuclei of confrontation" in *all* those social areas where modern life has become intolerable and the future a glimpse into the possible. Who would not want to exchange the reality for the possible, in the schools, the suburbs, the supermarkets, the bars, the bedrooms, as well as the factories?

We have no scenario. We do not know what the revolution will look like. We only know it is protracted, a "mounting fugue of attacks on political crimes of all sorts, on all fronts, at all levels of aspiration, from all sectors and classes, so that repression can never rest, never find a fixed or predictable target."[12] Who knows what waits for us at the end of this adventure, what bizarre architecture of revolutionary community we will have laid the foundation for? The end of action is not so important as how the "now" is negotiated, for it is in the moment here that choices present themselves. We would do well to choose wisely for after us come millions for whom it will not be possible to undo what we have done.

"I was enlisting. I think that's a great privilege."

The movement in Canada. Of Canada. An international event situated in the specifics of a Canadian place. In its Canadian particularity, reflecting the realities — both inspiriting and dismal — of the nation as a whole. The Canadian movement: seemingly overwhelmed by the American example yet fighting for its native life.

It was said: "We thought like Europeans and acted like Americans." In this there was some truth. The material of the civil rights movement, the anti-Vietnam war movement, the draft resistance and the countercultural movement was, throughout the Western world but particularly in a country bordering on the United States, sensational, arousing and inspiring. There were lessons here, in civil disobedience, non-violence, collectivity. In peace houses coast to coast, Canadians sang the blues of the Southern blacks, re-created the SNCC debates, practised curling up in a foetal position to ward off the boots and sticks of the police, and summoned up the courage to go out marching and get busted. In the hippie communes they smoked and elaborated California metaphysics, in the hippie streets they collected in the "liberation front" as though by rhetorical analogy they were in the Southeast Asian jungle, booby-trapping GIs. In the SDUs, they imitated the American constellation of "action freaks" spinning around the charismatic male leader, arrogant men who expected to be waited on, who always arrived late, never thought twice about inconveniencing others, publicly humiliated their "fellows" in brutal mind games, men who were "leaders" because of this power and not because they helped the group understand its milieu. Yes, here were Americanisms and the Canadian radicals were both exalted and debased by them, exalted by the example of their peers rising up in efficacious anger against the American machinery that pressed against the lives of all peoples, and debased by the self-contempt inherent in the imitative actions and ideas through which they identified with the syllabus of the "master race" of the United States of America.

On the other hand there were the Europeans — the British connection, the French connection, Aldermaston and the idea of nuclear disarmament,* the British Labour party and Fabian socialism, existentialism and Sartre and Camus, Fanon and Celine and Malraux. "The widespread growth and success of different revolutionary movements abroad has been the prime factor in the increase in socialist thought in Canada. . . ."[13] For later would come the other Europeans, Gramsci, Debray, Marcuse, and the Third World, most particularly Mao. Countervailing influences, then, to the Americans. A potpourri, an "undigested and perhaps undigestible" gourmet dinner of radical thought. An international generation of young intellectuals in search of roots and sources beyond the givens of middle-class existence.

Between the two models, the American and European, was, however, the real life of Canada. As early as 1966 the SUPA newsletter was reminding the readership that a too-close identification with the American left would obscure the unhappy (but irrefragable) fact that Canadian radicals were bred in the depressed culture of a colonized society.

> The querulousness among us, the pettiness, the conflict between personalities over non-issues. All of this showed a tremendous insecurity. Fanon says the Algerian intellectuals were afraid to write and to be criticized by their peers. How true for us too! A person like Tony Hyde, very articulate and insightful and an aspiring writer, was terrified at the prospect of actually putting something

---

*"The American movement was never unilateralist (that is, unilateral disarmament) to the extent that we were, and there was no American equivalent of the concept of 'positive neutralism' we had for Canadian foreign policy."

down and having somebody say, "Yeah, it's okay." How much did Art Pape write, or Liora Proctor or Myrna Wood or Joan Newman? We were scared.

It was important to face this condition, understand it, situate it in the structural realities of Canadian society by which *all* Canadians were defined. It may be, said the SUPA newsletter in 1966, that the base of a Canadian oppositional movement is not in a civil rights campaign, or in arguments with liberalism, or in an anti-war movement, but in the popular nationalism of Canada and Quebec and in a participatory democratic movement in the schools and universities. In such a supposition, still so tentative and suggestive, one can hear the creakings of the Americanized stage flats as they are shoved aside to reveal the scenario of Canada. After all, the struggle *to be in Canada* is ongoing, is proceeding every day, but only now and then in history is it given to people to answer to the very sharp questions of the nature of the place and to take a stand. The late Sixties were such a time. To say that the movement was "imported" is to demean the consciousness Canadians have had all along, however muted or mystified at times, that they live in a place of their own making.

In 1970 Toronto Workshop Productions presented a play, *Chicago 70* (about the conspiracy trial of the eight American activists arrested after the Chicago demonstrations in 1968), both in Toronto and New York. "I am told," wrote a reviewer, "that the two audiences responded quite differently to the show, the Canadians laughing more and the Americans arguing more."[14] One can account for this by quoting, as did the reviewer, Bertolt Brecht: "The man who laughs has not yet been told the terrible news." Or one can discern in the laughter the recognition that the situation was incongruous, out of place, absurd. The "terrible news" was of another country. We are not there, but here.

Americans seemed to have a real need to get their heads bashed in, to do something, anything, to "escalate" the confrontation — to what end none of them could really tell you, but no matter. The point, they said, was to go to Chicago and show the whole world that somebody in the godawful country *cared,* that you couldn't write the whole nation off so long as there were even one or two who were willing to get their heads bashed in, and so they did, thousands in Chicago. And then things got freakier and freakier until, a few years later, it was just one or two in an underground blowing up banks. That didn't happen here. Neither that kind of estrangement from a theoretical (intellectual) basis for their actions, nor that kind of irrecoverable hatred of their home. "We read books and talked a lot of theory. We weren't crazy." Listen, the Americans who knew us thought there was something a bit *strange* about us: their sensibilities were shocked by our, well, not quite Marxism perhaps, but by our socialist assumptions, a certain vocabulary, a new left stance, sure, but tempered with an ease with notions of "labour" and "class struggle" and "exploitation" that had come from the contact of the continentalist counterculture with the living socialist traditions of the Communist party and the CCF-NDP of Canada. They were there, the traditions, in the everyday life of thousands and thousands of our compatriots, and because of them there was something in the nature of our national life we honoured and held precious. It was in these traditions we were most un-American.

The charge that the identification with American issues cut Canadian radicals off from traditionally radical sections of the Canadian population[15] is naive. For one thing, the Canadian new left was never completely cut off from the old left (there was a marked overlap in membership of the new left and the NDP and Trotskyist parties, and there was continual debate among them). For another, there is more to the "radical tradition" in Canada than social democracy and the political affiliation of trade unions, as is shown by the new left's identification with the Wobblies, rural populism, the suffrage movement, cooperativism, Louis Riel and the resistance of the native people, the nationalist aspirations of Quebec and the challenges of regionalism to the centralist administration of Canada. For yet another, the charge fails to take into account the fact that, if the new left was estranged from the procedures of the NDP and the Canadian Labour Congress unions, they were no more so than the working class itself. Given that Canadian workers do not vote en masse for the NDP and were, in the late Sixties, beginning to form autonomous, breakaway unions outside the CLC, who was the new left to contradict them? For all their sympathy with the social democratic and union history of struggle in Canada and their admiration for the men and women who had gone before them, laying socialist tracks in the ideological wastes of Toryism and Liberalism, it was by no means obvious to the new left that the radicalization of the NDP was the only "logical" point of departure in building an anti-imperialist movement.[16]

The NDP. One loved it and one decried it. Here precisely was the agony of being in the Canadian movement, for at the same time that one was not, thanks to the social democratic tradition, sentenced like the Americans to rootless improvisations of radicalism, one was by the same token forced to come to terms with that tradition. To say the least, those terms were problematical. In 1933 the CCF had committed itself to "replace the existing capitalist system" with a new social order of democratic self-government and economic equality and had proposed disarmament, a humanized judicial system, the socialization of industrial enterprises, and a publicly organized medical system (among other proposals), all of which were projects close to the movement's heart of the Sixties. "The CCF was rooted in the Depression and the Depression had shown Canadians that capitalism couldn't deliver the goods. That's why it was important for us to make the link with the CCF." By the Forties the CCF had shown it was capable of winning political power, and by the Sixties it had struck a political alliance with the CLC. These achievements could not be sneered at by those with a sense of class.

> A lot of us had come out of social democratic working-class families and we knew that our parents had a belief, a *class* belief, in social democracy. We might have hated those NDP finks in Parliament but at the same time we knew they represented the aspirations of thousands of people.

And continued to do so, in spite of a record of retreat from the Regina Manifesto. By 1956 the aim of the eradication of capitalism had been set aside, replaced by the mere "subordination" of private profit and corporate power to "social planning" and the "working together" of public, cooperative *and* private enterprise in the people's interest. And, finally, by 1961 in the Declaration of the NDP, the notion of "public ownership" of enterprise had been replaced by "direct public accountability," the "class struggle" by "frustration," and "self-government" by "social and economic planning at all levels of government." It had also, by this time, under the red-baiting pressure of the Cold War, expelled its left wing into the wilderness of sectarianism and cynicism.

The NDP. Political institutions, said the movement radicals, can be as repressive as economic ones. Just look at this social democracy: compromise and brokerage in Parliament; day-dreams of social harmony and cohesion transacted, not in the bloody, ungovernable mess of revolution, but in the fastidious committees and commissions of legislation and planning; schemes of labour bosses' co-management of the economy with their erstwhile enemies, the politicians and the capitalists ("Everybody gets something here"), cosying up to the boys of Bay Street like their American union superiors up to the boys of Wall Street — the American union brass never could stomach socialism. Compromise, daydreams, schemes, all of it slicked over with unctuous moralizing on the misfortunes of the "people."

Not that the movement itself had been precisely revolutionary. It had had its moralistic moment of pious pronouncements on the "alienation" of the poor and oppressed, had gone on at some length about the need for new "sentiments" and new "perspectives" (had, in fact, gone into the NDP to lecture there about the "growing gap between the people and those who possess power"),[17] and had been generally, shall we say, ambivalent on the subject of the assignment of socialism to the working class. But by 1967 the movement was getting down to specifics, was thinking that maybe at the root of everybody's problems was "the problem of work" and that there was organizing to be done in the workplace as well as in the home and school and neighbourhood.[18] By 1968 the events in Paris had blown apart the radicals' complacent characterization of the industrialized and modernized working class as "integrated" and "conservative." "It was absolutely classic! We were sitting around reading Rosa Luxemburg on the mass strike and there on our TV screens was the general strike in France." And by 1969 the movement was theorizing about "workers' control" and "workers' self-management," all the while — and this was the genius of the movement — talking of participatory democracy, the absolute right to self-determination, individually and nationally, the free development of personality, the realization of ethics in action and all those other values by which you shall know the new left from the old.

And what then of the NDP? Fetishists of electoralism. A bureaucratic party, its decision-making authority centralized in an executive, its membership passively relegated to the manipulations of conventions. Silent on the nature of the "structural factors" underlying contradictions between "haves" and "have nots" and metropolis and hinterland, underlying "unemployment, waste, political corruption and commercialization of taste and values"[19] — *name it!* cried the movement. Obsessed with strategies of state power, large-scale government intervention, centralized planning: those hyperbolic ambitions of middle-level managers finally coming into their own. The nation-state as their very own sandbox. Blathering on about "control of Canada by Canadians," while all the time squelching that initiative to "assert ourselves by taking control of our lives directly, in our own names and without vanguards or representatives."[20] For the movement to embrace this in the name of a dream from the dust bowl of the Depression, in the name of a spurious Canadianism scared to look in the face of a new world, in the name of a perversely recalcitrant population, was to embrace inconsequence. "For as long as Canadian radicals persist in their commitment to the NDP . . . there will be no radical politics that is relevant to basic social change in Canada."[21]

That was written in 1965. Four years later, when the so-called Waffle Manifesto was issued, many radicals had still not cut the umbilical cord, as it were, but rallied around the Waffle on the left of the NDP, persuaded that a formation dedicated to transforming the NDP into a "truly socialist party," to the eradication of "alienation" and to "community democracy" was the continuation of the new left project, was indeed the maturation of a *movement* into a political organization. "People had become more serious, the Waffle seemed a culmination of our experience and the call to struggle in the trade unions an extension of our struggles in the community and the university. We thought that a captured NDP, transformed into a revolutionary party, was just what we needed." Certain Waffle themes were reminiscent of the new left — the democratization of the workplace, emancipation from American corporate capitalism, the notion of socialism as a *process* of socialist consciousness raising, and the construction of a mass base — and when the manifesto received the support of one-third of the delegates at the federal convention in October 1969 (four-fifths of its signatories were *not* academics!), it seemed it was only fools and rarefied purists who would turn down the opportunity to cultivate this base.*

Such "fools" and purists there were, however — new leftists who could no more sanction the Waffle than their own prehistory. They could see it coming: the debilitating battles with the party machinery (fights to gain control of riding associations, delegate selection, committees) would drain their blood and ruin them for the urgent task of building a grass-roots socialist movement throughout the cells of society. They twitched and winced at the Waffle Manifesto's claim that the "fundamental threat" to national survival was "external" (what of the threats to autonomy from within, from within liberalism and the bureaucracy and the corporate university?); at the irresolute declaration that in the interests of national unity Quebec's history and aspirations be "allowed" full expression and implementation (as though the national liberation of Quebec were not something that Québécois would simply *take*!); at the pusillanimous assertion that workers' "influence" be extended into every area of industrial decision making and that their "substantial power" determine the nature of their productivity (were these just pseudo-radical euphemisms for workers' co-management?). Not a word about

---

*More than 20 percent of Wafflers, by 1971, were students, half were under age thirty-five and the ratio of men to women was 3 to 1, compared to 7 to 1 in the party as a whole.[22]

the struggle for independent Canadian unions, for red power, for the liberation of women. Much, however, about national planning, public control and nationalization. We think, said the die-hard new leftists, we've been through this movie before.

There must be some other way of being a Canadian patriot, said the new left, some other strategems of liberation, than the propping up, the tarting up of the Canadian state. It was the intrigues of a technocratic imagination that required large-scale bureaucratic intervention into the economy and that insinuated that the critics of state institutions were "soft" on American capitalism. "What we need," wrote a social demo-crat back in 1964 (this was a very old tune), "is a strong and purposeful national economic policy designed to build Canada, to build it with native capital, to repatriate Canadian assets to Canadian control, and to herd the provinces back to the function of caring for local affairs."[23] Interesting verb that: to herd. The provinces, the regions, the peripheries, so many categories of undisciplined eccentrics to round up in the corral of the Head Office. To pull against the authority of the centre, to insist first on the assignment of identity and purpose to the immediate environs of experience was to be . . . un-Canadian. Scratch a Waffler and you find an Ontarian, a petit bourgeois centralist bereft of his employment, running the show. The movement had not come all the way from peace and anti-war work, denunciations of Canadian complicity in Vietnam, support of liberation struggles against American imperialism, revisions of confederation and celebrations of particularity — of self-generated collective being — to end up here, in the superannuated scenario of national superintendents.

Those who would not be Wafflers would be in the extra-parliamentary opposition. Here their ongoing program was to combat authoritarianism, to seek the national liberation of Canada through an insurgency movement on the campuses, to redefine the historic proletariat, to create new mobilized constituencies among youth, students, workers, professionals and farmers, to realize an independent Quebec, to accept the ethnic self-determination of all minorities, to combat male supremacy and to overcome psychological defeatism through direct actions and civil disobedience.[24] Now here was an

agenda worthy of the movement, here was acknowledgement of
the base of all youthful radicalism — the belief that the young
were capable of bringing about the transition from repressive
industrial society to a libertarian post-industrial society — and
here was the vision that only active, expressive, demystified
and uncoerced people could make the revolution. Here was
love of country in love of neighbourhood and comrade,
socialism in the self-activating community of classes and
partisans, emancipation in the open-ended reconstruction of
everyday life.

In 1969 the New Left Caucus had six principles: to build
socialism in Canada, to support the anti-imperialist struggle
around the world, to reject the parliamentary road to socialism,
to build an autonomous revolutionary student movement and
to support an autonomous women's liberation movement.[25] In
1969 the lines were drawn: one could choose the movement
and embrace the aggregate of one's experience and one's
wisdom, perpetually and inexhaustibly re-creating in the
process of struggle what was to be done, or one could slip into
the shelter of the party and embrace prescription and prede-
termination. Take your pick. One was never to know, however,
how the movement would have proceeded, and in what
measure its principles would have become its chronicle of
development, for within the year it had collapsed. 1970: after
the police, the beatings and the War Measures Act, the hardest
thing to bear was the nightmare that behind one's stumbling,
fatigued and frightened stride came no one at all.

II

PORTRAITS REVISITED

Gail Price Douglas:

She moved back to Edmonton, settled down with Ron, a potter, and opened up a small crafts store so she could sell her weaving and Ron his pots. It was a struggle. They had little money and the large, ambitious pieces she made for a gallery show burned her out. And these were hard to sell, they were so expensive.

Running a business has made her behave more, well, conservatively, than she would have liked. The things she has to worry about now go against the grain of the values she had supported back in the Sixties, back in the communal house in Vancouver. Worrying about profit. Making available the stuff that will sell. Trying to satisfy middle-class taste. Carrying more manufactured than handmade goods. Not even being able to wear her jeans when she goes into the store!

She turned thirty and the desire to have a baby overwhelmed her, taking her by surprise. Other things had always been more important than the idea of a family — work, travelling, relationships. She became pregnant and married. And now her artist's creativity goes into mothering. She likes to think her way of bringing up her daughter is freer than the way she was brought up, with more emphasis on the child's natural creativity, less on structure or discipline. And the child is being reared with a father around the house because he doesn't have a nine-to-five job. The mother, then, is not a full-time homemaker and mother. Sometimes she feels guilty about that, but for her own sanity she needs to be outside the house, among other stimuli. And they need the money. She has to work in that store. She didn't marry a doctor or lawyer. She married a potter.

So she expresses herself now in the store, and in their house, renovating and decorating it. This is not something her parents would have done; they bought new houses. But she likes the old houses, their workmanship and craftsmanship, the singularity of each of their old spaces.

The Sixties totally changed her life. Art is what keeps her sane, lightens things, keeps her unglued from the *status quo.* She had to go among the hippies to realize it, and what was evoked then will always be with her. The Sixties made her an artist.

Lydia Semotuk:

It was an invigorating time, the Sixties, but it was not a comfortable time. The period was not a good "fit" for her. Although it made her ask a lot of questions — if this isn't right, then I wonder what is — she could not see the answers anywhere. It was a testing time, a time when everything shakes down.

Out of all that shaking down and that loss of confidence, she had nowhere to go but up. Either that or become a basket case. She had been thrown into a whirlpool and went 'round and 'round, but she couldn't find any shore to land on because none looked safe. The lifeline that was finally thrown out to her was that of feminism. Feminism of her own making, the issues she'd work with, her own choice — issues pertaining to professional women and their work situations, because these were her own concerns too. She still sees that the world is entirely political, and what she means by that is that it all comes down to "influence manoeuvring," to power and powerlessness, to that insight of 1960 and the California gas chamber. So this is what she teaches the women in her women and management classes. If you're committed to working in the corporate world — and what isn't corporate these days? — then you have to figure out where the power is held and how to get a share of it. She doesn't think that's cynical. It's a given of the real world. The big question for women is: do you want to be part of that real world or do you want to change it? She would answer that you have to become part of it to change it. If you're not in, kid, you're out.

She doesn't know whether she'd still call herself a socialist, not knowing what that means these days. She'd say, rather, that she is a humanist. Justice and equality.

If the Sixties hadn't happened, she'd have ended up a schoolteacher, uptight, fearful, non-questioning, conformist.

Instead she asked a lot of questions. The period picked her up and shook her like a dog will shake an old sock and then set her down again in lots of painful pieces. And then it gave her a new life.

Robin Hunter:

He had been an open CCFer, willing to believe that the socialist commonwealth was going to be all sorts of different things, intellectually and emotionally. Post-revolutionary society was going to be a blank cheque they would write out themselves. After the struggle there would still be self-actualization to fulfill. When he first joined SDS, they had had a slogan "Toward a Community of Love," and most of the activists couldn't say it without blushing with embarrassment. But the idea was there: spirituality is politically relevant. The New Jerusalem on earth. Bill Irvine of the CCF believed that, having been a Methodist minister. Heaven forbid he should be ashamed of being like Bill Irvine.

The period of the Sixties had given him a chance to see a mass movement being created — in other words, a society in conscious process of change, people beginning to get new lives for old and linking that achievement up with the political things that had to be done.

He looks around. This society today is grinding people no less thoroughly than it was fifteen years ago, even more so, in fact. But understanding that you can be free can only really come about when you see other people getting free, and that's what was happening in the Sixties. He could *see* the struggles and partial gains of freedom. He could plug into the high energy and the alternatives that hadn't yet been worn out. The fronts of struggle have changed since then, and now, he says, it's a question of the working class stepping forward. And the housing situation. It's outrageous and people are beginning to realize it doesn't have to be that way, that they can live in housing co-ops, for instance. He lives in a co-op. A toehold, a clearing house to direct people to more resources.

He practises Buddhist meditation. He rides a bike. He delivers NDP pamphlets door-to-door and talks politics. He's thinking of doing a Ph.D. thesis on environmental law in Alberta, the science and bureaucracy of the matter. He'd still rather be a political scientist than anything else, although a friend has tried to persuade him to become a potter on Denman Island on the West Coast.

He'd like to marry again. He's getting a little old for it but still he would like to raise children. If he doesn't it'll be one of the great regrets of his life.

If only it hadn't taken so bloody long and so goddamn many stupid accidents and blindnesses for him to get to feel, finally, that he knows where he wants to be. It's almost as if the politics has been something to keep him busy, to keep him distracted from the real questions of existence. He doesn't want to believe this because then he'd be forced to think that his fury of political work was stupid, was beside the point, was dead-ended. His Buddhist friends, and those who have been through psycho-analysis, think this is precisely the conclusion he should come to. But he resists them. Politics has been one of the most emotionally gratifying parts of his life, has been rich and profuse with passion and illumination, and he will not gainsay it. When he is political, he is most human.

One step backward for every two forward. No more great leaps into the bright, unknown future. Just keeping on keeping on. His favourite song of the last few years is the Bee Gees' "Stayin' Alive."

III

IT'S MY FIGHT, IT'S MY LIFE

Generations define decades and later decades define generations, but there are some changeless things we've come to depend on: maple sugar in Quebec, White Spot hamburgers in Vancouver, Moosehead in Halifax, Goldeye in Winnipeg and John Diefenbaker in Prince Albert. As Dief goes, so goes the nation. But who remembered *that* in the Sixties? He was brought low, but he has arisen — and he forgives us. "The rebellious youth of the Sixties have gone back in the other direction," he told *Maclean's*. "They've put on some years and there's nothing like the change that comes with years." And that's what the Seventies are all about.

— *from "Getting on with the '70s"*
(Maclean's, January 1975)

In performing the post-mortem on the period 1964–70, it is important to sort out the errors and achievements of the movement from the forces which attempted to derail it. "In Canada the left is always blaming itself for everything that befalls it." Bombarded by the powerful ideological agencies of middle-class society* and interfered with by government and the police, the movement spent a lot of time sidetracked by the need to counter false information, to debate the pros and cons of government money, to fight the sudden and arbitrary application of repressive immigration, narcotics and assembly

---

*Even the middle class wasn't spared the effects of these agencies as when, in 1966, the controversial, and popular, CBC television program "This Hour Has Seven Days" was canned for attempting to "create within a deadening corporation, a small area of freedom, a breathing space."[1]

laws, and to smoke out informers and *agents provocateurs.*
("They were the ones in baseball jackets. They weren't Trots
so they had to be cops. The rule was: act as if everything you
were doing and saying was being watched and recorded.
Everything.")

At the University of Alberta, men purporting to be members
of the campus security staff hung around the doors of political
science classes and interrogated students about the instructors
and the course. There was a police attempt to keep Black
Panther Bobby Seale from attending the Montreal Hemispheric
Conference to End the War in Vietnam. "Disturbances on
Canadian university campuses were linked by the RCMP
yesterday to visits by militant agitators from the United States
. . . . 'At the present time with respect to the university milieu,
we have thirty-one of our [RCMP] regular members attending
Canadian universities, many of them in the field of sociology
and political science.' "[2] As far back as the days of CUCND,
the RCMP had increased the activities of its Security and
Intelligence Branch (now the Security Service) within the
movement, going as far as paying university secretaries for
"useful" information.[3] The Report of the Royal Commission
on Security, published in 1969, notes that the activities of
Communist subversives were "varied" and assisted by the fact
that "the communists are able to exploit and exaggerate
existing elements of social unrest and dissent . . . activities in
universities and trade unions appear at present to be of special
significance."[4] Not surprisingly, the RCMP was "nauseated,
disgusted, harassed and disappointed"[5] by such elements.

Nauseated and disgusted, the RCMP raided and ransacked
offices of draft-resisters' organizations, stationed patrol cars
outside their homes and photographed all who entered or left. It
turned information over to immigration authorities and the FBI
and even kidnapped and deported draft-resisters to the U.S.

> The RCMP in fact established its own policy on deserters,
> since the government did not give it any mandate to deport
> deserters unless it had gone through the established
> procedures of the deportation hearing and the deserters
> were found to be in Canada illegally. In this respect, the

RCMP was taking on a political role that displayed greater loyalty to the American FBI than to the formal policy of the Canadian government.[6]

High school and university newspaper staffs were harassed and, in some cases, shut down for material offensive to the administration. (In St. Catharines a teenager was sentenced to three months in reformatory for having the word "fuck" written on his blue jeans.) In 1967 the *Georgia Straight* had its license cancelled because it had allegedly sold copies to "children." In 1969 it was fined $1,500 and its editor $500 for "counselling to commit a criminal offense" (the paper had run an article on how to grow your own marijuana), and the judge put the editor on three months' probation. By February 1970 the paper had been subject to frequent searches and seizures, arrests (instead of summonses) and twenty-one various charges. Youths were actively harassed and sometimes arrested at rock concerts, at sit-ins, for lounging around, for narcotics possession. Adding insult to injury, the police made their charges on the basis of surveillance, unannounced raids, paid informers, blank warrants and discrimination against "hippies."

> . . . young persons view the sale of drugs as a service rather than a hostile activity. . . . Since they believe cannabis is harmless, youth scorn warnings and "establishment" drug education programs. Young persons view legal punishment and harassment for using drugs as political punishment.[7]

In Quebec, suspected Felquistes and their sympathizers were held for days at a time incommunicado, interrogated, beaten and humiliated. Although no direct link was ever proved between Pierre Vallières and the bomb that killed a union secretary at a shoe factory, he was sentenced, in view of his "clearly belligerent attitudes,"[8] to imprisonment in perpetuity. Groups and organizations contesting the Montreal civic elections in 1969 had their documents, files and printing machines seized. Pamphleteers and leafleters were harassed, arrested, thrown in jail. Anti-terrorist laws provided for the "illegalization" and suppression, in advance, of marches and rallies. A new form of search warrant came into use: "They're allowed to

seize anything written or unwritten, or printing machines, that
could put into the head of someone or *could* lead him to
conclude that he should engage in actions which *could* disturb
the peace. On that pretext, they've been seizing books, leaflets,
anything of the sort, any ideas or documents that oppose the
status quo."⁹ In 1970 the director of the RCMP Security
Service submitted to cabinet a twenty-one-page list of "Organizations Which Are Likely to Promote Violent Confrontation
with Authority" — heading the list was the Parti Québécois.
Burglaries, break-ins, mail tampering, acts of arson, blackmail
and frame-ups followed. Dirty tricks. The RCMP had suspected
the PQ was infiltrated by the FLQ.¹⁰

October 1970: the War Measures Act. Without indictment,
hundreds of innocent citizens, because their names had been
recorded in police files, were arrested and held without charge
for days and weeks, their homes raided, their reputations
smeared, their jobs in jeopardy. Across the country, censorship
regulations were redundant: intimidated, radicals kept their
silence, thereby censoring themselves.

It is said: the movement of the Sixties collapsed before the
exigencies of the Seventies, its brave words and bold gestures
smothered in the sludge of economic contraction and social
trepidation. It is said: the movement lost its nerve and forswore
its purpose. Look: the soft drugs of pleasure gave way to hard
drugs, gangs and violence; communes disintegrated; festivities
fell into the paws of hipster capitalists and community self-
help, into the bank accounts of OFY and LIP,* and many were
the countercultural mutineers who were snatched by suicide or
jail. Sexuality: rapes, abortions, unwanted pregnancies. One
was supposed to smash monogamy — to smash bourgeois
property relations — but in the censure of confessions of
ambivalence and suspicion, confessions that it hurt to be
violated, used and abused, pilloried between male egos in the
last-ditch stand of male supremacy in the movement ("This
wasn't politics, it was anything but politics"), it was the

---

*Opportunities for Youth and Local Initiatives Project, federally
funded.

movement itself that was almost smashed. And, of course, there were no homosexuals in the movement, no, absolutely not, revolution was a *man's* enterprise, well, maybe there was one but as soon as he came out of the closet, he quit the movement.

Look around: the heavy duty revolutionaries couldn't keep their personal lives together at all; at home they were martinets and Punchinellos; how was one to admire and emulate them while, in the meantime, one had babies now to feed and the tomatoes were ready to be picked? The choice: repression and bootless anger, or "cooling out" in therapy and sensitivity training, the self and its projects filling the available space defected by community; trapped in privacy, our loneliness is legitimized, and our mythologies of security in the isolation wards of the ego solace us. Who would not want to retreat there? Away from depression, bad trips and ennui.

Movement burn-out. Resources badly, stupidly used up. Out of the fastidious anxiety that "democracy" would be undermined by bureaucracy and discipline, four or five people did all the work. The decadence and degeneration of the leadership: the emigration of the membership into professions and academia. In the United States a mass student movement split into an old left faction and a terrorist faction, sharing between them the illusion of people's involvement and the frustration — one was at the end of one's radical tether — that the war was still not stopped, and still the police were murdering the black leadership and the CIA was plotting. In Canada the struggles for student control of the university had been bought off with co-administration and the new cadres never showed up: economic stagnation, cut-backs, over-population of graduates. Radicalism was apportioned between those who strode without a break into the strategies of social democracy and those who huddled closer together, poring over elaborate blueprints of social transformation both far in advance of and years too late for any social movement that would require them. But anything to stay out of the cold.

"If you're a socialist you must find yourself a political organization. Otherwise you're just a critic." And so they gravitated to the Waffle, to the Marxist-Leninist *groupuscules* and to the autonomous women's movement. Well, what were they supposed to do? Their base among the students had collapsed, and in any case many of them were no longer students themselves. And one must guard against that phantasm of political struggle where a clash with the police is said to be an "advanced political objective" when it was merely a fight, and a pause in that clash is thought to be a strategic defeat for the movement when it is merely the surcease of battering and bashing.[11] So here they were, the Wafflers in the civil service of social democratic governments, the Marxist-Leninists in democratic centralist covens of structure! discipline! program! and the feminists in the women's movement where, because it had the "franchise" on the woman question, the question became ghettoized. So it all has been said. One can leave it at that, or think again.

Bertolt Brecht: "To him who does not know the world is on fire, I have nothing to say." The movement knew it. Knew it for the future as well as for its past, knew it in the accomplishments it laid down like a track to the fire line. This is what the movement had done:

On acid one had had a glimpse of a paradise lost, had taken the sounding of a joy a thousand times stronger than what one had ever felt before. It was the same joy, the same illumination, as that fantasy of marching to Parliament Hill under a thousand red flags, and in this com-passion, this sharing of passions in the hours of hallucination and meditation and analysis around the circle of fellow devotees, one had undertaken to match within one's person that explosion of consciousness that had detonated within the generation. You could say that the attention to, the reverence for, the inner life and the vitality of the spirit was an attempt to "decondition" the personality, strip it of the excrescence of joyless, morbid bourgeois culture, and render it worthy of the revolution. You could say that such regenerated personalities *socialized* their perceptions in the escalating movement to defend the physical environment from the pollutions of industry. Here was a movement with an assignment that would take people up against the fences and gates of the very same enterprises they had already challenged and held accountable for the Bomb and the war in Vietnam.

The oppressed constituency of women organized themselves in a broad sisterhood of insurgency and called into question — such questions, unheard-of questions! — the totality of assumptions from which the body politic of capitalist society derived its legitimacy. You who would be powerful and maintain your power must answer to the women; you who would be liberators must count the women among yourselves. This too would be a movement for decades to come. And the gays, the women and men living outside the internment camp of heterosexual relations, they too would be answered to, for, along with the women's liberationists, they were impugning the bourgeois transactions of property, sexuality and family — the "holy trinity" of social chastisement.

From within the movement's concern to decentralize, to localize and to particularize unfolded the twin impulses of regionalism and ethnicity — the sensibility of the place and the person outside the English-French duality and the critical commentary upon that duality. They too are community, they who are rooted in the local and the native; there is a political and cultural authenticity in the devolution away from the nation-state and the capital city into the autonomous settlement. It is *here*, under our feet, that we have identity and purpose, it is here we know who we are, what needs to be done and where home is. And it is from this place that we will hold back the barbarians.

It was the Québécois, rising up angry, who threw into disequilibrium the ethnic stratification of the country and who posed for all minorities the questions of survival in the face of assimilation. The Québécois showed that that assimilation could be reversed through political mobilization around the demand for access to the resources by which the ethnic community could sustain its particularity. It was time to repudiate the "gratitude" of the immigrants for whom it had been enough that they be left in peace. It was time instead to challenge the insipid Anglo domination of Canadian life and to demand the social and political power due the immigrants for the prodigious labour with which they had paid for citizenship. And from the movement too had come the optimistic expectation that the technological society had humane as well as infernal capacities, that, under pressure, the "modern environment" could be made to generate the "inefficient," non-standardized ethnic other.[12]

If it was the "historical task" of the international students' movement to end the war in Vietnam,[13] then it was successful, for in the face of violent censure abroad, massive sabotage at home and the demoralization of the army, the United States could not prevail against the people of Vietnam and would be compelled to pull out before it had accomplished what it had meant to do. In the world-wide actions against the draft, against the purveyors of munitions and defoliants, against the Joint Chiefs of Staff and the president, in their actions of championship, succour and esteem of the Vietnamese, the youth of the movement broke the climate of ideological consensus in the mainstream of Western society and reversed the defection of their generation from political life. The generation was back now in the thick of it, fighting for the lives of those who at the edges of the empire were undermining the domination of the imperialists, and fighting for their own lives, struggling to come clear of how they had been reared and by whom and with what ideas, struggling with the consummate burghers of the Western world for the right to a different kind of citizenship. And when they had done so, they said it had been the best of their lives that had been invested and that they were very, very grateful to have been young in 1965.

"There's no such thing as 'Come the revolution. . . .' It's not true that one day you are not in the revolution, the next day you are and the day after that it's all over. That's not the way it works." It works, said the movement, first at the level of individual moral revolt ("This is stupid and evil and morbid") and the refusal to conform ("I will not and you cannot make me do it or say it or believe it"). From there, in the laboratory of collective action, it assumes the proportions of human freedom, the liberation of us all, in civil society, right here and now: politics. The system has invaded every aspect of our lives, and so to say we have the inalienable right to realize ourselves and to control our development is to say the system must withdraw and give way to a new order. The reordering is radical, for it is total. Down with political monotheisms, delegated authority, exclusivity and the division of political labour. From now on we are involved in a multiplicity of structures and actions, direct self-government, coalitions and collaborations.[14] From now on, we know something we didn't when we started out. "I'll never be fooled again." So this too the movement had accomplished.

And, of course, the unfinished business of the movement required that it regenerate itself when the conditions were ripe: some would say in the Eighties. The very incompleteness of the business meant that the struggles were ongoing, if only in an attenuated manner compared to the massiveness and universality of the movement in the Sixties — but ongoing nevertheless. Student protest, student action, student mobilization in Iran, Colombia, Nicaragua, El Salvador, Mozambique, Soweto, Brazil, have rolled back imperialist encroachments or at least have stalled them. Students in Canada have protested fee hikes and joined with unions in the fight against wage controls. French, British, Canadian, American students have been at the sites of resistance to nuclear power, nuclear weapons, uranium mining and 2,4-D spraying.

What is to be done? Get one step ahead of the boys and girls who, busy and unremarked, are computerizing the economy and culture of the technological society finally come into its full flower. Escalate the pressure on the energy corporations to divulge their operations, expose the shabby economics of Canadian dependency, reverse the pillage of the Third World, victim of our consumerism. Politically revitalize the working-class movement wherever it shows itself, for without such revitalization no serious opposition is possible, as even the most dramatic of the confrontations had shown in the Sixties. Devise a strategy, ah, yes, that again, and still: how to get from here to there, knowing what we know now. After the demonstration — what? and why? Finally, render radicalism ordinary, liberate it from the false achievement of eruptions into the extraordinary, ground it rather in the patient labour of working with the undramatic and unheroic realities of ordinary life: radicalism's "realism and sanity would be grounded in nothing more than the ability to face whatever comes."[15] To face, for instance, the likelihood that we will always be tempted to walk the line of least resistance — accepting reforms to the *status quo* — because it is so hard, so wearying, so dispiriting to sustain in great loneliness a vision of society that no one else discerns: we are the crazies, seeing ghosts. To face the truth that it is not given us now to make the revolution, except in our imagination, for the situation does not present itself — it is not our fault! — until such time as a thorough collapse in the system of production means no one can sell, no one can buy, no one can be paid, as in the Thirties, nearly — as in the Eighties? At which point our world will have to go to war or make the revolution. "'But no will, no courage, no ingenuity can force this eventuality."[16]

In the meantime there is much work to be done and there are opportunities to be secured to broadcast the good news about the revolutionary possibilty to come. In the meantime let no one be cheated of her and his sense of loss, the grievous deprivation in the life of the woman, the Indian, the Québécois, the immigrant, the file clerk, the fisherman, for it has been said that it is this pain of the irreparable and the irrevocable — you have taken what is mine and you have squandered it — that drives people to the barricades. In the meantime it is important not to forget what we have done, not to let the power-brokers erase from our thinking the images of our resistance and our inventions, for in that blank space they write in accommodation and assent.

Do not forget that at a time when the political parties of the opposition, the workers' movement, the arts and the media all declined the assignment to shove the system up against the wall, it was we, the kids and the students for God's sake, who showed up for the dress rehearsal, who were present at the crisis of modern capitalism, and routed its assumptions: how and for what we would be educated, for whom and why we would work, how we would be sexual and with whom we would build a family, what modes of logic and reverie we would employ and to what ends. "The experimental patrimony of psychological, social and political liberation which enriches the . . . New Left is only the vanguard of the base from which the forces of freedom will grow in the coming decades."[17] Remember! Like the person who says the glass is not half-empty but half-full, let us emphasize not the ways in which the ruling class prevailed but the ways in which its hegemony was circumscribed.[18] Remember! The system can wage a war but it cannot control the consequences, political and social, of that war; it cannot reverse the fact that the rich get richer and the poor get poorer; it cannot eradicate sexism, racism and Anglo chauvinism, because upon these processes it structures its authority. It can only in the very short run control us ideologically: in the ruptures of liberal education we become "conscious" of what is really going on and from there become contestants. By what we did and what happened to us in the Sixties, all of these limitations were demonstrated.

The period was the "peak" experience of our generation, and it is important, while all about us insist that we failed and were absorbed into the consensus, to remember that there was a moment, an hour, a day when we were successful, when the system could not, even though just for a day, proceed with impunity. When, in the years to come, all about us say it cannot happen, we will know, it did happen.

> Fidel said that what made the revolution in Cuba possible was all of the rebellions that had failed. That in those rebellions people had had a glimpse of what liberty might be and kept this secretly in their minds and hearts. So that when the revolution did occur there were people to go into its service who knew they had a part to play, who knew they were not hapless objects of history but its conscious subjects. That's the kind of "failure" the Sixties movement was.

Photographs. Ranks of soldiers thrust their bayonets at people in blue jeans and coloured stockings. Tanks roll down a street past a mailbox and a stop sign. Above the simian heads of soldiers with snouts of gas masks, a young woman floats a balloon. Another young woman, with a rifle of her own, step-marches a GI down the Ho Chi Minh Trail. Like the motion of a field of grain in the wind, a mass of students dances down the boulevard, their red banners floating like ribbons. In a non-descript room in a village in the Andes, men dressed as officers of the army point at the holes in the chest of the cadaver from which the life of the revolutionary bled. Che. Even dead, a countenance of incorruptibility. "Let me say at the risk of seeming ridiculous," he had written, "that the true revolutionary is guided by great feelings of love." And so we had been ridiculous with love, with joy, with the first free labour of our young lives. We should be so ridiculous again.

NOTES

INTRODUCTION

1. "Previewing the 1960's," *Maclean's*, November 1959.
2. *Canada Yearbook 1965–66* (Ottawa: Queen's Printer, 1965), p. 104.
3. Ibid., p. 151.
4. Philip Resnick, *The Land of Cain* (Vancouver: New Star Books, 1977), p. 59.
5. Massimo Teodori, *The New Left: A Documentary History* (Indianapolis: Bobbs-Merrill, 1969), p. 4.
6. Ibid., p. 81.
7. Theodore Roszak, *The Making of a Counter Culture* (New York: Anchor Books, 1969), p. 15.
8. Resnick, *Land of Cain*, p. 133.
9. Albert Goldman, "The Emergence of Rock," in Theodore Solotaroff, ed., *New American Review #3* (New York: New American Library, 1968), p. 121.
10. Allen Ginsberg, "Howl," *Howl and Other Poems* (San Francisco: City Lights Books, 1966), p. 17.
11. C. Wright Mills, "The New Left," in Irving Horowitz, ed., *Power, Politics and People* (New York: Oxford University Press, 1963), pp. 251–52.
12. Erich Fromm, *Marx's Concept of Man* (New York: Frederick Unger, 1963), p. 107.
13. "Report of Scientists' Committee for Radiation Information," in Seymour Melman, ed., *No Place to Hide* (New York: Grove Press, 1962), p. 98.
14. Philip Resnick, "Canadian War Industries and Vietnam," *Our Generation*, vol.5 no.3, p. 16ff.
15. Robin Hunter, untitled, unpublished paper, Edmonton, 1978.
16. Robert Scheer and Maurice Zeitlin, *Cuba: An American Tragedy* (Harmondsworth: Penguin, 1964), p. 245.
17. John Warnock, *Partner to Behemoth* (Toronto: New Press, 1970), p. 196.
18. Gary Moffatt, *History of the Canadian Peace Movement until 1969* (St. Catharines: Grape Vine Press, n.d.), p. 96.
19. Norman Mailer, *The Armies of the Night* (Harmondsworth: Penguin, 1968), p. 99.
20. Scheer, *Cuba: An American Tragedy*, p. 118.
21. Che Guevara quoted in Régis Debray, *Revolution in the Revolution?* (New York: Grove Press, 1967), p. 107.
22. Hunter, p. 5.

PART I
CHAPTER I

1. "The Alliance System," *Report of the CUCND Seminar,* Queen's University, Kingston, February 1964, p. 120.
2. "The University and Social Action in the Nuclear Age," CUCND pamphlet, Toronto, 1964, p. 5.
3. Tony Hyde, "The Student Union for Peace Action: An Analysis," unpublished paper, n.d., p. 7.
4. John W. Foster, "You Gotta Do When the Spirit Says Do," unpublished paper, Toronto, 1965, p. 5.
5. James Harding, "An Ethical Movement in Search of an Analysis," *Our Generation,* vol.3 no.4 / vol.4 no.1, p. 22.
6. "SUPA Says No to the Cold War and to the Society It Creates," SUPA pamphlet, n.d., unpaginated.
7. "SUPA: A Statement of Purpose," SUPA pamphlet, n.d., unpaginated.
8. Pat Uhl, "The Student Radicals and Community Organizing," *Canadian Alternatives*, vol.1 no.1, p. 80.
9. Foster, "You Gotta Do," p. 4.
10. "SUPA: A Statement of Purpose."
11. Students for a Democratic Society, *The Port Huron Statement* (New York: SDS, 1962), p. 62.
12. *SUPA Newsletter*, June 1965, p. 2.
13. Jim Mayor, "Society Endangers a Way of Life," *Freedom Now* (Canadian Friends of SNCC newsletter), vol.1 no.5, p. 10.
14. Peter Boothroyd, "Report on the Kootenay Project," unpublished paper, Edmonton, 1965, p. 9.
15. Foster, "You Gotta Do," p. 8.
16. Margaret Daly, *The Revolution Game* (Toronto: New Press, 1970), p. 6.
17. Ted Folkman,"Phase Two of SUPA," *SUPA Newsletter*, n.d., p. 19.
18. *SUPA Newsletter*, vol.3 no.1, p. 25.
19. Jim Harding, "We Take Ourselves Too Seriously," *SUPA Newsletter*, n.d., p. 30.
20. Folkman, "Phase Two of SUPA," p. 19.
21. Anatol Rapaport, "Have the Intellectuals a Class Interest?" *Our Generation*, reprint, n.d., p. 37.
22. Harding, "An Ethical Movement in Search of an Analysis," p. 28.
23. James Harding, "Values, Analysis and Action for the NDY," report to the National NDY Convention, 1966, p. 5.
24. *SUPA Newsletter*, vol.3 no.10, p. 3.
25. Folkman, "Phase Two of SUPA," p. 21.
26. *New Left Committee Bulletin*, vol.1 no.1, p. 1.
27. Hyde, "Student Union for Peace Action," p. 13.

28. James Laxer, "The Americanization of the Canadian Student Movement," in Ian Lumsden, ed., *Close the 49th Parallel Etc.* (Toronto: University of Toronto Press, 1970), p. 281.
29. "The Dissolution of SUPA," *New Left Committee Bulletin*, vol.1 no.1, p. 6a.
30. Dimitrios Roussopoulos, "Who We Are," *SUPA Newsletter*, vol.3 no.1, p. 17.
31. Malcolm Reid, ". . . And a Tale about Their Anglo Friends," *McGill Daily*, 5 April 1979, p. 9.
32. Hyde, "Student Union for Peace Action," p. 13.

PART I
CHAPTER II

1. Jean-Paul Sartre, "Genocide," in Mitchell Goodman, ed., *The Movement Toward a New America* (New York: Alfred Knopf, 1970), p. 160.
2. Bernard B. Fall, *Last Reflections on a War* (New York: Doubleday, 1967), p. 198.
3. Daniel Ellsberg, "The Curious Case of the Tonkin Gulf Telegrams," in Lynda Obst, ed., *The Sixties* (New York: Random House/Rolling Stone, 1977), pp. 128–29.
4. David Halberstam, "The War Will Be Over by Christmas," in Obst, ed., *The Sixties,* p. 90.
5. John Gellner, "Canadian Business as Usual in Saigon," *Saturday Night*, May 1968, p. 23.
6. Fall, *Last Reflections,* p. 200.
7. Len Giovannitti, *The Man Who Won the Medal of Honor* (Toronto: Popular Library, 1976), p. 45.
8. Richard Boyle, *GI Revolts* (San Francisco: United Front Press, 1973), p. 36.
9. Ron Kovic, *Born on the Fourth of July* (New York: Pocket Books, 1977), p. 21.
10. Philip Resnick, "Canadian War Industries and Vietnam," *Our Generation*, vol.5 no.3, pp. 22–23.
11. Ibid., pp. 28–29.
12. *Globe and Mail*, 6 November 1967.
13. Resnick, "Canadian War Industries," p. 24.
14. James Steele, "Canada's Vietnam Policy: The Diplomacy of Escalation," in Stephen Clarkson, ed., *An Independent Foreign Policy for Canada?* (Toronto: McClelland & Stewart, 1968), p. 76.

15. Ibid., p. 72.
16. Renee Goldsmith Kasinsky, *Refugees from Militarism* (New Brunswick: Transaction Books, 1976), p. 59.
17. Ray Davie,"The Military-Industrial Complex, the Defence Research Board, and You," *Carillon,* n.d., 1969.
18. Steele, "Canada's Vietnam Policy," p. 71.
19. Claire Culhane, *Une québécoise au Vietnam* (n.p.: Editions Québécoises, n.d.), p. 19.
20. Charles Taylor, *Snow Job* (Toronto: Anansi, 1974), p. 83.
21. Steele, "Canada's Vietnam Policy," p. 74.
22. David Lewis Stein, "The Night of the Little Brown Men," *City Boys* (Ottawa: Oberon, 1978), p. 99.
23. Dennis Lee, "Civil Elegies," *Civil Elegies and Other Poems* (Toronto: Anansi, 1972), p. 48.
24. Ian Adams, "How We Win Their Hearts and Minds," *Maclean's,* February 1968, p. 14.
25. Gary Moffatt, *History of the Canadian Peace Movement until 1969* (St. Catharines: Grape Vine Press, n.d.), p. 5.
26. Richard Price, "The New Left in Alberta," in Dimitrios Roussopoulos, ed. *The New Left in Canada* (Montreal: Black Rose Books, 1970), p. 43.
27. Moffatt, *Canadian Peace Movement*, p. 166.
28. Charles Hanly, *Revolution and Response* (Toronto: McClelland & Stewart, 1966), p. 33.
29. "That Was a Teach-in That Was — Or Was It?" *Maclean's*, 15 November 1965.
30. Hanly, *Revolution and Response*, p. viii.
31. Ibid., p. 51.
32. Ibid., p. 65.
33. "Open Letter to the 27th Parliament and the Government of Canada," *Our Generation,* vol.3 no.4 / vol.4 no.1, p. 93.
34. Robert Mahood, "The SUPA Sit-In," *Canadian Alternatives,* vol.1 no.2, p. 54ff.
35. Tony Hyde, "The Student Union for Peace Action: An Analysis," unpublished paper, n.d., p. 12.
36. Mahood, "SUPA Sit-In," p. 55.
37. "Open Letter to the 27th Parliament," p. 97.
38. Robin Murray, ed., *Vietnam: No. 1 in the Read-In Series* (London: Eyre & Spottiswoode, 1965), p. 147.
39. Fall, *Last Reflections*, p. 186.
40. Ibid., p. 187.
41. Herbert Aptheker, *Mission To Hanoi* (New York: International Publishers, 1966), p. 63.
42. David Gathier, "The New Left's View of American Imperialism," *Commentator,* February 1969, p. 17.
43. Allen Ginsberg, "From these States," in Theodore Solotaroff, ed., *New*

American Review #11 (New York: Simon & Schuster, 1971), p. 9.
44. From the Vietnamese national poem by Nguyen Du (1765–1820).
45. Resnick, "Canadian War Industries," p. 27.

PART I
CHAPTER III

1. "Vietnam, Professors and Draftdodgers: An Interview with Morton Brown, PSA Department," *Student Advocate,* Simon Fraser University, n.d., p. 1ff.
2. Renee Goldsmith Kasinsky, *Refugees from Militarism* (New Brunswick: Transaction Books, 1976), p. 64.
3. Ibid., p. 294.
4. Ibid., p. 86.
5. Toronto Anti-Draft Programme, ed., *Manual for Draft-Age Immigrants to Canada* (Toronto: Anansi, 1970), p. 46.
6. Kasinsky, *Refugees,* p. 81.
7. Roger Neville Williams, *The New Exiles* (New York: Liveright, 1971), p. 363.
8. Ibid., p. 107.
9. *Red, White and Black Newsletter,* 26 February 1970.
10. *Manual for Draft-Age Immigrants*, p. 10.
11. "War Resisters in Exile: The Memoirs of Amex-Canada," Amex-Canada, vol.6 no.2, p. 16.
12. "Police Raid Vancouver Homes," *BC Newsletter*, no.6, p. 14.
13. Williams, *New Exiles,* p. 330.
14. Lorne and Caroline Brown, *An Unauthorized History of the RCMP* (Toronto: James, Lewis & Samuel, 1973), p. 112.
15. Ibid., p. 113.
16. *Toronto Star*, 7 May 1969.
17. Kasinsky, *Refugees*, p. 128.
18. Williams, *New Exiles,* p. 346.
19. Ibid., p. 352.
20. From the film by Anthony Bannon et al, *Citizen of What Country?* (Toronto, 1970).
21. Dennis Lee, "Civil Elegies," *Civil Elegies and Other Poems* (Toronto: Anansi, 1972), p. 19.

PART II
CHAPTER I

1. Clark Kerr, *The Uses of the University* (New York: Harper & Row, 1966), p. 87.

2. Ibid., p. 124.

3. Students for a Democratic Society, *The Port Huron Statement* (New York: SDS, 1962), p. 9.

4. *The Trouble in Berkeley* (Berkeley: Diablo Press, n.d.), p. 65.

5. Mario Savio, "An End to History," in Seymour Lipset and Sheldon Wolin, eds., *The Berkeley Student Revolt* (Garden City: Doubleday, 1965), p. 219.

6. Robert Favreau, "The Quandary of UGEQ," in Tim and Julyan Reid, eds., *Student Power and the Canadian Campus* (Toronto: Peter Martin, 1969), p. 108.

7. Situationist International, *On the Poverty of Student Life* (Berkeley: Contradiction Press, 1972), p. 23.

8. Donald McKelvey, "The State of SDS," *SUPA Newsletter,* vol.3 no.10, p. 15.

9. Philip Resnick, "The New Left in Ontario," in Dimitrios Roussopoulos, ed., *The New Left in Canada* (Montreal: Black Rose Books, 1970), p. 96.

10. Dimitrios Roussopoulos, "Towards a Revolutionary Youth Movement and an Extra-Parliamentary Opposition in Canada," in Roussopoulos, ed., *New Left in Canada,* p. 133.

11. Julyan Reid, "Some Canadian Issues," in Reid, ed., *Student Power,* p. 7.

12. John Porter, *The Vertical Mosaic* (Toronto: University of Toronto Press, 1965), p. 95.

13. *Varsity*, 17 January 1968.

14. Jim Harding, unpublished paper to 32nd CUS Congress at the University of Guelph, 1968.

15. Resnick, "New Left in Ontario," p. 106.

16. Jean-Louis Ferrier, "Marcuse Defends His New Left Line," in Harold Jaffe and John Tytell, eds., *The American Experience: A Radical Reader* (New York: Harper & Row, 1970), p. 137

17. James Harding, "From the Midst of a Crisis," in Gerald McGuigan, ed., *Student Protest* (Toronto: Methuen, 1968), p. 99.

18. Noam Chomsky, "Knowledge and Power: Intellectuals and the Welfare/Warfare State," in Priscilla Long, ed., *The New Left* (Boston: Porter Sargeant, 1969), p. 177.

PART II
CHAPTER II

1. *Gateway*, 22 November 1968.
2. George Reamsbottom, "Student Motion in B.C.," *Our Generation,* reprint, n.d., p. 91.
3. "The Parts That Were Left Out of the Kennedy Book," *Realist*, May 1967, p. 18.
4. Paul Rockwell, "How We Became Revolutionaries," in Tariq Ali, ed., *The New Revolutionaries* (Toronto: McClelland & Stewart, 1969), p. 294.
5. Daniel and Gabriel Cohn-Bendit, "The Battle of the Streets," in Carl Oglesby, ed., *The New Left Reader* (New York: Grove Press, 1969), p. 259.
6. R. Gregoire and F. Perlman, *Worker-Student Action Committee: France May '68* (Detroit: Black and Red, 1970), p. 11.
7. "The Appeal from the Sorbonne," in Oglesby, ed., *New Left Reader*, p. 269.
8. Andrew Wernick, "Blowin' in the Wind: CUS in Winnipeg," *Canadian Forum*, September 1968, pp. 132–33.
9. Cohn-Bendit, "Battle of the Streets," p. 265.
10. James Harding, "What's Happening at SFU?" *Our Generation*, vol.6 no.3, p. 63.
11. Editorial, *Our Generation*, vol.6 no.3, p. 8.
12. Gene Marine, "Chicago: The Trial of the New Culture," in Rolling Stone, ed., *The Age of Paranoia* (New York: Pocket Books, 1972), p. 243.
13. *The Quebec Liberation Movement* (Toronto: Hogtown Press, n.d.), p. 12.
14. Stanley Gray quoted in Andrew Porter, "The Night the Québécois Took On McGill," *McGill Daily,* 5 April 1979, p. 8.
15. Jim Harding, "The Strike at SFU," reprint, n.d., unpaginated.
16. Kathleen Gough, "The Struggle at SFU," *Monthly Review*, May 1970, p. 36.

PART III
CHAPTER I

1. Nat Hentoff, "The Playboy Interview: Bob Dylan," in Craig McGregor, ed., *Bob Dylan, A Retrospective* (New York: Morrow, 1972), p. 39.
2. Mitchell Goodman, ed., *The Movement Toward a New America* (New York: Alfred Knopf, 1970), p. 374.

3. Henry Malcolm, *Generation of Narcissus* (Boston: Little, Brown, 1971), p. 166.

4. Robert Hunter, *The Storming of the Mind* (Toronto: McClelland & Stewart, 1971), p. 87.

5. Ibid., p. 124.

6. Leonard Wolff, ed., *Voices from the Love Generation* (Boston: Little, Brown, 1968), p. 76.

7. Peter Stansill and David Zane Mairowitz, eds., *BAMN: Outlaw Manifestos and Ephemera* (Harmondsworth: Penguin, 1971), p. 72.

8. "Final Report of the Slocan Valley Community Forest Management Project" (no other information available), p. 4:41.

9. Jack Batten, "The Dread Hippie Menace," *Maclean's*, August 1967, p. 51.

10. Ibid., p. 50.

11. Bill Usher and Linda Page-Harpa, eds., *For What Time I Am in This World: Stories from Mariposa* (Toronto: Peter Martin, 1977), p. 191.

12. *Countdown: A Subterranean Magazine* (New York: New American Library, 1970), p. 21.

13. John Sinclair, *Guitar Army* (New York: Douglas Book Corp., 1971), p. 32.

PART III
CHAPTER II

1. Theodore Roszak, *The Making of a Counter Culture* (New York: Anchor Books, 1969), p. 168.

2. Robert Hunter, *The Storming of the Mind* (Toronto: McClelland & Stewart, 1971), p. 84.

3. *It's Your Turn: A Report to the Secretary of State by the Committee on Youth* (Ottawa: Information Canada, 1971), pp. 39–41.

4. John Sinclair, *Guitar Army* (New York: Douglas Book Corp., 1972), p. 179.

5. John and Margaret Rowntree, "The Political Economy of Youth," *Our Generation*, reprint, n.d., p. 170ff.

6. Ibid., p. 184.

7. Herbert Marcuse, "On Revolution," in Alexander Cockburn and Robin Blackburn, eds., *Student Power* (Harmondsworth: Penguin, 1969), p. 372.

8. Gary Snyder, "Why Tribe," in Harold Jaffe and John Tytell, eds., *The American Experience: A Radical Reader* (New York: Harper & Row, 1970), p. 259.

9.   Irwin Silber, *The Cultural Revolution: A Marxist Analysis* (New York: Times Change, 1970), p. 35.
10.   Irwin Silber, "The Great Middle-Class Cultural Revolution," in Times Change Press, ed., *Hip Culture* (New York: Times Change, 1970), p. 42.
11.   Leonard Wolff, ed., *Voices from the Love Generation* (Boston: Little, Brown, 1968), p. 269.
12.   Larry Haiven, "Festival Scene II," *Varsity*, 26 September 1969, p. 6.
13.   Ibid.
14.   Ritchie Yorke, *Axes, Chops and Hot Licks* (Edmonton: Hurtig, 1971), pp. 219–20.
15.   Ibid., p. 206.
16.   Jack Batten, "Canada's Rock Scene," *Maclean's*, February 1968, p. 42.
17.   Kaspars Dzeguze, "What 'Hair' Is Doing to a Bunch of Otherwise Ordinary Canadian Kids," *Maclean's*, April 1970, p. 51.
18.   Hunter, *Storming of the Mind*, p. 23.
19.   Henry Tarvainen, "Che. . . Just Doing His Thing," *Varsity*, 27 October 1967.
20.   Hunter, *Storming of the Mind*, p. 166.
21.   Warren Hinckle, "A Social History of the Hippies," *Ramparts*, March 1967, p. 26.
22.   Silber, *Cultural Revolution*, p. 31.
23.   Pat Uhl, "In Response to Stan Gray," *Canadian Alternatives*, vol.1 no.1, p. 60.
24.   James Harding, "Hippies and the New Left," unpublished paper, n.d., p. 14.

PART IV
CHAPTER I

1.   Stokely Carmichael, "What We Want," in Harold Jaffe and John Tytell, eds., *The American Experience: A Radical Reader* (New York: Harper & Row, 1970), p. 82ff.
2.   "Program of the Black Panther Party," in Mitchell Goodman, ed., *The Movement Toward a New America* (New York: Alfred Knopf, 1970), p. 212.
3.   Stokely Carmichael, "A Declaration of War," in Goodman, ed., *New America*, p. 178ff.
4.   Eldridge Cleaver, "Soul On Ice," in Jaffe and Tytell, eds., *American Experience*, p. 54.

5. Ian Adams et al., *The Real Poverty Report* (Edmonton: Hurtig, 1971), p. 69.
6. Dick Fidler, *Red Power in Canada* (Toronto: Vanguard, 1970), p. 4.
7. Ibid., p. 3.
8. Edgar Dosman, *Indians: The Urban Dilemma* (Toronto: McClelland & Stewart, 1972), p. 15.
9. Fidler, *Red Power in Canada*, p. 4.
10. M. Patricia Marchak, *Ideological Perspectives on Canada* (Toronto: McGraw-Hill Ryerson, 1975), p. 29.
11. Howard Adams, *Prison of Grass* (Toronto: New Press, 1975), p. 191.
12. Heather Robertson, *Reservations Are for Indians* (Toronto: James, Lewis & Samuel, 1970), p. 14.
13. Richard Price, "The New Left in Alberta," in Dimitrios Roussopoulos, ed., *The New Left in Canada* (Montreal: Black Rose Books, 1970), p. 46.
14. John Ferguson and Barry Lipton, "Exploitation and Discrimination in the Alberta Beet Fields," *CUS National Supplement,* 20–24 October 1969, pp. 4–5.
15. Dosman, *Indians: The Urban Dilemma*, p. 179.
16. Harold Cardinal, *The Unjust Society* (Edmonton: Hurtig, 1969), p. 139.
17. Peter Stansill and David Zane Mairowitz, eds., *BAMN: Outlaw Manifestos and Ephemera* (Harmondsworth: Penguin, 1971), p. 185.
18. Howard Adams, *Prison of Grass*, pp. 204–5.
19. Cardinal, *Unjust Society*, p. 108.
20. Duke Redbird quoted in Marty Dunn, *Red on White* (Toronto: New Press, 1971), p. 115.
21. Jon Ruddy, "Portrait of the Artist as a Young Half-Breed," *Maclean's*, June 1970, p. 41.
22. Fidler, *Red Power in Canada*, pp. 8–9.
23. Howard Adams, *Prison of Grass*, p. 210.

PART IV
CHAPTER II

1. Sojourner Truth quoted in Betty Friedan, *The Feminine Mystique* (New York: Dell, 1963), p. 88.
2. *Report of the Royal Commission on the Status of Women in Canada* (Ottawa: Information Canada, 1970), p. vii.
3. Judy Bernstein et al., "Sisters, Brothers, Lovers. . . Listen. . . ," *Women Unite!* (Toronto: Canadian Women's Educational Press, 1972), p. 31ff.

4.   Judy Gill et al., "Sexual Myths," *Women Unite!*, p. 164.
5.   *Report on the Status of Women,* p. 263.
6.   Bob Bossin, "My First Real Honest-to-God Big-Time Campus Sit-in — We Win!" *Maclean's*, June 1970, p. 26.
7.   Women's Liberation News Service, "University of Toronto Women Win Daycare," *Pedestal*, April 1970, p. 2.
8.   Eleanor Wright Pelrine, *Abortion in Canada* (Toronto: New Press, 1972), p. 32.
9.   Women's Liberation Movement, "Brief to the House of Commons," *Women Unite!*, p. 117.
10.   Bonnie Kreps, "Radical Feminism," *Women Unite!*, p. 75.
11.   *Report on the Status of Women*, p. 154.
12.   Ibid., p. 65.
13.   Ibid., p. 309.
14.   Wynton Semple, "They'll Have to Start a War or Something. . . ," unpublished paper, n.d., p. 5.
15.   *Report on the Status of Women*, p. 21.
16.   M. Brady et al., "Working Women's Association: A Short History," Vancouver, n.d.
17.   *Yellow Journal*, vol.1. no. 8.
18.   Jerry Rubin, *We Are Everywhere* (New York: Harper & Row, 1971), p. 109.
19.   "Redstockings Manifesto," in Mitchell Goodman, ed., *The Movement Toward a New America* (New York: Alfred Knopf, 1970), p. 50.
20.   Ernest Mandel, *The Revolutionary Student Movement: Theory and Practice* (New York: Pathfinder Press, 1971), p. 12.
21.   Jerry L. Avorn. *Up Against the Ivy Wall* (New York: Atheneum, 1968), p. 118.
22.   Peter Stansill and David Zane Mairowitz, eds., *BAMN: Outlaw Manifestos and Ephemera* (Harmondsworth: Penguin, 1971), p. 141.
23.   *Manifeste des femmes québécoises* (Montreal: Editions l'Etincelle, 1971), p. 53.
24.   "A Prison Interview: Huey Newton," in Carl Oglesby, ed., *The New Left Reader* (New York: Grove Press, 1969), p. 232.
25.   "Does My Liberation Mean Not Your Liberation?" *Off Our Backs*, reprint, Detroit, n.d., unpaginated.

PART V
CHAPTER I

1.   Dennis Lee, "Civil Elegies," *Civil Elegies and Other Poems* (Toronto: Anansi, 1972), p. 56.

2. Tony Hyde, "The Student Union for Peace Action: An Analysis," unpublished paper, n.d., p. 14.
3. Charles Taylor, *Snow Job* (Toronto: Anansi, 1974), p. 24.
4. Philip Resnick, *The Land of Cain* (Vancouver: New Star Books, 1977), pp. 106–7.
5. John Porter, *The Vertical Mosaic* (Toronto: University of Toronto Press, 1965), p. 231.
6. George Grant, *Lament for a Nation* (Toronto: McClelland & Stewart [Carleton Library], 1965), p. 96.
7. Ibid., p. 41.
8. Ibid., pp. 15–16.
9. Gad Horowitz, "On the Fear of Nationalism," *Canadian Dimension*, vol.5 no.6, pp. 8–9.
10. Gad Horowitz, "Conservatism, Liberalism and Socialism: An Interpretation," *Canadian Journal of Economics and Political Science*, vol.32 no.2, p. 147ff.
11. Barry Lord, " 'mericans," in Al Purdy, ed., *The New Romans* (Edmonton: Hurtig, 1968), p. 150.
12. Resnick, *Land of Cain,* p. 41.
13. Grant, *Lament for a Nation*, p. 76.
14. Daniel Drache, "The Canadian Bourgeoisie and Its National Consciousness," in Ian Lumsden, ed., *Close the 49th Parallel Etc.* (Toronto: University of Toronto Press, 1970), p. 17.
15. Kari Levitt, *Silent Surrender* (Toronto: Macmillan, 1970), pp. 63–64.
16. Ibid., p. 77.
17. Resnick, *Land of Cain*, p. 70.
18. James Steele and Robin Mathews, "The Universities: Takeover of the Mind," in Lumsden, ed., *49th Parallel*, p. 171.
19. Robin Mathews, "The Americanization of Canadian Universities," *Canadian Dimension*, vol.5 no.8.
20. Ibid.
21. Mathews, "Takeover of the Mind," p. 172.
22. Robin Mathews and James Steele, eds., *The Struggle for Canadian Universities* (Toronto: New Press, 1969), p. 4.
23. Ibid., pp. 19–20.
24. Ibid., p. 7.
25. Ibid., p. 125.
26. Peter Warrian, "From Colonized to Colonizer," in John Redekop, ed., *The Star-Spangled Beaver* (Toronto: Peter Martin, 1971), p. 77.
27. Dave Godfrey and Mel Watkins, eds., *Gordon to Watkins to You* (Toronto: New Press, 1970), p. 130.
28. Ibid., p. 135ff.
29. James Laxer and Art Pape, "Youth and Canadian Politics," in Dimitrios Roussopoulos, ed., *Canada and Radical Social Change* (Montreal: Black Rose Books, 1973) p. 53.
30. Philip Resnick, "The Dynamics of Power in Canada," in Roussopoulos, ed., *Radical Social Change*, p. 183.

31. New Left Caucus, "Statement of Purpose," unpublished paper, n.d.
32. Resnick, *Land of Cain*, p. 169.
33. Godfrey and Watkins, eds., *Gordon to Watkins*, p. 103ff.
34. Hal Draper, "The Two Souls of Socialism," *Our Generation*, vol.6 no.3, p. 69.
35. Gerald Caplan and James Laxer, "Perspectives on Un-American Traditions in Canada," in Lumsden, ed., *49th Parallel*, p. 313.
36. Draper, "Two Souls of Socialism," p. 82.

PART V
CHAPTER II

1. M. Patricia Marchak, *Ideological Perspectives on Canada* (Toronto: McGraw-Hill Ryerson, 1975), p. 26.
2. Evelyn Puxley, *Poverty in Montreal* (Montreal: Dawson College Press, 1971), p. 5.
3. Ibid., p. 16.
4. Hubert Guindon, "Social Unrest, Social Class and Quebec's Bureaucratic Revolution," in Samuel D. Clark, ed., *Prophecy and Protest: Social Movements in Twentieth Century Canada* (Agincourt: Gage, 1975).
5. Hubert Aquin, *Prochain Episode* (Toronto: McClelland & Stewart [New Canadian Library], 1972), pp. 70–71.
6. Daniel Latouche, "Violence, Politique et Crise dans la Société Québécoise," in Laurier LaPierre et al, eds., *Essays on the Left* (Toronto: McClelland & Stewart, 1971), p. 179.
7. Joyce Kolko, *America and the Crisis of World Capitalism* (Boston: Beacon Press, 1974), p. 49.
8. "A Prison Interview: Huey Newton," in Carl Oglesby, ed., *The New Left Reader* (New York: Grove Press, 1969), p. 225.
9. Léandre Bergeron, *Petit Manuel d'Histoire du Québec* (Montreal: Editions Québécoises, 1971), p. 231.
10. *The Quebec Liberation Movement* (Toronto: Hogtown Press, n.d.), p. 229.
11. Bergeron, *Petit Manuel*, p. 232.
12. Ivan Avakumovic, *Socialism in Canada* (Toronto: McClelland & Stewart, 1978), p. 5.
13. Pierre Vallières, *White Niggers of America* (Toronto: McClelland & Stewart, 1971), p. 269.
14. Robert Chodos and Nick auf der Maur, eds., *Quebec: A Chronicle 1968–72* (Toronto: James, Lewis & Samuel, 1972), p. 43.
15. Jeff Sallot, *Nobody Said No* (Toronto: James Lorimer, 1979), p. 16.

16. Pierre Vallières, *The Assassination of Pierre Laporte* (Toronto: James Lorimer, 1977), p. 135.
17. Pierre Gravel, *A Perte de Temps* (Toronto: Anansi, 1969), p. 40.
18. Vallières, *White Niggers of America*, p. 281.
19. Philip Resnick, *The Land of Cain* (Vancouver: New Star Books, 1977), p. 192.
20. Gravel, *A Perte de Temps*, p. 26.

PART V
CHAPTER III

1. Leonard Mayers, "Lawlessness in Lotusland," *Commentator*, September 1970, p. 16.
2. Denis Smith, *Bleeding Hearts. . . Bleeding Country* (Edmonton: Hurtig, 1971), p. 81.
3. Ibid., pp. 56–57.
4. Pierre Vallières, *The Assassination of Pierre Laporte* (Toronto: James Lorimer, 1977), p. 156.
5. Daniel Latouche "Violence, Politique et Crise dans la Société Québécoise," in Laurier LaPierre et al., eds., *Essays on the Left* (Toronto: McClelland & Stewart, 1971).
6. Robert Chodos and Nick auf der Maur, eds., *Quebec: A Chronicle 1968–72* (Toronto: James, Lewis & Samuel, 1972), p. 50.
7. Smith, *Bleeding Hearts*, p. 47.
8. John Gellner, *Bayonets in the Streets* (Toronto: Collier-Macmillan, 1974), p. 116.
9. Chodos and auf der Maur, eds., *Quebec: A Chronicle*, p. 51.
10. Ibid., p. 68.
11. Ibid., p. 56.
12. Smith, *Bleeding Hearts*, p. 85.
13. Women's Liberation Movement Quebec Collective, "Les Patriotes, les Révoltés, les Québécois: A History of the Quebec Struggle," in Victoria College SAC and University of Toronto SAC, eds., *Quebec in Crisis*, October 1970, p. 9.
14. Chodos and auf der Maur, eds., *Quebec: A Chronicle,* p. 67.
15. Smith, *Bleeding Hearts,* p. 86.
16. Marc Laurendeau, "Les vrais évènements d'octobre," *L'Actualité,* November 1978, p. 92.
17. Richard Fidler, *RCMP: The Real Subversives* (Toronto: Vanguard, 1978), p. 15.
18. *Le journal jaune*, vol.1 no.9, p. 16.

PART VI
CHAPTER I

1. C. Wright Mills, "The New Left," in Irving Horowitz, ed., *Power, Politics and People* (New York: Oxford Unviersity Press, 1963), p. 257.
2. Stanley Rothman, "Intellectuals and the Student Movement: A Post Mortem," *The Journal of Psychohistory,* vol.5 no.4, p. 555.
3. Herbert Marcuse, *One-Dimensional Man* (Boston: Beacon Press, 1964), p. 4.
4. Carl Oglesby, "Notes on a Decade Ready for the Dustbin," in Mitchell Goodman, ed., *The Movement Toward a New America* (New York: Alfred Knopf, 1970), p. 737.
5. Theodore Roszak, "Youth and the Great Refusal," in Goodman, ed., *New America,* p. 86.
6. Paul Chamberland quoted in Malcolm Reid, *The Shouting Sign-painters* (Toronto: McClelland & Stewart, 1972), p. 142.
7. Roszak, "Youth and the Great Refusal," p. 88.
8. Peter Stansill and David Zane Mairowitz, eds., *BAMN: Outlaw Manifestos and Ephemera* (Harmondsworth: Penguin, 1971), p. 148.
9. Denise Levertov, "Let Us Sing Unto the Lord a New Song," *To Stay Alive* (New York: New Directions, 1971), p. 73.
10. Ellory Popoff, "The Divergence of Radicalism: The Old and New Left," *Canadian Alternatives,* vol.1 no.1, p. 10.
11. Murray Bookchin, *Listen, Marxist!* (New York: Times Change, 1971).
12. Oglesby, "Notes," p. 743.
13. Norman Penner, *The Canadian Left: A Critical Analysis* (Scarborough: Prentice-Hall, 1977), p. 249.
14. Paul Levine, "Theatre Chronicle: Chicago 70," *Canadian Forum,* July-August 1970, p. 175.
15. James Laxer, "The Americanization of the Canadian Student Movement," in Ian Lumsden ed., *Close the 49th Parallel Etc.* (Toronto: University of Toronto Press, 1970), p. 275ff.
16. See Gerald Caplan and James Laxer, "Perspectives on Un-American Traditions in Canada," in Lumsden, ed., *49th Parallel,* p. 305ff.
17. James Harding, "Values, Analysis and Action for the NDY," unpublished report to the National NDY Convention, 1966.
18. "Outline for the Working Place of the Left," *New Left Committee Bulletin,* vol.1 no.1, p. 13.
19. From the New Party Declaration, 1961.
20. Dimitrios Roussopoulos, "Towards a Revolutionary Youth Movement and an Extra-Parliamentary Opposition in Canada," in Dimitrios Roussopoulos, ed., *The New Left in Canada* (Montreal: Black Rose Books, 1970), p. 149.

21. Stanley Gray, "Old Left, New Left," *Youth Revolt and the New Left, Canadian Dimension Kit #2*, n.d., p. 18.
22. Philip Resnick, *The Land of Cain* (Vancouver: New Star Books, 1977), p. 230.
23. H.C. Pentland, "Is Canada Possible?" *Canadian Dimension*, vol.1 no.8, p. 5.
24. Roussopoulos, "Towards a Revolutionary Youth Movement," p. 138ff.
25. Andy Wernick, "A Guide to the Student Left," *Varsity*, 24 September 1969.

PART VI
CHAPTER II

1. Robert Fulford, "The Lesson of Seven Days," *Canadian Forum*, May 1966.
2. Dorothy Eber, *The Computer Centre Party* (Montreal: Tundra Books, 1969), p. 282ff.
3. Lorne and Caroline Brown, *An Unauthorized History of the RCMP* (Toronto: James, Lewis and Samuel, 1973), p. 107.
4. Ibid., p. 109.
5. Ibid., p. 125.
6. Renee Goldsmith Kasinsky, *Refugees from Militarism* (New Brunswick: Transaction Books, 1976), p. 227.
7. "It's Your Turn," *A Report to the Secretary of State by the Committee on Youth* (Ottawa: Information Canada, 1971), p. 47.
8. Malcolm Reid, *The Shouting Signpainters* (Toronto: McClelland & Stewart, 1972), p. 286.
9. Stanley Gray, "The Struggle in Quebec," unpublished paper delivered at Glendon College, Toronto, October 1969, p. 8.
10. Richard Fidler, *RCMP: The Real Subversives* (Toronto: Vanguard, 1978), p. 12.
11. Vittorio Rieser, "The Struggle Against Capitalism in Italy: A Political Manifesto," in Tariq Ali, ed., *The New Revolutionaries* (Toronto: McClelland & Stewart, 1969), p. 207.
12. W. Roman Petryshyn, "The Emergence of a Generation Entelechy: The Ukrainian Canadian Student Movement," unpublished paper, p. 32.
13. Jerry Rubin, *Growing (Up) At 37* (New York: Warner Books, 1976), p. 94.
14. Massimo Teodori, *The New Left: A Documentary History* (Indianapolis: Bobbs-Merrill, 1969), p. 37.
15. Tom Hayden, "The Ability to Face Whatever Comes," in Harold

Jaffe and John Tytell, eds., *The American Experience: A Radical Reader* (New York: Harper & Row, 1970), p. 441.

16. Carl Oglesby, "Notes On a Decade Ready for the Dustbin," in Mitchell Goodman, ed., *The Movement Toward a New America* (New York: Alfred Knopf, 1970), p. 145.

17. Teodori, *New Left*, p. 90.

18. *Monthly Review* editorial, "The Old Left and the New," *Youth Revolt and the New Left, Canadian Dimension Kit #2*, n.d., p. 42ff.

BIBLIOGRAPHY

Unlike the Americans, Canadian writers and publishers have not exhibited the capacity to be endlessly fascinated with the recent history of their own society, not even with the period known as "the Sixties" — the most turbulent period since the Thirties. American material on this period has been produced in an unbroken stream of memoirs, anthologies, scrapbooks, novels, plays and poems, oral histories and photo-essays, as well as the to-be-expected journalistic accounts, theoretical essays, critical interpretations, scholarly treatises, and social and cultural histories. Canadian material, on the other hand, is patchy.

If one goes looking in people's basements, through back issues of newspapers and magazines, and on the shelves of used book stores, one can find a hodge-podge of contemporary material (speeches, pamphlets, newsletters, correspondence, news clippings, short articles and ephemera) that fills in some gaps or illustrates a point. There are some books (mostly out of print now) that were written in response to some of the more sensational events — the influx of the draft-resisters, the occupation of the Computer Centre at Sir George Williams University, the phenomenon of the CYC. There was the heroic effort of the people around *Our Generation* magazine and Black Rose Books to anthologize the theoretical and analytical writing being done by Canadian movement activists of the time. There are two or three recent broad reviews of left-wing politics in post-war Canada — in which an account of the "new left" takes up a few pages. And there are a number of fine anthologies collected around specific themes — the Americanization of Canada, radicalism in Quebec, the women's liberation movement — as researched by academics, some of them ex-activists of the Sixties.

But there is not to be had any sustained and generalized interpretive and analytical treatment of the period (it is indicative of the "insecurity" of colonized intellectuals, I suppose, that they confine themselves to essays and anthologies), almost nothing in the way of social and cultural histories (as opposed to theses in political economy), and disappointingly little said in literature (Quebec literature excepted). As for a socio-economic *theory* of the period, I like to think it may yet be generated by some of the people who had much to say at the time, in speeches, meetings, newsletters and magazines; for Canadian movement activists, no less than their American and European counterparts, were creative and innovative in thought and deed, and have not forgotten.

The bibliography which follows is a selection (from among 150 titles) of the most useful and/or historically important books that I consulted in the course of my research. As for the more than 150 articles, pamphlets, essays, et cetera, that I also consulted, I refer the reader to the footnotes for details.

CANADIAN SOURCES

Adams, Howard. *Prison of Grass*. Toronto: New Press, 1975.

Adelman, H., and Lee, Dennis, eds. *The University Game*. Toronto: Anansi, 1968.

Aquin, Hubert. *Prochain Episode*. Toronto: McClelland & Stewart (New Canadian Library), 1972.

Avakumovic, Ivan. *Socialism in Canada*. Toronto: McClelland & Stewart, 1978.

Bottomore, T.B. *Social Criticism in North America*. Toronto: CBC, 1966.

Brown, Lorne and Caroline. *An Unauthorized History of the RCMP*. Toronto: James Lewis & Samuel, 1973.

Canadian Dimension Kit No. 2. *Youth Revolt and the New Left*. Winnipeg: Canadian Dimension, n.d.

Cardinal, Harold. *The Unjust Society*. Edmonton: Hurtig, 1969.

Chodos, Robert, and auf der Maur, Nick. *Quebec: A Chronicle 1968–72*. Toronto: James, Lewis & Samuel, 1972.

Clark, Samuel D., et al., eds. *Prophecy and Protest: Social Movements in Twentieth Century Canada*. Agincourt: Gage, 1975.

Daly, Margaret. *The Revolution Game*. Toronto: New Press, 1970.

Eber, Dorothy. *The Computer Centre Party*. Montreal: Tundra Books, 1969.

Fidler, Richard. *RCMP: The Real Subversives*. Toronto: Vanguard, 1978.

Godfrey, Dave, and Watkins, Mel, eds. *Gordon to Watkins to You*. Toronto: New Press, 1970.

Grant, George. *Lament for a Nation*. Toronto: McClelland & Stewart (Carleton Library), 1965.

Gravel, Pierre. *A Perte de Temps*. Toronto: Anansi, 1969.

Hunter, Robert. *The Storming of the Mind*. Toronto: McClelland & Stewart, 1971.

Kasinsky, Renee Goldsmith. *Refugees from Militarism*. New Brunswick: Transaction Books, 1976.

LaPierre, Laurier, et al., eds. *Essays On the Left.* Toronto: McClelland & Stewart, 1971.

Lee, Dennis. *Civil Elegies and Other Poems.* Toronto: Anansi, 1972.

Levitt, Kari. *Silent Surrender.* Toronto: Macmillan, 1970.

Lumsden, Ian, ed. *Close the 49th Parallel Etc.* Toronto: University of Toronto Press, 1971.

Marchak, M. Patricia. *Ideological Perspectives on Canada.* Toronto: McGraw-Hill Ryerson, 1975.

McGuigan, Gerald, ed. *Student Protest.* Toronto: Methuen, 1968.

Moffatt, Gary. *History of the Canadian Peace Movement until 1969.* St. Catharines: Grape Vine Press, n.d.

Moore, Brian. *The Revolution Script.* Richmond Hill: Pocket Books, 1972.

Penner, Norman. *The Canadian Left: A Critical Analysis.* Scarborough: Prentice-Hall, 1977.

Porter, John. *The Vertical Mosaic.* Toronto: University of Toronto Press, 1965.

Purdy, Al, ed. *The New Romans.* Edmonton: Hurtig, 1968.

Reid, Malcolm. *The Shouting Signpainters.* Toronto: McClelland & Stewart, 1972.

Reid, Tim and Julyan, eds. *Student Power and the Canadian Campus.* Toronto: Peter Martin, 1969.

Report of the Royal Commission on the Status of Women in Canada. Ottawa: Information Canada, 1970.

Resnick, Philip. *The Land of Cain.* Vancouver: New Star Books, 1977.

Roussopoulos, Dimitrios, ed. *Canada and Radical Social Change.* Montreal: Black Rose Books, 1973.

The New Left in Canada. Montreal: Black Rose Books, 1970.

Smith, Denis. *Bleeding Hearts... Bleeding Country.* Edmonton: Hurtig, 1971.

Stein, David Lewis. *Scratch One Dreamer.* Toronto: McClelland & Stewart, 1967.

Taylor, Charles. *Snow Job.* Toronto: Anansi, 1974.

Teeple, Gary, ed. *Capitalism and the National Question in Canada.* Toronto: University of Toronto Press, 1972.

Toronto Anti-Draft Programme. *Manual for Draft-Age Immigrants to Canada.* Toronto: Anansi, 1970.

Vallières, Pierre. *White Niggers of America.* Toronto: McClelland & Stewart, 1971.

Warnock, John. *Partner to Behemoth.* Toronto: New Press, 1970.

Women Unite! Toronto: Canadian Women's Educational Press, 1972.

Yorke, Ritchie. *Axes, Chops and Hot Licks.* Edmonton: Hurtig, 1971.

OTHER SOURCES

Ali, Tariq, ed. *The New Revolutionaries.* Toronto: McClelland & Stewart, 1969.

Bourges, Hervé, ed. *The Activists Speak.* London: Jonathan Cape, 1968.

Cliff, Tony, and Birchall, Ian. *France: The Struggle Goes On.* London: Socialist Review Publishing, 1968.

Cockburn, Alexander, and Blackburn, Robin. *Student Power.* Harmondsworth: Penguin, 1969.

Cohn-Bendit, Daniel and Gabriel. *Obsolete Communism: The Left-Wing Alternative.* New York: McGraw-Hill, 1968.

Debray, Régis. *Revolution in the Revolution?* New York: Grove Press, 1967.

Dickstein, Morris. *Gates of Eden: American Culture in the Sixties.* New York: Basic Books, 1977.

Fall, Bernard. *Last Reflections on a War.* New York: Doubleday, 1967.

Fanon, Frantz. *The Wretched of the Earth.* New York: Grove Press, 1966.

Free. *Revolution for the Hell of It.* New York: Pocket Books, 1970.

Gobin, Richard. *The Origins of Modern Leftism.* Harmondsworth: Penguin, 1975.

Goodman, Mitchell, ed. *The Movement Toward a New America.* New York: Alfred Knopf, 1970.

Goodman, Paul. *Growing Up Absurd.* New York: Vintage, 1960.

Jacobs, Paul, and Landau, Saul. *The New Radicals.* New York: Vintage, 1966.

Jaffe, Harold, and Tytell, John, eds. *The American Experience: A Radical Reader.* New York: Harper & Row, 1970.

Kerr, Clark. *The Uses of the University.* New York: Harper & Row, 1966.

Lipset, Seymour, and Wolin, Sheldon, eds. *The Berkeley Student Revolt.* New York: Doubleday, 1965.

Long, Priscilla, ed. *The New Left.* Boston: Porter Sargeant Publishing, 1969.

Mairowitz, David Zane. *The Radical Soap Opera.* Harmondsworth: Penguin, 1974.

Marcuse, Herbert. *One-Dimensional Man.* Boston: Beacon Press, 1964.

Murray, Robin, et al., eds. *Vietnam: No. 1 in the Read-In Series.* London: Eyre & Spottiswoode, 1965.

Obst, Lynda, ed. *The Sixties.* New York: Random House/Rolling Stone Press, 1977.

Oglesby, Carl, ed. *The New Left Reader.* New York: Grove Press, 1969.

Rolling Stone, ed. *The Age of Paranoia: How the Sixties Ended.* New York: Pocket Books, 1972.

Roszak, Theodore. *The Making of a Counter Culture.* New York: Anchor Books, 1969.

Sale, Kirkpatrick, *SDS.* New York: Random House, 1973.

Sinclair, John. *Guitar Army.* New York: Douglas Book Corp., 1972.

Solomon, David, ed. *LSD: The Consciousness-Expanding Drug.* New York: G.P. Putnam's, 1966.

Stansill, Peter, and Mairowitz, David Zane, eds. *BAMN: Outlaw Manifestos and Ephemera 1965–70.* Harmondsworth: Penguin, 1971.

Students for a Democratic Society. *Port Huron Statement.* New York: SDS, 1962.

Teodori, Massimo. *The New Left: A Documentary History.* Indianapolis: Bobbs-Merrill, 1969.

Watts, Alan. *The Joyous Cosmology.* New York: Vintage, 1962.

I also made use of the SUPA newsletter, *Canadian Alternatives, Our Generation, Saturday Night, Maclean's, Canadian Forum, Canadian Dimension,* some CUS publications, the University of Alberta *Gateway,* University of Regina *Carillon,* University of Toronto *Varsity, Georgia Straight, Yellow Journal* and *Pedestal.* Among American journals and magazines, I found *Monthly Review, Ramparts* and *Rolling Stone* particularly helpful.